Multiliteracy Play

Also available from Bloomsbury

Transition and Continuity in School Literacy Development, edited by Pauline Jones, Erika Matruglio, and Christine Edwards-Groves
Digital Media Use in Early Childhood: Birth to Six, Lelia Green, Leslie Haddon, Donell Holloway, Sonia Livingstone, Brian O'Neill, and Kylie Stevenson
Digital Personalization in Early Childhood, Natalia Kucirkova
Transformation, Embodiment, and Wellbeing in Foreign Language Pedagogy: Enacting Deep Learning, edited by Joseph Shaules and Troy McConachy
Language Learning Strategies and Individual Learner Characteristics: Situating Strategy Use in Diverse Contexts, edited by Rebecca L. Oxford and Carmen M. Amerstorfer

Multiliteracy Play

Designs and Desires in the Second Language Classroom

Chantelle Warner

BLOOMSBURY ACADEMIC
LONDON • NEW YORK • OXFORD • NEW DELHI • SYDNEY

BLOOMSBURY ACADEMIC

Bloomsbury Publishing Plc, 50 Bedford Square, London, WC1B 3DP, UK
Bloomsbury Publishing Inc, 1359 Broadway, New York, NY 10018, USA
Bloomsbury Publishing Ireland, 29 Earlsfort Terrace, Dublin 2, D02 AY28, Ireland

BLOOMSBURY, BLOOMSBURY ACADEMIC and the Diana logo are
trademarks of Bloomsbury Publishing Plc

First published in Great Britain 2024
Paperback edition published 2025

Copyright © Chantelle Warner, 2024, 2025

Chantelle Warner has asserted her right under the Copyright,
Designs and Patents Act, 1988, to be identified as Author of this work.

For legal purposes the Acknowledgments on pp. viii–ix constitute an
extension of this copyright page.

Cover image © Thatphichai Yodsri/Getty Images

All rights reserved. No part of this publication may be: i) reproduced or transmitted
in any form, electronic or mechanical, including photocopying, recording or by means
of any information storage or retrieval system without prior permission in writing from
the publishers; or ii) used or reproduced in any way for the training, development or
operation of artificial intelligence (AI) technologies, including generative AI technologies.
The rights holders expressly reserve this publication from the text and data mining
exception as per Article 4(3) of the Digital Single Market Directive (EU) 2019/790.

Bloomsbury Publishing Plc does not have any control over, or responsibility for,
any third-party websites referred to or in this book. All internet addresses given
in this book were correct at the time of going to press. The author and publisher
regret any inconvenience caused if addresses have changed or sites have ceased
to exist, but can accept no responsibility for any such changes.

A catalogue record for this book is available from the British Library.

A catalog record for this book is available from the Library of Congress.

ISBN:	HB:	978-1-3503-3837-1
	PB:	978-1-3503-3841-8
	ePDF:	978-1-3503-3838-8
	eBook:	978-1-3503-3839-5

Typeset by Integra Software Services Pvt. Ltd.

For product safety related questions contact productsafety@bloomsbury.com.

To find out more about our authors and books visit www.bloomsbury.com
and sign up for our newsletters.

Contents

List of Figures	vi
List of Tables	vii
Acknowledgments	viii
Introduction	1

Part 1 Designs and Desires

1	Designs: Multiliteracies as a Paradigm for Language-Culture Study	23
2	Desires: Affect and Aesthetics in Literacy and Language Learning	63

Intermezzo: Second Language Literacy as Designs and Desires — 101

Part 2 Play and Poetics: Toward a Critical-Affective Approach to Multiliteracies

3	Learning by Designs and Desires: Toward a Playful Pedagogy of Multiliteracies	107

Introduction to the Classroom-Based Chapters: Multiliteracy at Play — 133

4	Poetic Play in a German Language-Culture Classroom	135
5	Translation Play in a Spanish Language-Culture Classroom	151
6	Speculative Play in an Italian Language-Culture Classroom	169

Conclusion: A Critical-Aesthetic Multiliteracy Pedagogy for the Language-Culture Classroom — 183

Notes	191
Bibliography	195
Index	221

Figures

1	Three-part model of design	29
2	Pedagogical acts/knowledge processes	32
3	Language figure	103
4	Types of design play	118
5	Sample from Yazmin's PSA	158
6	Sample from Julieta's PSA	165
7	Sample from Carla's presentation slides	176
8	Tommaso's masks	179

Tables

1	Sample reading activities and corresponding pedagogical acts	45
2	Comparison of learning activities in multiliteracy models	47
3	Linguistic and visual metafunctions in Halliday's and Kress/van Leeuwen's frameworks	54
4	Curriculum overview for "Gateway to German Studies: Encounters in Language"	85
5	Learning activities in multiliteracy pedagogies/learning activities at play	132
6	Overview of Alcázar Silva's (2022) curriculum for "Introduction to Translation and Interpretation: Social Justice and Practice"	154

Acknowledgments

I have had the fortunate opportunity to play with the ideas in this book alongside many amazing students, colleagues, and friends over the years. I am incredibly grateful to students in the German language program at the University of Arizona for teaching me about languages and language education every bit as much as I taught any of them. I also want to thank the students of Spanish and Italian whose creativity inspired my thinking and whose work is showcased in Chapters 5 and 6.

Guiding each of these language classrooms was a graduate student teacher-scholar, whose own pedagogical designs and desires shaped the languaging and learning of their students and my understanding of what multiliteracy can look like. These graduate students have been my thought partners, my critical friends, and my collaborators over the last more than a decade. I want to thank all the graduate assistant teachers in German Studies for the many cohort meetings and class visits that have been my fieldwork and playground, with special recognition of Laurie Clark, Richmond Embeywa, Björn Kaspar, Kristin Lange, Patrick Ploschnitzki, Diane Richardson, and Chelsea Timlin, for their willingness to experiment with me. Borbi Gaspar, whose Italian classroom is the case study for Chapter 6, has been my co-conspirator and colleague now for longer than she was my student, and she has continually reminded me why the work we do as university-level language educators is important, powerful, and quite often even fun. Sara Alcázar Silva's Spanish translation class is showcased in Chapter 5; much of what I know about the seriousness of play and the power of symbolic competence comes from my conversations with her. Amanda Schufflebarger's work on critical creativity is woven into my own theoretical thinking around multiliteracy play, and she has shown me in so many ways what it means to teach and research with integrity.

As a co-director of the Center for Educational Resources in Culture, Language and Literacy (CERCLL) for the last several years, I have had the tremendous opportunity to learn from people in a wide range of positions who are doing the work of building and strengthening language and culture education. I cannot possibly name them all, but the classroom teachers, project leaders, presenters, language advocates, Department of Education staffers, and teacher educators, whom I have met through this work, have taught me so much about the rich ecosystem within which classroom-based practice is located. I am particularly indebted to CERCLL's core team, Beatrice Dupuy and Kate Mackay, for welcoming me to the table and providing a rich little microcosm for intellectual thinking around multiliteracies and intercultural learning. Through CERCLL, I was also able to connect with Carl Blyth and Joanna Luks, who became my collaborators for the *Foreign Languages and the Literary in the Everyday* project. So much of my current thinking around play and poetics has developed over our conversations in Austin and elsewhere.

I also want to acknowledge the support I received through an ACTFL Research Priorities Award, for the study described in Chapter 4, and the generosity of the editors of *Second Language Research and Practice*, who allowed me to reproduce images included in Chapter 6.

Finally, I want to shout out my appreciation to the Bloomsbury editorial team, especially Laura Gallon and Maria Giovanna Brauzzi, for their guidance and patience.

Introduction

Language Learning—An Aesthetic Education?

Several years ago, I was teaching an introductory seminar on second language teaching and learning for first-year graduate students, who were pursuing degrees in a range of modern language, literature, and culture departments across campus. Because the course was specifically intended for graduate students who were just starting out as or would soon serve as the primary instructors for beginning and intermediate language courses in their respective programs, teaching methods were a primary focus, although the course curriculum also attempted to provide a basic foundation in second language learning theories. One of the earliest assigned readings was Krashen's well-known and much-cited article on the affective filter (1982), which always resonated with the cohorts of very early or pre-service teachers in their first year of MA and Ph.D programs, who could readily grasp how emotions like anxiety and excitement must saturate their professional fields. After all, such feelings were practically bouncing off the walls of the seminar room. Following our discussion of Krashen, we made our way through a series of readings chosen to capture the evolutions over the past several decades in proficiency-based and other meaning-oriented approaches to second language teaching and learning. From Hymes' (1972) theories of communicative competence and the associated pedagogical frameworks developed by second language studies scholars (e.g., Breen and Candlin 1980; Canale and Swain 1980; Omaggio-Hadley 1986) into discussions of interculturality as a communicative competence (e.g., Byram 1997) or a reflective-critical discourse practice (e.g., Diaz 2013; Kramsch 1993, 2006; Levine and Phipps 2011) and then into discussions of literacy and language teaching (e.g., Kern 2000; Paesani Allen and Dupuy 2015; Thorne and Reinhardt 2008), a recurring theme was that language learning—and consequently *good* language teaching—relies on engagement with meaningful language use. In a reading journal entry, one of the students in the class, Sasha,[1] pointed to something that had long been an unarticulated discomfort of my own and which echoed a discussion in second language education that has received increasing attention in recent years. Sasha questioned how language education, as represented by the articles we had read, could both promote meaningful language use and simultaneously compel educators to diminish any negative feelings that students might experience. Noting that meaningful language is often infused with a range of affective responses outside the classroom, she argued that "students should be put in uncomfortable situations to perform. Because even though it may prove very difficult, the classroom is still the safest environment where there is the least amount of judgment and criticism." At the heart of Sasha's critique was a question: how could contemporary scholarship on second language teaching preach the importance of meaning-centered approaches and not recognize that meaningful acts of language use are often ineluctably rich with affect?

Over the last couple of decades, a growing body of scholars in second language teaching and learning and applied linguistics has paid renewed attention to those affective dimensions of language and culture learning, with many arguing that the personal, subjective, and aesthetic aspects of learning a new language are not a bug in our internal language acquisition systems, but rather an essential and significant feature of language as it is lived, through human relations with one another, the world, and themselves (e.g., Levine 2020; Lytra et al. 2022; Phipps and Gonzalez 2004; Ros i Solé 2016; van Lier 2004). Across their different theoretical frames and points of emphasis, there is a shared argument in these conversations that language teaching must start from the lifeworlds of language learners and other language users (Rowsell and Pahl 2020, 1; Phipps and Gonzalez 2004; Ros i Solé 2016) while expanding their imaginative potential through the translingual exploration of "not only new words, but also new worlds" (paraphrasing Kern 2000), both actual and imagined. This kind of humanistic approach to language education necessarily bears ethical implications because it engages with the values and ascriptions of meaning inherent in people's interpretations within lived experiences of language and communication (see also Leung and Scarino 2016, 89), as these come into play in intersubjective encounters between people in different and often unequal subject positions (Kramsch 2011, 360; Kramsch, Zarate, and Levy 2008). In characterizing language learning as **not** most centrally a new way to talk about what the world is, but rather as new ways to express and think about what the world means, there is potential for envisioning how it might be otherwise. This principle that language shapes not only how we communicate, but how we make *sense* (read: meanings and feelings) of human activities and our environments has led some in language education to argue that the second language-culture classroom is an ideal space for realizing humanistic learning goals, including those related to social justice and peace building (e.g., Levine 2020, 76–99; Oxford et al. 2020). Such an approach to language teaching and learning precludes assertions that the teacher's role is to mitigate any and all emotions that are not unambiguously positive; along with the joys and pleasures come the sensations of duress, discomfort, and even pain experienced when stepping into meanings and affective spaces where we are not at home (see Boler and Zembylas 2003; Zembylas 2015).

Discourses around language learning are often caught in a set of binary oppositions—between instrumental and interpretive, practical skill and humanistic inquiry, critical thinking and personal response. Approaches to language and culture teaching and learning that center affect and aesthetics also deliberately work to deconstruct these dichotomies by recognizing that what is being enacted even in the most seemingly practically oriented instances of language use is not just the exchange of information, but also "the experiences, lifeworlds, and ethical values of the participants" (Leung and Scarino 2016, 88). Accordingly, Kramsch has argued that *communicative competence*, which has dominated pedagogical paradigms for second language study since the 1980s, ought to be augmented with a notion of *symbolic competence*, including a focus "on what words index and what they reveal about social identities, individual and collective memories, emotions and aspirations" (2011, 357). To echo the point Sasha made in her reflection journal, feeling our way through things is as innately human as language itself, and affect and aesthetics are central to language and culture education, not instead of or in spite of but enmeshed with any understanding of language learning as oriented toward language *use*.

If a practical education is concerned with developing a capacity to act in the world, the ways in which people move others and are themselves moved by language and other culturally shaped systems of meaning are necessarily part and parcel of such a model of language teaching. Arguing for the place of the humanities in the era of globalization, Spivak (2012) rewrites Schiller's (1795) case for an aesthetic education, sharing in his belief that the kinds of play found in (but not only in) literature and art allow one to shuttle between rationality and emotionality, while also "sabotaging" (Spivak 2012, 2) his case that this enables a form of transcendent freedom. For Spivak, the hope of an aesthetic education is that it can help us learn to live with the double binds of society. While she is not positioned within conversations around additional language learning per se, Spivak's idea of an aesthetic education is intimately wound up with a model of linguistic diversity; her overarching argument is that although we are necessarily always located in a perspective, by entering into the texts of others' worlds (Spivak 2012, 433) we can challenge the illusion of uniformity that globalization fosters and gain insight into multiplicity of languages and meanings at play in the world. The resulting double subjectivity and the forms of affect that emerge when one's own perspective is provisionally set aside but not rescinded are similar to Kramsch's theorization of the multilingual subjectivities of language learners, whom she characterizes as possessing heightened reflexivity and aesthetic sensibility (Kramsch 2009). Understood as pedagogical practice that fosters individuals' capabilities as multilingual subjects, language teaching and learning must be understood as not provisionally but inherently a kind of aesthetic education, where a sensibility to the perceptions, senses, and emotion that underlie expressions and ascriptions of meaning is both a means and an end.

Multi-perspectives in Second Language-Culture Teaching

It is no coincidence that attention to affect and aesthetics in language in second language studies runs parallel to a booming interest in multilingualism, multiliteracies, and multimodality. Inspired by a set of intersecting discussions in education and applied linguistics that have developed over the last two decades, there has been a steady paradigm shift toward approaches to language education, which envision language as a dynamic repertoire of resources for making meaning in and out of the world (e.g., Kramsch 1993, 2006; van Lier 2004). The pedagogical frameworks that have developed from this body of work have collectively emphasized that language learners are not most importantly acquiring new words but diverse ways of making meaning—through language and other culturally embedded semiotic systems, such as images, gestures, and sounds (e.g., Kern 2000; Paesani, Allen, and Dupuy 2016; Swaffar and Arens 2005). Because of this attention to the multiplicity of both potential meanings and modalities, many scholars have adopted the term "multiliteracies" from the New London Group's 1996 education manifesto as a shorthand for these approaches. I will adopt both the jargon and general theoretical framework of multiliteracies as a conceptual foundation for the pedagogical perspective of *multiliteracy play* espoused in this book, while also offering the critique that current models of what multiliteracies look like in practice need to more fully attend to the affective and aesthetic dimensions referenced in the previous section. Chapter 1 presents a detailed discussion of how multiliteracies has been taken up as a concept in second language studies, tracing its genealogy from educational scholarship, and Chapter 2 introduces additional conceptual frameworks for thinking about affect. However, to position the current intervention in these broader discussions within the larger context of contemporary discussions of applied linguistics and language development, it helps to recognize that multiliteracies is one of a cluster of what we might call *multi*-perspectives that have shaped the field of second language teaching over the past few decades and to consider the conceptual implications of this paradigm.

What has been described as a multilingual *turn* (May 2013) in applied linguistics and language education is characterized by an increased focus on plurality and hybridity (e.g., Blommaert 2010; Canagarajah 2013; Gramling 2021; Kubota 2016). This intellectual trend cannot be fully attributed to the shifting socio-political landscape, as it has evolved over the last few decades; however, the crossing of geographical boundaries both physically, through patterns of mass migration that began to take shape in the late twentieth century, and virtually, through the rise of digital communications media has certainly influenced how scholars talk about multilingualism and its relation to other forms of semiodiversity including multimodality. As with all "turns" and "shifts" in academic discourse, however, changing paradigms do not mark a complete break from what has come before (Dupuy and Michelson 2019). Ongoing conversations about disciplinary bifurcations and contestations point to the persistence of many of the same dichotomies that have held fast since the 1990s.

Freire (2007[1970]) has asserted that methodological failings can always be traced back to the ideologies that underlie them. Taking stock of the current moment, we can identify three different intersecting levels or domains across which these ideologies operate:

- Language ideologies
- Learning ideologies
- Learner ideologies

In what follows, I trace each of these ideologies, connecting them back to the discourses of the mid-1990s, the climate within which this broader "multi/plural turn" (Kubota 2016) in language education and applied linguistics was first percolating, in order not only to show (in the last section of this chapter) how multiliteracies pedagogies attempt to resolve or at least sit astride these discussions, but also to draw attention to some aspects of literacy and language learning that I believe have remained under-examined or have evaded critical prodding in contemporary discussions.

Language Ideologies

One of the most pernicious dichotomies in second language studies is that between native speakers/non-native speakers. This binary is assumed in theoretical concepts from applied linguistics, such as "interlanguage" (Selinker 1972) and educational paradigms that have tended to place learners on a trajectory where the goal is a construct called "native-like competency" (Kramsch 1993, 9; compare NCSSFL/ACTFL 2017; European Council 2001, 2018). The ideal of native-ness has been heavily critiqued in the ensuing years alongside challenges to modernist notions of languages and language use as bounded and individuated (see Kubota 2016, 474). This segregationist (Harris 1998) view of language can be found in the metaphor of "language acquisition," which positions language as a thing in the world that can be possessed, as well as in the constitution of language programs and departments around a single language. Programs in Chinese and Arabic, where the question of which of many possible languages is being taught under these designations, reveal quickly—perhaps even more quickly than their European linguistic counterparts—how ill-fitting this reification of language truly is; but there is always an implicit standardizing process behind the identification of *a language* as unitary (Liddicoat 2005). As Liddicoat and Scarino (2013) note, "This standardized, regularized variety becomes *the* language and education focuses on the dissemination of this language to both native speakers and to new learners" (12).

Given the close correlation between standardization and structural ideologies of language, it also stands to reason that more recent moves toward pluralism and multiplicity represent not only a quantitative but also a qualitative difference in conceptualization. Pluralizing view of language can be found in a range of terms and concepts that have established themselves as part of the shared parlance of applied linguistics and second language studies during the 2000s, e.g., code-switching, -mixing, and -meshing (Canagarajah 2006; Rampton 1999); metrolingualism (Otsuji and Pennycook 2010); translanguaging (Creese and Blackledge 2015; García and Sylvan 2011; Li 2018 and 2022). These concepts stress not only variation in language but also fluidity between what are often identified as bounded languages. The unboundedness and interwovenness of languages are often indexed by a preference for terms like *languaging*, which positions language as an activity rather than an object (e.g., Swain and Watanabe 2013; Phipps and Gonzalez 2004), and *repertoire*, which places language among other semiotic resources in a constellation of conventionalized but imminently adaptable meaning-making practices. (There are some clear conceptual affinities between this and the notion of *design* from the New London Group, which is discussed in detail in Chapter 1.) While it would hardly be inaccurate to describe all these concepts under the header *multilingualism*, they also capture activities for which that label may be too "abstract, exclusionary, coarse, or programmatic to attend adequately" (Gramling 2021, 28). This is especially the case because *multilingualism* comes with its own dichotomous companion—*monolingualism*—and this very contrast re-assumes that languages are enumerable and discrete.

When languages are understood not as closed linguistic systems but as embedded in and interdependent from human activity, language use and learning begin to be viewed more holistically and spatially. For example, ecological models consider the semiotic environments or ecosystems (Kramsch 2008; Kramsch and Steffenson 2008; Thorne, Fischer, and Lu 2012; van Lier 2004) within which languaging activities take place. Summarizing these models as they have developed within second language acquisition and applied linguistics research, Kramsch (2008) notes that they all view language learning as "an emergent phenomenon, triggered by the availability of affordances in the environment, heavily dependent on an individual's perception of these affordances and his/her willingness to participate actively in their use" (23). Drawing heavily on the critical theories of Deleuze and Guattari (whose theories on affect are discussed further in Chapter 2), Pennycook (2017, 2018) has proposed the concept of *epistemic assemblages* as an alternate view for understanding languages. For Pennycook, "[t]his opens up alternative ways of thinking that focuses not so much on language use in particular contexts—as if languages preexist their instantiation in particular places, having been carried around by people as mobile language containers—but rather on the ways in which particular assemblages of objects, linguistic resources and places come together" (Pennycook 2018, 129).

Li's (2011, 2018, 2022) notion of *translanguaging space* similarly brings multimodality and multisensorality together with translanguaging practices in ways that resonate with both ecosystem and assemblage framings but emphasize the transformative potential of meaning making. "Translanguaging is not simply going *between* different linguistic structures, cognitive and semiotic systems and modalities, but going *beyond* them," Li writes.

> The act of Translanguaging creates a social space for the language user by bringing together different dimensions of their personal history, experience, and environment; their attitude, belief, and ideology; their cognitive and physical capacity, into one coordinated and meaningful performance ... and this

> Translanguaging Space has its own transformative power because it is forever evolving and combines and generates new identities, values and practices.
>
> (Li 2011, 23)

Translanguaging as conceptualized by Li is simultaneously a practice and a perspective; it can entail visible behaviors like "code switching" and "code meshing" but in shifting attention from discrete, standardized languages to individuals' full repertoire of semiotic resources and meanings, it also incorporates a much wider scope of what counts as multilingualism. The transformative potential of translanguaging for Wei is not in the ability to mediate between systems, but in the translingual, transmodal assemblage that becomes more than its parts. (See also Futro 2022 for an example of these concepts put into pedagogical practice.)

Looking at this collection of pluralizing conceptualizations of language and language use with all their nuances and incongruities as part of a broader trend, a thread that runs through them is a close association with poststructuralist and postcolonial epistemologies (Kubota 2016; McNamara 2012; Makoni and Pennycook 2005; Pennycook 2010). McNamara (2012), noting this same connection, suggests a relationship between poststructuralism's questioning of stable truths and structures and a sustained critique of current social, political, and cultural forms, which brings with it an ethical commitment to social justice (477). Advocating for what he calls a "human ecological approach," Levine (2020) makes a similar case; in his view, understanding language as a complex system, used by people who are themselves complex systems interacting within complex social systems, allows educators to see the transformative power of even seemingly mundane aspects of language, in that they are indexical of larger cultural discourses and hierarchies of meaning. This aligns with an earlier point made by Phipps and Gonazalez (2004) that languages—and therefore language learning—"are always a social justice issue" because they are part of "the richness of human being" (xv).

Multi-perspectives, for all their flair of progressivism, are not necessarily incongruous with modernist frameworks. Multilingualism and pluricompetences often show up in both professional and public discourses around language learning and teaching to describe more a diversified portfolio of skills (see de Costa 2019; Heller 2010; Warner, Gaspar, and Diao 2021) than the manifold, complex human activities described by the various scholars cited in this section. Scholars such as Kubota (2016) and Flores (2013) have cautioned that notions of hybridity and celebrations of multilingualism are not de facto subversive, but rather often reinforce privileged statuses and neoliberal, individualistic forms of diversity, which actually perpetuate racism and other forms of discrimination. Within this view, languages are valued first and foremost as commodities that secure economic, diplomatic, and self-fulfillment benefits for the individuals who speak them and for the nation states they serve (Heller 2010; Heller and McElhinny 2017). Gramling (2020) has noted that tech industries have also experienced a "multilingual turn" in recent decades, but one characterized more by glocalization and "translatable linguistic commodities" (25), than the rich lived experiences of human beings. Gramling (2021) builds on this point to argue that multilingualism may be in need of *right-sizing* "for the needs and experiences people actually express interest in it" (45); in educational contexts, multilingualism, as something that can be taught, fostered, or developed would need to account for the norms and discourses through which languages and language learning are viewed, as well as the subjective desires—"the manifestation of the world-making desires and social needs"—people bring with them into the classroom (48).

The disruption of modernist and monolingual ideologies is thus not a de facto effect of multiplicitous views of language, but is tied intimately to ideologies of language use, and consequently language learning, and with our understandings of the language learners engaged in this pursuit.

Learning Ideologies

Understandings of language and models of language learning develop in tandem, but not always symmetrically. The history of the last few decades of second language teaching and learning has been dominated by two tensions that Kramsch (1993) characterizes as dichotomies between *grammar and communication* (4–5) and *language and culture* (8–9). At the core in both cases are the structuralist, modernist ideologies referenced in the previous section, but paradigms of language learning have also been shaped by tendencies in modern language education since the 1980s to valorize *doing* over *thinking*, and moreover to hold these in stark contrast to one another. This can be found in the US-American proficiency movements and in the European "direct methods" for language teaching, as well as in the broader frameworks for communicative language teaching that dominate contemporary pedagogies in many parts of the world. For the purposes of the current discussion of multiliteracies pedagogies, changing ideologies in relation to second language literacy development can serve as a case study of how these ideologies weave through evolving understandings of language learning.

In the 1970s and 1980s, discussions of second language reading were dominated by comprehension-oriented models. In the United States, a significant influence was the research of Krashen, which treated reading as first and foremost an important source of comprehensible input (e.g., Krashen et al 1984; Krashen and Terrell 1983). The primary purpose of reading comprehension according to this model is to foster the natural acquisition of language, and thus reading was disconnected from the social contexts of use which functional approaches attempt to integrate. As communicative language teaching became a dominant paradigm in the 1980s, many scholars acknowledged the social nature of reading, but positioned it primarily in the service of functional communication skills, that is, students' "ability to cope with the written messages that surround them in a foreign country and that affect their behavior" (Phillips 1978, 281). Whether it is the acquisition of new structures and vocabulary or as a tool for getting around, comprehension-oriented models of reading share a sense that texts are something to get through as a means to other ends, what Kramsch describes as a dichotomy between reading-to-learn and learning-to-read (1993, 6–7).

Vocabulary knowledge and linguistic complexity were often highlighted in discussions of text selection and pedagogy in these early discussions, but beginning in the mid-1980s studies began to focus attention on another aspect of reading in a new language, namely the role of background knowledge (see Bernhardt 1991). Drawing from research in first language reading and English as a second language contexts, scholars (e.g., Carrell 1984; Rumelhart 1980) make a case for more "top-down approaches" to literacy, which entailed in essence a recognition that people attempt to understand new information, be it written or spoken, by first trying to fit it into what they already know about the world. This includes topical background knowledge (e.g., Nunan 1985), but also cultural schema related to language use (e.g., Pritchard 1990). As Bensoussan (1986) argued, "Language proficiency alone does not guarantee the understanding of a text. The reader also needs to be aware of the differences between written texts in the foreign and the native language" (1986, 400). Within these discussions we can find some elements of literacy as social practice and even an emergent interest in how meanings are designed in different linguistic communities, but there is still a tendency to treat the structure of language as relatively prescriptive and as distinct from communicative or cultural content.

In the 1990s, a shift in thinking began to take place within which the socially and culturally situated nature of texts became less of another hurdle to comprehension and more of an important locus for different dimensions of learning. Kramsch's work was emblematic and influential for this as were many of the same applied linguistic and anthropological theories that were inspiring concurrent scholarship in education and literacy studies. Prominent among them are Halliday's (1978) systemic functional linguistics and work in linguistic anthropology by Hymes (1972). As language was being conceptualized as dynamic, complex, and socially embedded, there was a growing sense that comprehension alone was not a satisfying learning goal, accompanied by an interest and emphasis in the role of interpretation and analysis in language learning. As Widdowson (1978) argued, interpretation underlies all forms of language use: "You cannot talk ... without interpreting, but you can interpret without talking" (67). Two seminal works on from the early 1990s similarly advocate for an emphasis on interpretation in second language curricula: *Reading for Meaning: An Integrated Approach to Language Learning* (1991) by Swaffar, Arens, and Byrnes and Kramsch's already mentioned *Context and Culture in Language Teaching* (1993). Both books advocate for discourse perspectives, connecting form to culturally instantiated meanings and, echoing Widdowson, point to the need for more integrative or holistic approaches to second language reading that synthesizes cognitive, text-linguistic, and social dimensions. These publications give early voice to the concerns about curricular divides that become more consistently thematized in the 2000s; by emphasizing interpretation, analysis, and reflection from the beginning levels of instruction and by attending to the discursive (i.e., linguistic) construction of the cultural, historical, and literary studies content that makes up many upper-division programs these scholars also propose frameworks for connecting the common interests of the scholars and educators working in these domains. As Swaffar has elsewhere argued, whatever their differences, these disciplines are connected a shared concern with larger questions of how "individuals and groups use words and other sign systems in context to intend, negotiate, and create meanings" (Swaffar 1999, 157).

Discourse or meaning-oriented approaches effectively deconstruct the assumed binary between practical and interpretive or reflective learning by advocating for reflective doing. Although they are rarely explicit, there are some connections here to discussions in applied linguistics and language education around the role of language awareness (Carter 2003; Svalberg 2007 and 2012). In contrast to early research on language awareness (e.g., Schmidt 2001), not only the learners' noticing is being engaged, but their awareness of form-meaning connections, to polysemy and levels of meaning, to the social and cultural discourses they index, and to the ways in which language shapes realities in sometimes more conventional, sometimes more subversive ways.

A direct implication of the emphasis on interpretation and reflection was a new potential role for texts. As there was a growing sense that comprehension alone was rather satisfying as a learning goal, there was a need to slow down student engagements with language, and to make space for analysis and careful contemplation. Texts (including instances of entextualized spoken language), on account of their transmissibility and their relative stability, are ideally suited for attending to these activities.

This re-engagement with texts in language curricula also relates closely to another conversation prominent in scholarship advocating for literacy-oriented language curricula; one of the most common critiques voiced as part of an argument for integrating literacy and multiliteracies into second language pedagogy is that it helps to rebalance an overemphasis on oral language use that has developed within communicative language teaching since the 1980s (e.g., Kern 2000; Kern and Schulz 2005; Paesani, Allen, and Dupuy 2016) and has its roots in traditions of structural linguistics (Ong 1982, 5). Of course, reading and writing were not altogether missing from even the earliest work on communicative language teaching (e.g., Lee and vanPatten 1995; Omaggio-Hadley 1986); however, one result of language learning ideologies that prioritize comprehension and fluency, and relegate literacy to the functional service of these communicative goals, has been an underemphasis on the differences between orality and literacy (Ong 1982). Without falling prey to another dubious dichotomy, we can view orality and literacy as distinct modalities, which are often associated with specific genres and social practices, even if there is also movement and interdependence between orate and literate language use in the flow of activity (see Kern and Schulz 2005). At the same time, attention to oral and written modalities, not as distinct skills, but as differently mediated modalities of language, also makes it possible to recognize the potential of hybrid practices. For example, some scholars (Bredella and Delanoy 1996; Kern and Schulz 2005; Kramsch 1993, 2011; Hallet 2009) have argued that literature offers opportunities for exploring the stories and discourses of a language community and language features that are absent from or underrepresented within more propositional genres, including spoken language varieties as they are represented in the direct discourse of characters. Digital literacy practices also actively disrupt clear divides between spoken and written language conventions by introducing orate forms of speech into everyday written forms of communication like text messages and chats (Kern 2014).

Understandings of literacy as social practice recognize that second language literacy is not only about "what texts mean in an absolute sense, [but] what people mean by texts" and also "what texts mean to people who belong to different discourse communities" (Kern 2000, 2). The second point here, emphasizing differences between socially inculcated ways of making meaning, draws a direct connection between second language and intercultural learning (see Liddicoat and Scarino 2013 for a wider history of these discussions). Models of intercultural communicative competence, most notably those inspired by the early work of Byram (1997), had already contributed to an established tradition of considering intercultural learning as integral to language learning; the continuing effect of this work can be seen readily in the descriptors formulated in the Common European Framework (2001) and its companion volume (2018), both published by the European Council, and in the most recently released NCSSFL-ACTFL Can-do Statements (2017) used widely in North America. However, conceptualizations of literacy and of discourse as a set of relationships, of patterned linguistic and other semiotic practices that are tied together and reflect particular communities and their affinities have developed in tandem with critical poststructuralist (re-)theorizations of interculturality that are less concerns with *cultural facts*, including relative stable notions of cultural practice, and are more concerned with culture as dynamic symbolic systems through which people mutually create and interpret meanings (e.g., Liddicoat 2004; Liddicoat and Crozet 2000; Liddicoat and Scarino 2013; Kramsch 1993; Risager 2006, 2007). Social practice in such a view is not an established, predetermined set of ways of speaking and acting, but rather "a situated process of dealing with the problems of social life" (Liddicoat and Scarino 2013, 21). This also entails, as Kramsch has compellingly and continually argued, a recognition that language and other ways of making meaning do not simply respond to but actively shape cultural contexts (see Kramsch 1993 and 2011; Kramsch and Whiteside 2008). As we will discuss in the next section, this view of language and culture also brings with it, perforce, particular ideas about the positionality of language learners.

Learner Ideologies

One of the core pedagogical principles in contemporary language education is that teaching should be learner centered. Centering the learner may be widely accepted as the clear and common good in contemporary language pedagogy; however, it sometimes seems that there are about as many diverse interpretations as to what exactly this means or entails as there are individual learners. These range from learner-centeredness as a general curriculum development orientation (e.g., Nunan 1985, 2012) to an impetus to foster learner autonomy and differentiation (e.g., Benson 2012) to awareness that classrooms inevitably include a diverse body of learners (e.g., Anya 2020; Lau 2016; Warner, Gaspar, Diao 2021). Learner-centered language teaching has found theoretical validation in communicative and proficiency-oriented language learning as active participation, interaction, and engagement in real-world tasks became pedagogical desiderata, as well as in learning models grounded in sociocultural theory and constructivism, which center the learners' active role in knowledge construction. However, in addition to setting up a false binary that encourages educators to side-step questions of what choices might contribute to *learning-centered teaching* (Johnson 2022), discussions of learner-centered teaching tend to conceive of learners as relatively generic, thereby reducing their humanity to their role as those who learn (Firth and Wagner 1997).

As Liddicoat and Kern (2011) demonstrate through their brief history of perspectives on the learner in methods of language instruction, as early as the audio-lingual methods of the 1950s and 1960s, learners were positioned as speakers, but it was with the advent of linguistic anthropological influences, including perhaps most saliently Hymes' theories of communicative competence, that they were also viewed as social actors. The pedagogical implication was that *learners* must be given opportunities to occupy a range of different speaking roles in different social situations; whereas *learners as speakers* were often relegated to what Goffman (1981) has described as animator roles, giving voice to rote learned, chunks of language, *learners as speaker/actors* are given opportunities to author the form and content of their utterances. Liddicoat and Kern (2011) also note that the notion of speaker/actor upsets ideas that learning happens along established, standardizable trajectories in a linear progression "insofar as it emphasizes the contingencies, subjectivity and flexibility of the speaking subject" (20).

Attention to the diversity and heterogeneity of language learners has replaced the deceptively fixed signified "the learner" in much of pedagogical and applied linguistic theory and hearkened more of a "first-person perspective" (Busch 2017, 50) in second language studies and applied linguistics. Norton's theories of identity, investment, and imagination have been highly influential in this body of work. For Norton, identity must be defined relationally; it involves "how a person understands his or her relationship to the world, how that relationship is structured across time and space, and how the person understands possibilities for the future" (Norton 2013, 45). Drawing on Bourdieu's (1977) sociological concept of symbolic capital and on feminist theorist Weedon's

(1987) poststructuralist understanding of subjectivity, Norton argues that when learners invest time, energy, emotions, labor, etc., in a language they do so as part of a process of ongoing self-construction (see Norton 2013; Norton and Darvin 2015). Identity construction is itself caught up in struggles for symbolic and material resources and recognition, where language classrooms are not neutral spaces, but instead often reflect and refract other social power structures. These include those garnered by specific languages and the kinds of symbolic capital that might be afforded by identifying—or not identifying—as a speaker of those languages, even as this tendency for people to invest in language-specific identities in their social worlds is at odds with the poststructuralist anti-entity views discussed in the previous section on ideologies of language.

Kramsch's previously mentioned conceptualization of the multilingual subject shares some of the same theoretical inspirations as Norton's identity model—and indeed both scholars have mutually influenced one another's work. Kramsch's work on subjectivity developed from the thinking she began in *Context and Culture in Language Teaching* (1993), where she started to consider the complexity, fluidity, and ofttimes ambivalence of the positions taken up by teachers and learners in the hybrid "third space" of the classroom. Kramsch (2009), like Norton, is concerned with how one's sense of self is ensnared in struggles for recognition and cultural capital, but she also emphasizes the potential of the imagination in constituting oneself as a subject. This allows her to devote more attention to the tactics and forms of subversion that multilingual subjects take up in interaction with their environments, but also to the place of the aesthetic and affective dimensions of meaning making and language use in our sense of sense of ourselves vis-à-vis others.

Reflecting on the scholarship on language and identity and subjectivity that has developed in recent decades, Ros i Solé (2016) notes that fields of second language acquisition/development and applied linguistics have only just begun "to build a view of the language subject grounded on contemporary understandings of the learner as a human being" (14; see also Dervin and Risager 2014; Levine 2020; Phipps and Gonzalez 2004), which has also meant that the complexity of learners' social and personal lives has been severely neglected. Applied linguistics and language education, like many other fields, has in recent years faced a long overdue reckoning with the extent to which racialized identities and intersectional identities have been historically excluded from research and inquiry. There has consequently been a growing understanding of the broad range of ways race shapes language learning experiences (e.g., Anya 2020 and 2022; Anya and Rudolph 2019; Kubota and Lin 2009; Rosa and

Flores 2017). Parallel to and at times at intersection with this work is a growing body of scholarship on how LGBTQ+ identities are frequently made invisible through language educational materials and teaching practices (e.g., Coda 2017; Liddicoat 2009; Paiz 2018, 2019). This is particularly pronounced in the case of trans, non-binary, and gender non-conforming individuals, whose identities are sometimes deliberately erased in the name of linguistic and cultural conventions (Knisely 2020 and 2021; Knisely and Paiz 2021). As these scholars and others make abundantly clear, how we account for the "diverse diversities" (Dervin 2015) of language learners must be at the heart of any pedagogical model.

Attention to learner identities and subjectivities consequently raises questions about what kind of multilingual subjects students in modern language classrooms desire to be—and whether the forms of advocacy language programs and agencies tend to adopt speak to their imaginations (see Gaspar 2020; Warner 2011 and 2018). In promotional materials and public policy documents, language learners, especially those in anglophone-dominant countries, are often positioned first and foremost as enterprising multilingual subjects, whose ability to adapt to different linguistic and cultural contexts will enable them to live and work across the globalized markets of late capitalism (Flores 2013; Heller and McElhinny 2017); however, recent studies of US-based learners of languages other than English show that this commodity-centered framing is often at odds with learners' experiences and desires, which are frequently far less calculating than market-driven discourses of language learning might suggest (see Anya 2020; Looney and Lusin 2019; Warner, Gaspar, and Diao 2021). Flores (2013) has argued that neoliberalism manifests itself in individual subjectivities by promoting the ideal of an *enterprising-self*—"an autonomous, flexible, and innovative subject" who is able to rapidly adapt (503). As indicated earlier, there is evidence that the neoliberal takes on language and multilingualism that are complicit in the construction of language learners as primarily *enterprising subjects,* reducing the complexity of their multilingual lives to consumers and entrepreneurs, have contributed significantly to the maintenance and intensification of inequities related to race and class (see Anya 2020; Flores 2013; Kubota 2016).

An alternative positionality is offered by Phipps and Gonzalez (2004) in their book *Modern Languages*, where they propose a more pointedly provocative version of the speaker/actor notion discussed by Liddicoat and Kern (2011), envisaging learners as first and foremost *languagers:*

> "Languagers," for us, are those people, we may even term them "agents" or "language activists," who engage actively with the world, and for whom language

learning [teaching/researching] is a way of embarking on the risky business of stepping out of one's habitual ways of speaking and acting in order to engage with others whose modes of speech and action are other.
(Phipps and Gonzalez interview with Crosbie 2005, 295)

Phipps and Gonzalez's characterization of the qualities possessed by *languagers* resonates with Kramsch and Whiteside's (2008) description of symbolic competence as a desideratum for language learning. They define symbolic competence as the ability to position oneself as a multilingual subject, that is, to understand the cultural memories evoked by symbolic systems, to perform and create alternative realities, and to reframe and shape the multilingual game in which one invests (662). Kramsch and Whiteside's (2008) notion of symbolic competence, which is also developed further in work from Kramsch (2011), relates to the subjective spaces inhabited by language learners and other multilingual subjects. As such there are some overlaps with Li's previously mentioned concept of translanguaging space, as an evolving, open constellation of potentials "where teachers and students can go between and beyond socially constructed language and educational systems, structures and practices to engage diverse multiple meaning-making systems and subjectivities, to generate new configurations of language and education practices, and to challenge and transform old understandings and structures" (24).

The Current Intervention: Multi-perspectives at Play

As an example of one of the *multi*-perspectives within contemporary second language studies described in the previous section, multiliteracies frameworks—which are discussed in greater detail in Chapter 1—have brought attention to the diversity of modes, media, language varieties, and discourses involved in what we often shorthand as language learning. A core concept in these discussions is the idea of meaning design, the idea that languages are dynamic, culturally shaped systems of resources for engaging with and making sense of the world. This invites a model of language teaching and learning, which centers acts of meaning design and positions learners as not only decoders or interpreters of language but more importantly as users, as themselves designers of meaning. This chapter introduces this framework and provides a brief history of its development, with particular attention to how multiliteracies has been taken up within language and culture education as a way of realizing the kinds of ideological shifts clustered together in this introduction; however, an underlying argument in this book is that academic turns are never breaks with the concepts and practices that have come before. Thus, even as this book opens by making a strong case for multiliteracies frameworks and the notion of meaning design as helpful heuristics within second language and culture education, Chapter 1 sets up a parallel claim that design, when treated as standards or conventions, can fall back into a prescriptivist paradigm in which the dynamic, manifold, and emergent qualities of the concept get lost. Relatedly, learner subjectivities become reduced to exactly that, and the subjective desires of the individuals in and beyond the classroom are too quickly conflated with the goals and intentions embedded in tasks and genres.

Chapter 2 focuses on subjective desires as they manifest through affective and aesthetic dimensions of language and literacy practices in a second language. A guiding question for this discussion is what gets missed in multiliteracies frameworks when we attend to designs at the expense of these desires. Following an overview of how affect has been theorized within the fields of applied linguistics and second language teaching and learning, I identify two main ways of thinking about affect in relation to language and literacy studies: as an unarticulated flow of intensities and sensations that move us and as an emotional stickiness that accrues through histories of contact between people, objects, and signs. For the former, I lean on scholarship inspired by the affect theories of Deleuze and Guattari, including work from affective literacy studies (e.g., Leander and Boldt 2013; Ehret 2021) that responds directly to multiliteracy theories; for the latter, I draw from the affect theory of Ahmed (2004) and scholars in applied linguistics, notably Benesch's (2017) critical perspectives on emotions in language teaching. Although these forms of affect work on different time scales, they both come into play as subjective desires through which people form aesthetic and emotional relationships with languages, texts, and literacy practices. Through two vignettes from a German as a second language classroom, I then demonstrate how these dimensions of affect manifest in instructional contexts as complex personal responses to design tasks.

The second section of the book takes up the notions of design and desires from the first two body chapters as a foundation for language-culture teaching education that locates meaningfulness in not only designs and teachable ways of designing meaning, but also in desires, our aesthetic and affective responses to language and literacy as they are lived. In answer to the question, how can we attend to those dimensions of language use and learning that resist planning, I propose pedagogies that integrate "play," understood here as both a creative, tinkering, sometimes subversive engagement with language and culture and as an essential feature of language systems, which are much more plastic and flexible than language textbooks or standardizing frameworks of assessment often convey. The opening part of this section introduces this notion and connects it to previous work on language play and language learning. The body of this chapter is divided between three dimensions of play, which run parallel to the model of design proposed in the original conceptualization of multiliteracy theory (New London Group 1996): play as the creative manipulation of the material aspects of language (e.g., sound, structure, sight, etc.), play as a bracketing off of ordinary life including everyday language and literacy activities, and play as transformative potential.

The next three chapters are located in the classroom, exploring examples from university-level language-culture classrooms where teachers and curriculum designers worked to integrate pedagogies, which encouraged multiliteracy play of some form. In the methodological spirit of affective literacy studies research and poststructuralist applied linguistics, these three chapters offer what Leander and Boldt described as "strategic sketch[es]" (2013), of moments within language classrooms that are not intended to be absolute or even "thickly" described (Geertz 1973), but instead to attune moments of unexpected intensity and heightened attention in the midst of teaching and learning activities. My access to these vignettes comes in part through the teacher-scholars who were serving as instructors for the classes, in their positions as graduate student instructors, and in part from learner compositions and reflections. In some moments, especially in the second and third of these chapters, which come from Spanish and Italian language-culture classes where the instructor was also the primary curriculum designer, I will work to integrate the voice and perspective of the instructors overtly. In the first of the chapters, where the student examples come from a German language-culture program where I was serving as the language program director at the time, my voice as the curriculum designer is present, but it has also been shaped through many dialogues with the instructors, who were my collaborators and, in many cases, also my most constructive critics. While there are certainly many choices in task design, pedagogical practice, and student composition that I—in the role of close collaborator and mentor for all of these classrooms—would like to believe are exemplary, the goal is not to present a set of best practices, but to highlight different elements of multiliteracy play that can serve as points of reflection for an ongoing conversation about how designs and desires become entangled students' wild and precious multilingual lives.[2]

The concluding chapter brings together the ideas developed throughout the rest of the book, identifying three principles of a pedagogy of designs and desires: the centering of learners' subjectivities, including their affective and aesthetic entanglements, which are being redesigned through learning a new language; making space for indeterminacy and affective dimensions of language and literacy activities; viewing language-culture education as an inherently hopeful, in that it asks of learners and teachers that they maintain an openness—an openness to meanings, sensations, the world, and their ways of thinking, feeling, and moving within it being different from what they are or what they are expected to be. As a stance for learning and teaching new languages, multiliteracy play is a way of connecting with this potential.

Part One

Designs and Desires

1

Designs

Multiliteracies as a Paradigm for Language-Culture Study

Both within the field of education, where it was first theorized, and within the field of second language teaching and learning, where it has had a significant uptake in the past two decades, the conceptual framework of *multiliteracies* came with the promise of paradigm shifts (see Dupuy and Michelson 2019). While the impulses and feelings of dissatisfaction driving scholars and practitioners to embrace multiliteracies as a core critical concept for theorizing language development and teaching practices overlap in many ways, second language teaching (and specifically the teaching of languages other than English, a.k.a. LOTEs) likewise has a particular genealogy that has shaped the kinds of conceptual work that notions of literacy and multiliteracies do in these fields (see Introduction). This chapter teases out these distinct but intersecting histories in order to explicate some of the most important contributions that multiliteracies and the associated concept of language use as meaning design have made to contemporary understandings of language teaching and learning, as well as some potential conceptual limitations for instructed language learning that they have imposed. The chapter then ends with a call for an expanded multiliteracies pedagogy for the language and culture classroom that places a weightier emphasis on the affective and aesthetic lives of learners and centers their desires alongside their attention to designs.

Multiliteracies as a Paradigm Shift in Language Education

Diversifying Literacy: Multiliteracies in Education Theory

Sociocultural Models of Literacy as Practice

As a core concept in educational theory and policy, literacy stepped into public and professional discourse in the 1970s as a contested signifier. In the introduction to their book *New Literacies: Everyday Practices and Social*

Learning (2011), education scholars Lankshear and Knobel (2011, 4) identify five interconnected factors that led literacy to take hold in educational discourses in the United States and several other anglophone countries during the 1970s and 1980s: (1) the rise of critical pedagogy inspired in particular by the thoughts of Paolo Freire and a related growing sense of class-consciousness; (2) the "literacy crisis" of the 1970s; (3) increasing academic and public recognition of the connections between literacy, economic growth, and social well-being—motivated in part by an awareness of the disparity with which the literacy crisis impacted different communities; which led to (4) the emergence of new institutional cultures of accountability within school systems and the rise of literacy as an arch-indicator for professional accountability; and (5) the spread of sociocultural theory within academic discourses of education.

The narratives of national "literacy crises" in countries like the United States, Britain, Canada, Australia, and New Zealand and a belief that literacy would be a strategic component in the development of countries in Africa, Asia, and Latin America were both shaped by social and economic shifts associated with post-industrialization and late capitalism. Like many public discussions of education, concerns about literacy were driven partly by empirical evidence and partly by moral panic, and they contributed substantially to the rise of regular standards-based testing through which schools were increasingly evaluated based on students' performance in literacy and math (sometimes among other subjects) (Lankshear and Knobel 2011, 9). Despite scholarly arguments cautioning against unfounded presumptions that literacy is determinative in social and cognitive development (Street 1984), literacy assessment developed into one of the societally sanctioned ways in which education programs could demonstrate effectiveness and prove their worth.

At the same time as public narratives of "crisis" were fueling the standardization of literacy education and assessment, professional understandings of the concept were being expanded through scholarly work in critical pedagogy and sociocultural theory. From different vantage points, both drew attention to inequities, to the situatedness of literacy (as practices), and questioned de-contextualized notions of functional literacy as a desired goal for learning. Freire's work was profoundly influential for education movements in the late 1970s and 1980s (e.g., Freire 2007[1970], 2021[1988]); among other impacts, Freire's ideas brought literacy from the realms of informal (i.e., home) education where it had previously been relegated and in doing so decentered remedializing notions of "basic" education by interrogating whose language practices had been positioned as standards. Literacy, Freire argued, must always relate to the personal and potential lives of people. "Reading the word and learning how to write the word so one can later read it are preceded by learning how to 'write' the world, that is, having the experience of changing the world and of touching the world" (Freire and Macedo 2005[1987], 9).

Heath's seminal study of early literacy development *Ways with Words: Language, Life and Work in Communities and Classrooms* (1983) can be understood at least in part as an ethnographic realization of Freire's critical literacy theories. Brice's research showed how different ways of "taking from books," that is, making sense of texts and relating those meanings to the world, are socialized within communities (defined in her study in terms of local geographies, socioeconomic disparities, and racialized identities). In the 1980s and early 1990s, sociocultural theories of literacy, such as Heath's, drew from recent work in linguistic anthropology (e.g., Hymes 1972) to conceptualize the intersections between linguistic development, social practices, and worldviews (e.g., Heath 1983; Scollon and Scollon 1981; Scribner and Cole 1981; Street 1984). As the preferred idiom, *literacy* in this body of work pointed to a deliberate break from reading research that was securely grounded in psycholinguistic frameworks. Instead, literacy in a sociocultural purview was to be understood as a social practice, that is, as "socially recognized ways of generating, communicating, and negotiating meanings" (Lankshear and Knobel 2011, 33). Thus, literacy in this sociocultural sense is located not in the minds of individuals, but in the relations between language users, texts, and contexts of use, i.e., what people do with literacies (see Barton and Hamilton 1998, 6).

One of the implications of this shift in thought was greater attention to everyday literacy practices as diverse, legitimate ways of knowing and engaging with the world. Ethnographic studies such as Heath's (1983) shed light on the diversity of everyday literacies even within close geographical range through an examination of how children from three communities within the same town learned to use language in ways that interacted with and in some cases were at odds with the expected literacy practices of their schools. As Ong meticulously documented in his 1982 book on the differences between oral and written language within their sociological contexts of use, if writing restructures consciousness in important ways, then it stood to reason that different ways of engaging with texts and textuality would structure thought in different ways. Literacy then can be understood to entail not only culturally neutral processes of decoding, as is implied in the binary distinction literate-illiterate, but what Hasan (2002) described as *invisible semiotic mediation*, i.e., unself-conscious ways in which everyday discourse mediates our dispositions, including how we tend to respond to particular situations, our beliefs about the world around us, and our sense of our place within it.

Literacy in a sociocultural view is always already embedded in a complex web of social practices, values, identities, interactions, tools, and contexts (for more comprehensive overviews of this history, see Gee 2007[1990], Chapter 3; Lankshear and Knobel 2011, Chapter 1). Relatedly, there are often social rules about who can engage with or be recognized as legitimately executing certain literacy practices (Barton and Hamilton 1998, 13). These rules can be more codified, as is often the case with legally recognized documents like a Supreme Court ruling, or more informal, as indexed in debates around the translation of Black American writer Amanda Gorman's poem "The Hill We Climb" after its recitation at President Joe Biden's inauguration in 2020.[1] In either case, however, the power of the texts is in direct relation to the recognized authority of those who composed them, and this power can be subject to contestation.

With the shift to sociocultural models of literacy also came an insistence that literacy is not a singular cognitive ability or a functional skill-set that one either does or does not possess; instead, scholars in education began to talk of *literacies* as a way of indexing the multiplicity of practices (Scribner and Cole 1981; Barton and Hamilton 1998) through which social actors engage with the world through and in relation to reading and writing and *new literacies studies* became a shorthand for the field of inquiry that advocates for such an approach (e.g., Gee 2007[1990]; Street 1984). Amidst the rise of digital communications media and composition technologies in the 1990s, this notion of *new literacies* increasingly represented not only the reality that literacy is not universal or ideologically neutral, but also an acknowledgment of the screen as our dominant text structure in the current era (Cope and Kalantzis 2000; Kress 2003). This new digital revolution brought with it both new "technical stuff" and new "ethos stuff," to borrow from Lankshear and Knobel's (2007) distinction between the functional affordances of media and the ethical-dispositional nature of technology-mediated literacy practices, e.g., that they are potentially more *participatory, collaborative,* and *distributed* (ibid, 7–9). These two aspects are not synonymous, but they are interconnected; for example, the technical capacity to remix a sample from an existing composition enables a more participatory relationship to the literacy practices one encounters, which in turn allows for the production of new creations that are more overtly collaborative and de-centers the place of an original author. At the same time, as Bolter (1990) identified early on, the relative ephemerality of digital texts that allows them to be remixed has also meant that they are not assumed to transparently represent a logical, objective truth (cf. Ong 1982) in the way that printed books have been in other moments of human history; this has repercussions for how we engage in not only the articulation but also interpretation of new literacy practices. Bolter's observation resonates differently but no less poignantly in 2022, amidst discourses of *truthiness* and enhanced technologies for deliberately doctoring digital artifacts such as photos and films—a set of conditions that have led some scholars to assert that we are coping with a "post-truth" society (McIntyre 2018).

Pluralizing Literacy: The Multiliteracies Framework of the New London Group

Building on the backdrop of sociocultural theories of literacy described in the previous section and prompted by further sociopolitical developments within the 1990s, an international collective of education and literacy scholars writing under the collective moniker the New London Group (NLG)[2] issued a manifesto in 1994 on education and literacy, titled "A Pedagogy of Multiliteracies: Designing Social Futures."[3] The "multi" in their portmanteau *multiliteracies* was intended to capture both the cultural and linguistic diversity of contemporary society in the historically predominantly anglophone countries within which the authors lived and worked, as well as the range of literacy practices that were emerging in the wake of digital, multimedia technologies. While this pluralization was already seen in earlier scholarship as is captured by notions such as *new literacies*, *multiliteracies* subsumes multilingualism and multimodality more deliberately into the very concept of literacy.

It is worth noting here how radically expansive the New London Group's model of literacy actually is. The rising interest in digital literacy practices has driven a lot of the work on multimodality in recent decades, resulting in a focus on the visual mode, which has perhaps also been the most accessible to traditionally text-centric fields such as applied linguistics and language studies; however, the New London Group's framework also included audio, gestural, and spatial modes (1996, 3), to which members of the group, Cope and Kalantzis (2005[1999], 2000), later added tactile and a clearer differentiation between written and oral linguistic modes. Multilingualism in the multiliteracies framework was intended to capture various linguistic, social, and cultural diversities and acknowledge the need for learners to be able to differentiate, negotiate between, and appreciate a plurality of voices and stances as presented through various media from around the world (Cope and Kalantzis 2000, 2009; Gee 2009; Kress 2003; New London Group 1996). Multilingualism here stood in for intralingual forms of diversity, including the sociolects associated with different discourse communities, social roles, identities, and affinities, as well as—although admittedly less stringently—distinct official or nationally recognized languages.

Of these two dimensions of the "multi" in multiliteracies, the attention to multimodality is often regarded as the most innovative aspect of the New London Group's proposed framework (see Mills 2010; Perry 2012); however, it is arguably the social, linguistic, and cultural diversity that they foreground most decisively in their manifesto. In reference to the second half of the title, "Designing social futures," the authors expound on the educational mission of a mutiliteracies pedagogy in the following way: "creating access to the evolving language of work, power, and community, and fostering the critical engagement necessary for them [learners] to design their social futures and achieve success through fulfilling employment" (1996, 60). This, they indicate, will involve "negotiating the multiple linguistic and cultural differences in our society" (1996, 60). Like much of the academic work in education and applied linguistics from the end of the twentieth and the beginning of the twenty-first centuries, the premise of the group's argument was that globalization and the rise of digital communications media have brought about social changes that language and literacy teaching have yet to address. They locate this within the context of "fast capitalism" and "post-Fordism" (New London Group 1996, 66; see also Gee 2018), which they characterize using terms that are echoed in Lankshear and Knobel's later depictions of new literacy practices as more participatory, collaborative, and distributed, including multi-skilled, hierarchically flattened forms of participation, and favoring commitment, responsibility, and motivation (66); however, the New London Group acknowledged that these new work-life cultures are also Janus-faced: on the one hand, the emphasis on creativity, adaptability, and innovation presents new educational and social possibilities, but it also opens up new potentials for exploitation and the continuation of social and discursive hierarchies that are made all the more sinister by hiding under platitudes of diversity. This is also emphasized in the New London Group's discussions of changing public and private lives in the 1990s, which they saw as driven by market forces of late-stage capitalism but also by the potential for civic pluralism and personal complexity that current sociopolitical environments afford. The result is a push and pull across the New London Group's manifesto between multiliteracies as competencies for contemporary work-life on the one hand and as a critical consciousness for imagining new social orders and realities on the other hand.

Echoes of the factors that Lankshear and Knobel identified as shaping the discourse around literacy in the late twentieth century (see the beginning of this chapter) reverberate through the New London Group's essay. It is in this tension between the pressure to respond to the new world order with its subsequent literacy crises and an insistence that education must empower students to be not only actuarial but also speculative that their most influential concept, the idea of *meaning design*, is born (New London Group 1996, 73–7). The word *design* in English is grammatically ambiguous—it can function as a noun referring to an organizing structure and as a verb referencing an agentful act of creation. The New London Group made use of this inherent duality in their heuristic of design, which they theorized as including three dimensions (see Figure 1). Language and other modes of communication are viewed as dynamic resources (Available Designs) for meaning making that undergo constant changes in dynamic acts of language use (Designing) as learners attempt to achieve their own purposes, thereby contributing again to the cycle of available designs (The Redesigned). At the same time, through their acts of meaning making, individuals *redesign* themselves, reconstructing and renegotiating their identities (New London Group 1996, 76).

Within the New London Group's model of design, meaning is not viewed as something that resides in texts but rather, designing meaning is understood as an active and dynamic process in which learners combine and creatively apply linguistic and other semiotic resources (e.g., visuals, gesture, sound, touch, spacing, etc.) with an awareness of "the sets of conventions connected with semiotic activity […] in a given social space" (i.e., discourses) (New London Group 1996, 74; see also Cope and Kalantzis 2009, 175–6; Gee 2002, 2007[1990]; Kress 2003). In addition to expanding the scope of available resources from more

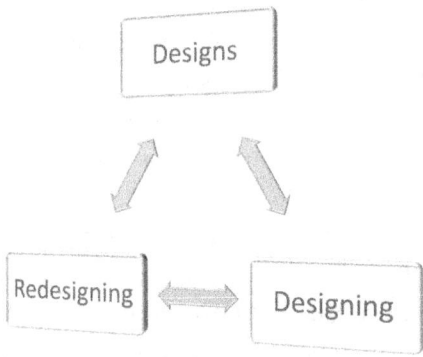

Figure 1 Three-part model of design.

traditional, linguacentric metalanguage such as *grammar* and *vocabulary*, the New London Group chose the term *design* to highlight the "creative intelligence" needed in contemporary society and the role of learners as social agents. As Cope and Kalantzis later wrote:

> To do something by Design is to do it with a peculiar intensity of focus, in a designerly way. Design is premeditated, a series of extraordinarily focused stages of thinking and action: conceptualization, enactment, evaluation. Design is reflexive, aware of the range of its potential applications. Design is contextually aware—of its antecedents, of the scope of present needs, and of possible future consequences. Design is respectful, open to alternative perspectives and practices. Design is resource prudent. Design is functional, creating things for the world which are usable, useful and enhance the quality of people's lives.
>
> (2011, 56)

Design, in particular through Redesigning, also has the potential to be subversive. Although there is a heavy focus on *participation* and *access* in the essay, the social futures they foreground are, after all, yet to be actively and emergently *designed*, as the title indicates. Gunter Kress, another member of the New London Group, describing what he sees as the contrast between Design and critique, proposes a connection between this transformative potential of (re-)design and broad societal and cultural transformations:

> While critique looks at the present through the means of past production, Design shapes the future through deliberate deployment of representational resources in the designer's interest. Design is the essential textual principle and pedagogic/political goal for periods characterized by intense and far-reaching change.
>
> (2000, 156)

Cope and Kalantzis (2009) are a little more tentative in their discussions of Redesigning, noting that change can be incremental or radical, it is only inevitable, and that ultimately teachers and students can be agnostic about whether they want to confirm or critique the status quo (174). If, as the New London Group proposed, the new normal is negotiating discourse differences, then this necessarily also implies a process of self-negotiation, involving highly personal questions of what kind of designer one wants to be in the world.

The New London Group's model of multiliteracies is securely located within the context of formal, i.e., instructed learning contexts, and this is most evident in a section of the article where they discuss what they theorize as the four core "pedagogical acts": *situated practice, overt instruction, critical framing,* and *transformed practice*. Although it is not directly cited as such, and in fact they are cautiously agnostic about subscribing to one theory, the pedagogy they proposed has clearly been influenced by the sociocultural theories of Vygotsky, and learning is situated within not only psychological but also "social, cultural, and material contexts" (see 1996, 82). The four acts they identify are thus each intended to focus on different dimensions of learning, and effective curriculum design will rely on the intentional integration of all four at various moments and in interactions with one another. *Situated practice* involves what is often called experiential learning, immersive learning in sociocultural settings and "heavily contextualized" in specific knowledge domains and discourses (84). *Overt instruction* includes active interventions on the part of teachers and other experts to focus the learners' attention on specific design elements or components of the activities that have been part of situated practice. This can include various forms of scaffolding that might help the learner to accomplish more complex tasks and both more implicit and more explicit forms of knowledge-building. Through *critical framing* learners are able to relate their emergent knowledge and competencies to historical, social, cultural, and political systems. This requires that teachers facilitate the kind of reflection that enables learners "to denaturalize and make strange again what they have learned and mastered" (87). *Transformed practice* recognizes that learning cannot involve a perpetual return to what one already knows and has experienced, i.e., to situated practice. Through the kinds of awareness honed through overt instruction and critical framing, learners are developing reflective practice, and they must also be given opportunities to demonstrate the ability to transfer this into new contexts embedded in their own goals and values (87).

Cope and Kalantzis, who were members and early organizers of the New London Group, have continued to develop the model across a series of publications outlining what they dub the "learning by design" approach. Among the amendments and additions that they make to the original multiliteracies framework, they revise the "pedagogical acts" to highlight the kinds of "knowledge processes" (also referred to as "design processes") that underlie each. They also divide each into two subcategories. Situated practice is reconceived as *experiencing*, which includes both *experiencing the known* and *experiencing the new*, and they advocate for curricula and teaching activities that weave both together. In place of overt instruction and critical framing, Cope and Kalantzis propose *conceptualizing* and *analyzing*. The former is inspired by Vygotsky's distinction between everyday spontaneous knowledge and scientific or systematic knowledge and recognizes that more complex knowledge building is supported through mental models, abstract frameworks, and transferable schemas, which can be either *conceptualized by naming* or *conceptualized by theorizing*. *Analyzing* entails the ability to relate what they have experienced and conceptualized to historical, social, cultural, and political systems previously denoted by *critical framing*, but Cope and Kalantzis distinguished between *analyzing functionally*, e.g., causal, logical, and textual connections, and *analyzing critically*, e.g., the evaluation of perspectives, interests, and motives, including one's own. Finally, *transformed practice* becomes two ways of *applying* the reflective practice gained through learning: *applying conventionally*, i.e., in ways that are more predictable and reproduce the status quo, and *applying creatively*, i.e., in ways that make "the world anew with fresh and creative forms of action and perception" (Cope and Kalanzis 2009, 19). As is the case with experiencing, in the act of applying, learners ideally weave between more familiar and more novel designs. An overview of the original new London Group's pedagogical acts alongside Cope and Kalantzis' knowledge processes can be found in Figure 2.

A final aspect of the New London Group's model that has had a significant impact on literacy education and more recently on second language studies is the role of metalanguage in articulating elements of design and dimensions of meaning. In comparison to the specificity of the pedagogical terminology, the vocabulary for design is left fairly open—a choice that is deliberate, because, as

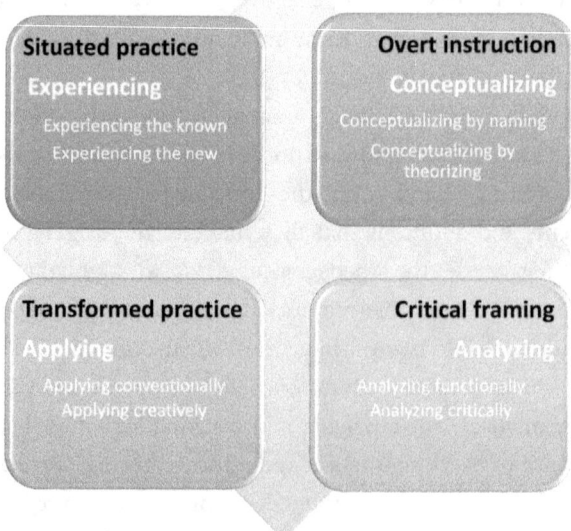

Figure 2 Pedagogical acts/knowledge processes.

they explain, metalanguage in such an approach "should be seen as a tool kit for working on semiotic activities, not a formalism to be applied to them" (77). Their reasoning for this is anchored in aspects of design and learning that are present in the pedagogical framework's critical and sociocultural foundations. They emphasize that a metalanguage for analyzing and conceptualizing design should be descriptive and functional, not prescriptive and constrained. This also informs a critique of the move toward standardization, which had been mounting in the decades prior to their 1994 manifesto—and which is the focus of ongoing debate (see also Garcia, Luke, and Seglem 2018, 76). The New London Group describes the stakes here in terms of literacy and power:

> [T]he primary purpose of the metalanguage should be to identify and explain differences between texts and relate these to the contexts of culture and situation in which they seem to work. The metalanguage is not to impose rules, to set standards of correctness, or to privilege certain discourses in order to 'empower' students.
>
> (77)

Despite these caveats, the New London Group's manifesto does include some tentative suggestions for a potential metalanguage for multiliteracies. They first note that the metalanguage must include key terms for larger orders of discourse such as "genres" and "related concepts such as voices, styles, and probably others" (77). Because their work has been influential for theorizing multimodal design elements, it is worth noting that Kress (1990), a member of the New London Group, and van Leeuwen (1993) are cited here (see also Kress and van Leeuwen 2020[1996]) along with Fairclough (1992), one of the founding theorists of critical discourse analysis. A selective list of "elements of linguistic design" then follows, which is summarized below:

- Delivery (e.g., intonation, rhythm)
- Vocabulary and metaphor (i.e., word meanings and colocation)
- Modality (here understood as the speakers' relationship to the message)
- Transitivity (the process and participants and how they are represented)
- Nominalization (the creation of nouns from other parts of speech, e.g., assess → assessment)
- Information structures (e.g., theme and rheme)
- Local and global coherence relations (e.g., organization structures)

Although he is not mentioned here by name, the influence of Halliday's (e.g., 1978, 1996, 2002) systemic functional linguistics (SFL) is apparent here in the choice of terms (e.g., transitivity, modality, and nominalization) (see also Introduction). A primary reason for this is already alluded to in New London Group's discussion of design as, at least in part, an alternative approach to traditional notions of grammar and vocabulary learning in language and literacy education. Halliday's SFL model emphasizes that language is functional, in that it enables us a means through which we can act on and interact with others and ways of understanding the physical and social world(s) we inhabit and our experiences within them, as well as systemic, because it is dynamically stable, which is to say that language users do not select from all of the available design resources each time anew but instead these tend to cluster together into constellations of meaning designs Halliday described as registers (see Halliday 1978). SFL remains one of the predominant metalanguages in multiliteracies scholarship (e.g., Lim 2018; Unsworth 2001, 2006; Colombi and Schleppegrell 2002) and has received extensive theoretical attention from scholars including notably Kress and van Leeuwen's already mentioned work on multimodality and Rose and Martin's (2008) genre-based model of communication in culture. Additional SFL-based research from second language studies is discussed in the next section. While the impact of SFL in the body of work that has amassed in association with multiliteracies is significant, in their original proposal, the New London Group was cautious about prescribing a singular jargon. Of the utmost importance is that the metalanguage supports "sophisticated critical analysis of language and other semiotic systems" (77) and motivates the students and teachers who work with it.

The impact of the multiliteracies framework and additional work around literacy and education that it inspired has been significant. In a special volume of the journal *Theory in Practice* on "Twenty Years of Multiliteracies: Moving from Theory to Social Change in Literacies and Beyond" (2018), the editors, Garcia and Seglem, laud the impact of the work started by the New London Group: "For researchers of educational technology, pedagogy, teacher education, school design, learning sciences, and sociocultural contexts of education, multiliteracies has not-so-subtly shifted the landscape of how and what is researched in schools today" (1). The group of scholars were brought together by a shared set of concerns about the inequities they saw in the moment and speculations about the potential futures, which new digital communications and mass mobility might afford, but to quote Luke, one of the original members of the New London Group who was interviewed in the volume, "What a difference two decades makes." For Luke, the current reality is one in which students and educators must contend with not only economic disparities but also "the stark effects of autocracy and plutocracy, renewed racism and sexism, ideological distortion and untruth, unethical and unjust social relations and conditions, and fundamental issues around freedom, policing and public safety, control and surveillance" (74). Luke's words here hearken back to the work of Freire and others and remind us that the social worlds to which literacy education must respond are given but not determined; the question for educators is what capabilities and resources will prepare the students in our classrooms to design alternate futures within which they and others can thrive. The subsequent section of this chapter, which now turns to the uptake of multiliteracies in LOTE second language learning, will build toward an additional question: what role can the learning of additional languages play in these acts of design?

Multiliteracies and Second Language-Culture Learning by Design

The New London Group's pedagogy of multiliteracies was conceived as a "statement of general principle" (1996, 89) for education, but their call to recognize the diversity and social situatedness of literacy was also heard by scholars and teachers in second language teaching and learning over the last decade. The uptake of multiliteracies pedagogies[4] in second language studies coincides with a general trend in the field toward more socioculturally oriented frameworks that in many ways parallels the developments in education theory discussed in the first part of this chapter, but second language studies, despite its transdisciplinary inclinations, is also a field of its own with its set of discussions and discourses that are distinct from education (see Douglas Fir Group 2016).

Within second language teaching and learning, the notion of multiliteracies entered educational discourses against the backdrop of not only new reading research (e.g., Bernhardt 1991; Swaffar, Arens and Byrnes 1991) but also—and perhaps more acutely—the predominant paradigm of communicative language teaching (see Paesani, Allen and Dupuy 2016; Paesani and Menke 2023). Multiliteracies pedagogies are, within this context, treated in various moments both as a departure and as a further realization or expansion of the communicative language teaching that has dominated the preceding decades. Both multiliteracies pedagogies and communicative language teaching emphasize meaning making; however, the former actively critiques any assumption that *getting one's meaning across* or *reading for gist* might serve as the primary pedagogical objective of language and culture study.

Furthermore, the emphasis on multiliteracies or literacy-oriented language teaching more generally is often framed as a direct commentary on the tendency within communicative language teaching to rely too heavily on oral modes of communication and to privilege instances of propositional language use where there is an assumed singularity of meaning and intent. Proponents of the multiliteracies framework in language and culture teaching emphasize that the goal of second language teaching is not simply to equip students with communicative skills, but more importantly to foster active and critical languagers (Phipps and Gonzales in Crosbie 2005, 295), who are capable of moving beyond literal meanings and of reflecting on the nuanced connections between semiotic form, meaning, context, perspective, and history.

The contrast between quintessential communicative language classrooms and those that deliberately integrate multiple literacies is illustrated well in Kern's seminal book *Literacy and Language Teaching* (2000). Kern presents two contrasting vignettes of class sessions focusing on an evergreen curriculum topic for beginning language learners, the family. In the first, the instructor begins class by peppering students with personal questions about their family members—numbers and ages of siblings—then prompting students to ask each other about familial relationships, followed by collectively reading a textbook passage containing stereotypical facts about French families. The second engages a range of literacy practices from comparing photos and letters received from students' respective pen pals to synthesizing family descriptions into family trees to asking students to critically reflect on the kind of information about families gleaned from the pen pal activity that might have been missing from the textbook passage. While both classes prioritize collaboration and communication, and both touch upon cultural dimensions of the topic, only in the second, Kern argues, are learners presented with opportunities to go beyond practicing "vocabulary and structures […] to explore a different world and to relate that world to their own thinking and experience" (2000, 15). In the first classroom, the content of language used sometimes pertains to the self and sometimes to others—those in the classroom or those represented in statistics about French culture—but it is primarily informational. In the second, language and culture manifest through literacy practices that themselves are shaped through historical and cultural expectations and in the situated relationships between students and pen pals. Kern's two vignettes illustrate a claim made by Cope and Kalantzis (2005[1999]), who wrote: "The Design notion … begins with a different notion of meaning and ends with a very different notion of culture" (204)—and arguably a very different notion of language.

In ways that parallel discussions within education, the concepts of literacy and multiliteracies in contemporary scholarship in second language studies do not represent discrete skills but rather a paradigm shift in how language and culture learning are thought (e.g., Byrnes, Maxim, and Norris 2010; Kern 2000; Kramsch 1994; Swaffar and Arens 2005). Across the many publications on multiliteracies and second language-culture teaching and learning that have appeared in the past decade and a half, especially in North American contexts, a common narrative emerges in which multiliteracies is positioned as an answer to a common curricular problem—the bifurcation of modern language departments and programs into basic language instruction in the first two years, which emphasizes everyday communicative skills and formal linguistic knowledge, on the one end and largely content-based courses on literature, history, and cultural studies on the other (e.g., Byrnes 1998; Maxim 2008, 2009; Geisler et al. 2007; Paesani, Allen, and Dupuy 2016; Swaffar 1999). This division of curricula in at least some institutions in North America is indexical of hierarchies and long held beliefs about languages and their relation to other areas of study (see Kramsch 1993, 7; Warner 2018), which find at least partial equivalencies in other parts of the world, e.g., in the separation of languages and literatures in academic programs (see Phipps and Gonzalez 2004, xv–xvii). The argument is that creating holistic curricula that merge language study with textual content (literature, film, advertising, etc.) and implementing instructional approaches that encourage students to interpret, analyze, and transform content in meaningful ways (e.g., Byrnes, Maxim, and Norris 2010; Geisler et al. 2007; Paesani, Allen, and Dupuy 2016; Swaffar and Arens 2005) creates a common tie that binds the diverse disciplines traditionally housed together in modern language departments, e.g., second language studies, literary studies, linguistics, cultural studies, and history around the question of, to quote Katherine Arens, "how do individuals and groups use words and other sign systems in context to intend, negotiate, and create meanings?" (Swaffar 1999, 157).

Beyond the matters of institutional politics that often motivate these discussions (see Warner 2018), scholarship in applied linguistics and second language studies also makes a language developmental case for literacy-based curricula. The underlying argument is that proficiency-oriented pedagogies in language education all too rarely account for language learning that goes beyond the level of the functional tourist. The effect is that curricula and programs do not articulate a potential trajectory from the early levels of language learning to more advanced capabilities (see Byrnes, Maxim, and Norris 2010; Byrnes and Sprang 2004; Ortega and Byrnes 2008). One of the most comprehensive expressions of this argument can be found in a 2010 monograph volume of the *Modern Language Journal* entitled *Realizing Advanced Foreign Language Writing Development in Collegiate Education: Curricular Design, Pedagogy, Assessment* and written by Byrnes, Maxim, and Norris. The opening chapters of the monograph explore the state of collegiate foreign language education and the relative lack of both scholarly and curricular attention to what kinds of pedagogical and assessment practices might best support advanced language development. Drawing from a curriculum development project implemented in a four-year undergraduate German program at Georgetown University, where all three authors were based at the time of writing, they then lay out an argument for literacy and more specifically writing development as an organizing principle for the language, literature, and culture curricula of modern language departments. For writing, they argue, "provides a maximally functional means for introducing learners, from the very beginning of their collegiate FL [foreign language] studies, to the integrated nature of language and cultural content, helping them (and teachers) to envision sophisticated goals and to pursue them right away" (Byrnes, Maxim, and Norris 2010, 197).

Across these publications from the last twenty years, a pervasive question to which multiliteracies and literacy-based pedagogies are positioned as the answer is how to develop articulated programs from the beginning language classes all the way to the final levels of study. In this role, the notion of multiliteracies has contributed meaningfully to a larger debate within North American language education about the identity of modern language programs and the connections between the disciplines housed within them, that is, between the humanities, linguistics, and language studies/applied linguistics. For the purposes of this discussion, however, I would like to disarticulate multiliteracies pedagogies from both this specific instructional context and the questions of curricular sequencing, in order to create a little more breathing room within which to consider what other lines of thinking multiliteracies' core concept of design might afford—and what pedagogies based in design might downplay. Recognizing that multiliteracies comes into second language teaching and learning with the promise of paradigm shifts, the overarching question here is then what kinds of pedagogical and conceptual thinking the multiliteracies notion of teaching by design has tended to encourage.

In the remainder of this chapter, we will look at three aspects of multiliteracies frameworks as they have been discussed and implemented in relation to second language and culture learning (specifically in the context of the teaching and learning of languages other than English): designs, designing, and designers. These are closely interconnected and deliberately align with the three ideological levels discussed in the introduction: language, learning, and learners. The guiding question here is how this trifecta of concepts has mediated thinking about language learning and teaching in recent years, including what types of pedagogical thinking and scholarship it has afforded, as well as the limits of learning by design as a framework for second language educational theory and practice.

Designs

Perhaps the most consequential and visible contribution of the New London Group's multiliteracies framework was its recognition that linguistic design elements do not exist in isolation from other modalities. For the field of second language and culture teaching, multiliteracies has been received as an invitation to consider the role of other modalities, especially the visual, within the scope of our work, and as a reminder of the extent to which languaging is always already a multimodal activity. In this regard, there are some clear overlaps between discussions of multiliteracies pedagogies and theoretical frameworks within applied linguistics that conceptualize language as manifesting as part of a larger semiotic repertoire (e.g., Busch 2012; Li 2018; see additional discussion in Introduction). Allen (2018) notes that multimodality can be incorporated at a variety of different levels, from learners analyzing the multimodal elements of a written text such as format and font to them engaging in the composition of their own complex multimodal compositions such as digital stories or comic strips (526). While the objects of multiliteracies pedagogies in second language teaching are often described as "authentic texts," it is the range of the texts and the attention to the multidimensionality of their designs that distinguish these approaches from communicative language teaching.

As we saw already in the education scholarship, multimodality in multiliteracies pedagogies is bound up in the increasing presence of digital communications media over the last couple of decades and the now-established place of digitally composed and circulated forms of cultural expression in contemporary life (Walsch 2010). As Lotherington and Jenson (2011) note, "Though multimodality does not necessarily utilize digital technologies, digital technologies enable 'modes to be configured, be circulated, and get recycled in different ways' (Jewitt 2009, 1), thus intensifying multimodal possibilities" (227). Both multimodality and digital technologies have been present in language classrooms separate from any discussions of multiliteracies or literacy-based teaching, but what it provided was support for exploring and assessing learning in relation to a range of vernacular digital genres (Thorne and Reinhardt 2008), including a sense of how the design functions of digital tools relate to the available designs that circulate. The range of digital literacy practices that are taken up as multimodal teaching and learning materials run the gambit from previously offline literacy practices that are now more frequently found online, e.g., recipe websites, advertisements, music, and art to literacy practices that are more deeply digital in their design, such as video games (Reinhardt, Warner, and Lange 2014; Sykes and Reinhardt 2012; Thorne and Reinhardt 2008) and social media (Chen 2013; Reinhardt 2019). A classroom-based study of a digital gaming unit piloted in an intermediate German language-culture class by Warner, Richardson, and Lange (2019) reminds us that the transposability of digital literacy practices into learning spaces is hardly neutral; the very experience of playing a game or engaging on a discussion forum is transformed when it is framed as a learning activity (see also Hanna and de Nooy 2003).

In addition to easing widespread access to cultural artifacts from the digital wild (Thorne, Sauro, and Smith 2015), attention to multimodal composing practices has expanded the repertoire of designs, with which learners are asked to engage, to include digital stories and video projects (Alcazar 2022; Kumagai et al. 2016; Oskoz and Elola 2016), blogs (Ducate and Lomicka 2008), and vlogs (video blogs) (Lopez et al. 2016). In line with Lankshear and Knobel's (2011) observation that new literacy practices break down traditional roles of authorship (74), the emphasis here is not on comprehension or analysis but on participation. As Reinhardt and Thorne (2019) write, "Since many digital literacies are by design participatory, activities to practice them can leverage the sharing, interaction, and collaborative engagement that new tools and online communities afford" (217). In this way, the digital enhances the inherently multimodal nature of semiosis by making it easier for teachers and students to access and create a wider range of available designs.

While the digital has dominated, the increased attention to multimodal designs in language teaching has also enriched the teaching of more analogue literacy activities. For example, Ryshina-Pankova (2013) reports on an advanced-level language-culture course on *Green Germany* where political posters, cartoons, and paintings were integrated to both enrich the thematic focus and develop learner's critical literacy by highlighting how a given perspective or mood is suggested through the visual design. In a study from a Spanish translation course for heritage language learners, Alcazar (2022) showed how students engaged in the analysis, conceptualization, and creation of bilingual public safety announcements negotiated the relationship between the images, the source text, and the translated text, and in so doing demonstrated an emergent awareness of how texts and images interact in multimodal genres that reach multiple audiences. The edited volume, *Films, Graphic, Novels, and Visuals: Developing Multiliteracies in Foreign Language Education—An Interdisciplinary Approach* (2013) edited by Elsner, Helff, and Viebrock, features a section on what they describe as "still images," i.e., graphic novels, street art, and film posters. Taken as a collection, the practice-oriented chapters in this section show how genres that blend verbal and visual can highlight the interconnectivity of modalities. In recognizing available designs as more often than not inherently multimodal, learners can be supported in drawing from their broader semiotic repertoire, thus allowing them to weave more functional tasks (i.e., describing, expressing an opinion) with intercultural reflection.

By giving design a place alongside textual attributes such as comprehensibility, practicality, or functionality, multiliteracies pedagogies for language education have also renewed interest in one of language learning's longest bedfellows—literary texts (compare Mills 2010). Literature, once the raison d'etre for language learning, was relatively absent in the audiolingual and direct methods en vogue in the United States and Europe in the 1970s and then found a supporting role in communicative language teaching pedagogies, as an example of comprehensible language and a means of enriching cultural themes and discussion topics. Of course, literature has never completely disappeared from language education, especially within European scholarship on second language studies (e.g., Bredella and Delanoy 1996; Carter and McRae 2014; Carroli 2008; Hall 2005; Paran 2008); however, the theoretical framework of multiliteracies and language teaching puts the design of these texts front and center in discussions of advanced language development and curricular sequencing (see Scott and Tucker 2001). Literary texts, as primarily linguistic designs, often include more nuanced vocabulary, extended discourse, and other language features that may be absent in other genres (Barette, Paesani, and Vinall 2010; Byrnes and Sprang 2004). They also enact the interconnectivity of orality and literacy by mixing features of both and redesigning spoken dialogue tendencies (i.e., dialect, slang, and other speech styles) into a written form (Kern and Schulz 2005; Simpson 2004).

A small but significant subset of studies looks at how learners engage in multimodal composing in response to and in the creation of literary writing, in particular poetry. Smith, Amgott, and Malova (2022) built upon Smith's (2014, 2018) earlier work to show how bilingual and emergent bilingual students in a high school English class engaged with a series of multimodal composing activities in response to literary texts—a hypertext poetry analysis, a persuasive podcast, and a video literary analysis. In their reflections on the activities, students in the study expressed that the opportunity to engage with different modalities enabled them to express aspects of their bilingual and bicultural selves, including affective responses. Students also reported that the process of collaboration with peers to design these various compositions created a more meaningful relationship to the literary texts. Schufflebarger Snell's (2016, 2019) work similarly shows that the opportunity to respond to poetry multimodally and multilingually enabled learners in a beginning-level community English class for adults with a migration or refugee background to express complex hopes and feelings in relation to their new lives in the United States. Schufflebarger Snell's examples focus on what she dubs "playful bricolage," i.e., the creative process of making use of the tools available to complete a task (Schufflebarger Snell 2019, 81). The poetic texts in Schufflebarger Snell's classroom effectively become a focal available design for students' creations, which playfully borrowed from the vocabulary, grammatical, and genre resources offered by the poems.

Narrative films occupy a place comparable to literary texts in contemporary cultural production and practice and have long been a mainstay in language and culture pedagogy; nevertheless, in contrast with literature, digital communications media, and even digital games, relatively little has been written on multiliteracies and the teaching of film (Kaiser 2018, 49). Kaiser himself proposes a multiliteracies approach to close-reading clips in second language and culture classrooms, to focus learners' attention to how the cinematography in tandem with other visual and linguistic elements functions as a meaning-making device in filmic works. Kaiser guides the reader through an analysis of two juxtaposing clips from a film, indicating how students could be invited in to do the same. Elsner, Helff, and Viebrock's (2013) volume, which was referenced earlier in the discussion of verbal-visual multimodality and "still" images, concludes with a section on "moving images," i.e., film, advertising, and television. Apart from Helff's chapter on documentaries, the focus of the chapters is overwhelmingly not on genre elements or the close analysis of visual elements, but on broader cultural and transcultural discourses as they are mediated through the confluence of modalities in film. The chapters by Hoof, Herzogenrath, Lütge, and Starck all emphasize the potential of film, as a widely, often globally circulated popular art form as a means of fostering critical literacy, e.g., around topics such as social justice and prison reform, environmental and cultural sustainability, and representations of gender in the media.

Across these publications the notion of *design* offers a tool for reconceptualizing language learning as inextricable from the rich, multiply modal semiotic environments, within which language is used. At the same time, attention to the designs that are made available and salient to learners in language and culture classrooms has encouraged scholars and practitioners to expand the scope of materials and modes of relevance to language teaching. The multiplicity of languages and cultures included in the original theorization of multiliteracies is often assumed to be intrinsic to the educational context; whether it is positioned as foreign, world, or second language learning, the implication is that a plurality of languages or at least their speakers is present. How these languages and other modalities enter the classroom is the focus of the next section.

Designing

We have already seen in the previous section that designs in multiliteracies-oriented language teaching are not relegated to a role of analytical object but instead become available designs for learners to take up in the act of designing. How learners are being invited to respond, i.e., to design meaning, as they work to understand and interpret the texts, compositions, and artifacts that are brought into the classroom matters just as much as the range and nature of the designs themselves. Within the context of instructed language teaching, two interconnecting aspects of how designing is conceptualized are most salient in the scholarly literature, each of which will be discussed in turn in this section. The first relates to how the pedagogy around designing is conceptualized, and the second to the metalanguage that is used to describe and analyze available designs.

Pedagogical Sequences for Designing

Allen and Paesani (2010) underscore that the integration of rich, authentic materials, i.e., the available designs, alone is not enough to evoke meaningful learning experiences; deliberate pedagogical principles and choices create the potential for the kind of reflective, critical, creative, and transformative engagements with texts that multiliteracies frameworks advocate. For educators and scholars in second language studies who are centrally concerned with teacher conceptual development and the multiliteracies pedagogies, the pedagogical acts proposed by the New London Group (1996) and later adapted by Cope and Kalantzis (2009) have offered a robust framework for intentionally connecting designing to pedagogical choices (e.g., Allen and Paesani 2010; Kern 2000; Paesani, Allen, and Dupuy 2016; Paesani and Menke 2023). The focus in these discussions is on showing how these pedagogical acts—situated practice/experiencing, overt instruction/conceptualizing, critical framing/analyzing, and transformed practice/applying—can be realized in second language education contexts.

As indicated in the previous section, multiliteracies concepts are often introduced in contrast to prevailing pedagogical frameworks. Kern (2000), whose work is a key influence for many of these later scholars, offers lists of sample learning activities for teaching reading as design (160) and writing as design (213), and relates these likely more familiar classroom practices with the pedagogical acts. Paesani, Allen, and Dupuy (2016) build off Kern's work to offer a similar set of lists but draw from pedagogical frameworks from within language education to also show how these pedagogical acts are often sequenced and integrated. For example, their chapter on "Teaching Reading as Constructing Meaning from Texts" first reviews four models of literacy-oriented reading instruction, namely Hedgcock and Ferris (2009), Kern (2000), Maxim (2006), and Swaffar and Arens (2005), and merges these into a five-part template, including (1) pre-reading, (2) initial reading, (3) detailed reading, (4) critical reading, and (5) knowledge application (154). By connecting each of these stages to typical pedagogical activities that occur in each and the pedagogical acts they evoke, these scholars show how these pedagogical sequences integrate various ways of learning, ranging from the more experiential to the more reflective, in the process of designing meaning. Paesani, Allen, and Dupuy (2016) also offer similar templates for teaching vocabulary and grammar as meaning-making resources, scaffolding oral language use, teaching writing as designing meaning through texts, and teaching video-mediated listening as constructed meaning from texts.

As an example, Table 1 provides an overview of the kinds of reading as design activities Kern (2000) and Paesani, Allen, and Dupuy (2016) categorized in their respective categories. Checkmarks represent classification in Kern's discussion, with a standalone checkmark [✓] indicating that this is a primary focus of the activity and a checkmark in parentheses [(✓)] that this is a secondary focus. An X designates an activity included in Paesani, Allen, and Dupuy's classification. As the table reveals, many teaching and learning practices cross categories or can facilitate different learning processes depending on the emphasis. For example, while both models identify readers' theater, the practice by which learners perform a reading of a text, as potentially critical framing, Kern

Table 1 Sample reading activities and corresponding pedagogical acts.

Literacy activities	Situated practice	Overt instruction	Critical framing	Transformed practice
Reading as design				
Predicting	X		X	
Instructional conversations	X		X	
Scanning for information	X			
Sequencing text elements	X			
Information mapping		X		
Directed Reading Thinking Activities	✓	(✓)	(✓)	
Reading journals	✓X		(✓)X	
Focusing on relationships	✓	✓X	(✓)	(✓)
Summary writing	(✓)	✓	✓	✓
Synonym substitution		X		
Textual Comparisons	✓	✓X	✓	
Multiple interpretations			X	
Critical focus questions	(✓)	(✓)	✓X	(✓)
Readers theater	X		(✓)	✓
Text elaboration				X
Retellings				X
Translation	(✓)		(✓)	✓

Inspired by Kern (2000, 160) and Paesani, Allen, and Dupuy (2016, 156).

positions it as a kind of transformed practice and Paesani, Allen, and Dupuy as situated practice. The difference here may lie in the relationship between the activity and critical framing and the placement within a lesson; are students being asked to perform a reading as one of their initial reading activities, so that this might activate the kinds of reflective noticing that can contribute to critical framing (situated practice) or are they being asked to critically analyze a text in preparation for performing it, after having already worked with the text more extensively (transformed practice). Activities that are on the threshold between two pedagogical acts thus underscore that the division between these categories is not absolute, but also how heuristics such as this be deliberately used in the classroom to transition between different moments in a learning sequence.

In other publications, second language scholars lean more on other models of pedagogical sequencing from within education and literacy studies. For example, Warren and Winkler (2016) relate Rothery's (1996) genre pedagogy cycle to the New London Group's pedagogical acts, noting that although there is not a one-to-one correspondence, there is some conceptual resonance between the two models. Rothery's (1996) teaching and learning cycle includes four distinct stages: negotiating field, which involves exploring students' prior knowledge of a given genre and the social field in which it tends to operate; deconstruction, where learners engage with model texts to conceptualize their communicative goals and the linguistic design resources through which these are realized; joint construction, during which students collaboratively create texts based on the models; and independent construction, when students are able to more independently work with a particular text type (Warren and Winkler 2016, 38). Ryshina-Pankova (2013) draws on Unsworth's (2001) cycle of literacy development in content-based teaching in her study of multimodal composing, which includes three stages: recognition literacy, during which general knowledge about a topic or a text is activated; reproduction literacy, where attention is drawn to specific design elements and how they construct meaning; and critical literacy, when students are asked to reflect on whose interests are served by a text and to what ends. While these models for enacting multiliteracies pedagogies vary in their choice or terms and key concepts, they all emphasize the iterative nature of literacy development and the importance of opportunities for modeling and reflection. (See Table 2 for an overview of these models.)

The need to bridge between more familiar pedagogical paradigms and multiliteracies concepts is a frequent area of attention in scholarship on learning and teaching languages by design. This concern is informed by prior research that has revealed the difficulties teachers may experience when putting new pedagogical paradigms and concepts into practice, but also act as critical interventions in the field of language education. In addition to establishing shared conceptual ground, connections to standardizing bodies, especially

Table 2 Comparison of learning activities in multiliteracy models.

New London Group (1996)*	Cope and Kalantzis (2009)*	Rothery (1996) [Warren and Winkler (2016)]	Unsworth (2001) [Ryshina-Pankova (2013)]	Shared aspects
Situated practice	Experiencing	Joint construction	Recognition literacy	Emphasis is on knowledge activation and experiential learning
Overt instruction	Conceptualizing	Deconstruction		Emphasis is on guided attention to design elements
Critical framing	Analyzing		Critical literacy	Emphasis is on which meanings are enacted, whose perspectives are represented, and whose interests they serve
Transformed practice	Applying	Independent construction	Reproduction literacy	Emphasis is on the application of new knowledge through literacy practices that have been redesigned

*These two frameworks are not treated as a sequence but have been ordered here to align most closely with other models.

the US-based professional organization American Council on the Teaching of Foreign Languages (ACTFL) and the frameworks promoted under their aegis are often cited in order to identify shared educational goals, while also expanding the scope of language learning (e.g., Byrnes 2008a; Troyan 2014; Zapata 2022, 23–4). For example, Paesani and Menke (2023, 124) deliberately and explicitly relate multiliteracies pedagogies to dominant discourses of proficiency-based language teaching and to communicative language teaching practices; using the heuristic of the four pedagogical acts, they show how communicative language teaching in the beginning and intermediate language classes, where educators reach the widest number of learners, tends to be over dominated by situated practice and overt instruction activities, whereas critical framing and transformed practice activities are integrated less systematically or relegated to the more advanced literature-culture courses. This has ideological consequences, as they note (Paesani and Menke 2023, 124), because it reinforces the myth that language is primarily a tool that can be wielded more or less skillfully, which in turn contributes to a belief that language learning is a neutral, practical but not an intellectually rich, emotionally and sociopolitically laden activity (Warner 2011).

There's no such thing as neutral education, Freire cautioned (2007[1970]). And multiliteracies pedagogical frameworks are inextricable from ideologies of language, and more concretely from the notion of *designing* as not just getting one's meaning across but reflectively, critically considering which meanings get across, how, from whom, in what contexts, and in what ways the scope of possible meanings might be transformed. At times this creates a push and pull between the ideologies of proficiency and (intercultural) communicative competence that underlie the frameworks shaping commercial textbooks, standardized assessment practices, and which are endorsed by institutionalized bodies (such as ACTFL or the Common European Framework of Reference) (see Warner 2020). The promise of a pedagogy based in multiliteracies pedagogies is not that it will enable educators to merely do better but that it will inspire them to do *differently*; that is, as a new framework it offers new models of language teaching but also ways of rethinking language and its relationship to other modes. This dimension of designing is the focus of the next section.

Metalanguages for Conceptualizing and Analyzing Designing

The New London Group (1996) intentionally left the question of which designs would be most relevant to learners and educators an open-ended one. While this has certainly enabled the adaptability and likely the longevity of their framework and much of the conceptual and empirical work it has inspired, for a field like foreign language education, with its deep roots in linguistically oriented disciplines, it left an unsatisfied yearning for systematic ways of focusing on form. The uptake of multiliteracies pedagogies in second language and teaching has thus contributed significantly to scholarship from education by continuing to hone metalanguage and models that can help practitioners, scholars, and ultimately learners to conceptualize and analyze how available designs manifest in language (and to an increasing extent in visual compositions) and to connect them to broader, multimodal systems of meaning making and to the cultural products, practices, and perspectives through which they manifest.

Many scholars follow Kern's (2000) lead, integrating more familiar terms and concepts, while encouraging educators and scholars to think of these as dynamic design resources instead of stable, rule-governed structures (see also Paesani, Allen, and Dupuy 2016, 29). Kern (2000) provided a model, which identified several of the most salient available designs for adolescent/adult second language learners: grammar, vocabulary, writing systems, declarative knowledge, procedural knowledge, stories, style, and text-type (62–3). Following suit, Paesani and Menke (2023) point to how grammatical forms, such as the past tense, are approached differently in communicative and in multiliteracies-oriented language teaching. "For instance, in multiliteracies pedagogy, instead of focusing on learning past tense forms to carry out the function of narrating, the focus might be on learning how past tense forms shape the chronology of a story and its related historical events" (27). Whereas both examples potentially involve language use in context, only the latter focuses on the design of meaning through grammar.

Another strand of scholarship develops a metalanguage from the model of systemic functional linguistics (SFL) developed by Halliday (e.g., 1978, 1996, 2002) and his collaborators (e.g., Hasan 2002; Schleppegrell 2004), which also inspired early work on multiliteracies within education. As a theory of vocabulary, grammar, and the relationship between the two, what Halliday describes as *lexicogrammar*, SFL has provided a valuable heuristic for conceptualizing these traditional elements of language teaching as design resources (e.g., Byrnes 2006, 2008b). "Because grammar is a meaning-making resource, learning 'the grammar' of a language is not about learning to adhere to rules, but learning to turn experience and human existence into meaning by using the resources that the grammar of a particular language makes available" (Byrnes 2009, 5). Within SFL, language forms are thus treated as resources for meaning. These manifest within social situations which can be analyzed in three dimensions: in terms of field, or what is going on (e.g., what's happening); tenor, who is taking part; and mode, what place language has (e.g., the medium). And these are then realized in language in relation to three metafunctions: the ideational, the construal of our experience and perception of the world; the interpersonal, the ways in which language shapes relationships with others through mood, attitude, etc.; and textual metafunctions, the organizing and structuring of language into a message (Halliday 1994). By viewing language as a social semiotic in this way, Halliday offers, as Byrnes notes, "the language field" the potential "to investigate the intricate link between culture and language or, in reverse, language and culture" (Byrnes 2008b, 115).

Second language studies has also been heavily influenced by the work of scholars such as Rose and Martin (2008), who built on Halliday's framework to develop a model of language and social context centered on the notion of genre. Genres, according to this framework, are configurations of design elements and the recurrent social purposes they realize (Martin 2002). These genres and the relations between them provide a way of "mapping culture," in that the genres, the shapes they take, and the kinds of contexts within which they are most at home are a way of tracing the contours of a culture's literacy practices (Rose and Martin 2008). Scholars within second language teaching and learning such as Byrnes et al. (2006, 2008), Ryshina-Pankova (2013), and Troyan (2014) have demonstrated how an explicit focus on genre can help educators to orient language teaching activities toward "the purpose of communication" (ACTFL 2017, 1), while also making space for critical reflection on the design of a wide range of text types and media. There is overlap between these discussions within second language studies, where the emphasis is on languages other than English (LOTE), and scholarship on English for specific purposes and academic literacy (e.g., Swales 1990; Tardy 2006); in contrast, however, to English language and literacy education, there is an assumption in the teaching of LOTEs that students may begin their language studies at institutions of secondary or tertiary education. A key focus in studies located in this context is thus on genre as a potential organizing principle for the intellectual content of the multiple kinds of courses present in language, literature, and culture programs.

Swaffar (2005), who is likewise concerned with the articulation of curricula in modern language, literature, and culture programs, has proposed that genres can be conceived along two axes, one ranging from informal to formal and the other from private to public (22). Swaffar's model draws attention to the interconnectedness of function/context, modality (e.g., spoken, written), form, and topic. So, for example, a personal letter to a friend and a business letter may share characteristics, but strikingly different sender-receiver relationships shape them; personal letters typically have a specific intended addressee (or set of addressees), whereas business letters are more impersonal and generic. A business letter is thus more likely to exhibit characteristics of what Bernstein (1971) described as *elaborated* code, including a higher level of detail such that the letter could "stand on its own" if forwarded to another office or representative; a personal letter, say to a friend or family member, would be more likely to be *restricted*, with inside references that take for granted a history of shared knowledge and experiences.

Genre was also a core concept for the Georgetown German curriculum reform project discussed in the previous section of this chapter (see also Byrnes, Crane, and Maxim 2006; Byrnes and Kord 2001). Through a series of reports, collaborators from this project demonstrate how the staging of genre-based tasks across a four-year program allowed for a curricular progression from primary to secondary genres, as proposed by Gee (2002). Connections between genre families, such as narratives, across the curriculum, also enabled representatives of different disciplines to find common ground and to articulate shared learning outcomes. Through the lens of genre, the design of meaning in various genres of narrative from oral personal recounts to written autobiographical testimonies to historiographies can be compared and contrasted. Focusing on genre moves and how they are realized in different acts and modalities of storytelling, students can be guided to critically examine the interrelations between context, genre, and language, while also developing their fluency, accuracy, and complexity in language use.

Troyan (2014, 2016) has shown that genre-based multiliteracies pedagogies can also be implemented in early grade levels—in the case of his study, a fourth-grade Spanish class—to support learners' writing development across a range of text types. Troyan (2016) also argues that the metalanguage of SFL and genre can be useful for language educators, in that it provides a more rigorous framework for making principled decisions about text selection "in a way that realizes the full meaning-making potential of authentic texts and contexts" (319). Troyan's aim is in part to expand upon existing standardizing frameworks, in his case those promoted through ACTFL, by offering a more systematic metalanguage that considers "the functions of language and the linguistic representation of content in authentic, written contexts" and applies those frameworks "in the design of curriculum, instruction, and assessment" (2016, 332). Troyan constructs his framework around the concepts of field, tenor, and mode, which Halliday and others have used to theorize the concept of a situation (also denoted as the register), and then connects these to a series of meaning-oriented questions that can be used to guide students' engagement with texts and their coinciding traditional language features (324). For field, for example, meaning-oriented questions focus on what is happening, who is taking part, and the circumstances around the situation, and these are expressed through verbs, nouns, adjectives, and adverbs. Tenor raises questions of the attitudes expressed and how the reader is engaged, and key language features that contribute to these levels of meaning include positive and negative word choices and the relative formality of the language. And mode related to how the text is organized, as realized linguistically through markers of cohesion and coherence. By drawing attention to these design elements, the instructor and students in Troyan's study were able to deconstruct model texts and co-construct an understanding of the genre at the center of their lesson, a description, before then independently composing their own texts.

Another aspect of SFL-informed genre-based pedagogies that has appealed to scholars in second language studies is that it offers a systematic model for responding to one of the evergreen questions in contemporary second language teaching—how do we teach language and culture (see Byram and Kramsch 2008)? In functional genre approaches, cultural context is modeled as a system of genres (Rose and Martin 2008). Through genres, understood as recurrent configurations of meanings, the social practices of a given culture are enacted (Martin and Rose 2008, 5). Maxim puts it in a similar but slightly different way, "The choices available within a genre are limited by the conventions that have become valorized for that specific communicative situation" (Maxim 2008). It is common in language education discourses to speak of "appropriateness," but Maxim's word choice here seems more revealing. To say that certain conventions are valorized recognizes that our sense of how language works is not only a matter of what is typical, but what is acceptable, what is good, what demonstrates a sense of awareness in relation to that speech situation and one's place within it. In short, not only cultural practices, but also cultural values are enacted through the choices made in designing meaning. In their proposal for a genre-based approach to comparative literature, Swaffar and Arens (2005) similarly emphasize attention to communication patterns in texts in the development of "cultural literacy" (see also Arens 2005), but also suggest that the work in comparative literary studies and culture studies often found at the more advanced levels of modern language departments necessitates a careful negotiation between the inclusion of text types that work toward typologies of cultural systems, communities, and discourses and the kinds of genres the students themselves are asked to design (176). This poses questions about who students are and with whom and where they might be engaging in designing in their new languages outside of the classroom.

Detailed metalanguages for designing in other modalities remain admittedly less robust than their linguistic counterparts, hence the focus thus far on verbal texts. However, Kress and van Leeuwen's (2021[1996]) model of SFL-based visual grammar and further developments of their framework within literacy education (e.g., Serafini, 2014; Unsworth 2006) have also inspired research in second language studies. For example, Ryshina-Pankova's (2013) critical literacy approach for working with images and film uses Kress and van Leeuwen's framework to develop a set of guiding questions, which can be applied to both static and video images (175). The following are translated from Ryshina-Pankova's original list in German:

- Where do you first look? Which elements attract you? Which elements are highlighted?
- How are the visual elements highlighted? Through exaggerated or understated size? Through color? Through a specific perspective? Positioning in foreground or background?
- What is the perspective? Normal view, bottom view/frog's eye perspective, top view/bird's eye perspective, close-up, distanced? What meaning does that have?
- What function do the colors have?
- How realistic is the image? Is it exaggerated or understated?
- How are various elements of the image connected to one another? (Vectors or lines that bind or separate, color coherence …)
- What is the role of language? Are there interesting syntactic patterns, metaphors, word plays, dialect words, rhyming, sounds?
- What is the relationship between language and image?
- How do the different linguistic and visual elements relate to the overarching communicative goal of the image?

Ryshina-Pankova exemplifies how the analytical metalanguage of SFL can be adapted to more "student friendly" guiding concepts and reflective questions, which students can use to analyze and conceptualize how meaning is designed in multimodal texts.

Table 3 Linguistic and visual metafunctions in Halliday's and Kress/van Leeuwen's frameworks.

	Linguistic metafunctions		
Halliday (1994)	Textual	Interpersonal	Ideational
	Visual metafunctions		
Kress and van Leeuwen (2021[1996])	Composition	Interaction	Representation
What is it?	The channels and design choices through which communication is carried out and made text	The interactants, their relationships to one another and their purposes	Relates to the topics and actions which language and imagery are used to express
Questions it poses?	What strikes you about the text or image? What stands out as defining for the text's structure?	How does the text make you feel? Do you feel addressed? Is there evaluative language?	What experiences or ideas are expressed? What perspectives, points of view, or beliefs are expressed? What types of action are represented?

Table 3 integrates both Halliday's metafunctions and parallel terms proposed by Kress and van Leeuwen (2021[1996]) for the analysis of images. The bottom rows of the table provide an overview of what these metafunctions are and the kinds of questions educators might ask of students—and themselves—in analyzing linguistic and visual texts.

Designing as Textual Borrowing

Across these pedagogical frameworks and conceptual metalanguages for teaching language and literacy as meaning design, there has been continuous importance placed on the role of authentic texts, that is, those not designed primarily for didactic or language practice purposes, as models of available designs as they are instantiated in socially situated, culturally constituted acts of meaning making. Through the experience of these texts and guided opportunities for interpretation and reflection, learners are designing meaning as active participants in literacy activities. A few studies have shown how textual borrowing, the re-appropriation of elements from a model text, can also be a helpful strategy for linking reading texts and attending to their available designs in the creation of new compositions (e.g., Allen and Goodspeed 2018; Maxim 2009; Warren and Winkler 2016). Maxim (2009) examined how the textual borrowing practices of six advanced German learners evolved over the course of a semester. Based on a mixed methods analysis of the original text and the learner compositions, as well as reflective interviews, Maxim's study shows how the students were negotiating between an impetus to "get things right" and a desire to develop their own voice in the new language, but also that their choices were sometimes driven by preconceived notions that truncated textual meaning. He concluded that greater attention to linguistic design could support students in becoming more conscientious textual borrowers. Warren and Winkler's (2016) study of three beginning-level German course sections lends support to Maxim's hypothesis. Two of the sections in Warren and Winkler's study explicitly focused on evaluation in a model text recounting a travel experience, while in the third students read a text from a travel site that featured overwhelmingly positive evaluation and this feature was not directly discussed. Analysis of the learner compositions revealed qualitative and quantitative differences between the two groups. The compositions of the students who explicitly paid attention to evaluation not only included a greater amount of evaluative language, but also were generally longer and generated more peer discussion (48). The authors concluded that the students not only borrowed more but also exhibited a greater willingness to communicate, perhaps because of the increased confidence that the careful attention to language had fostered in them.

Noting that research related to genre-based pedagogies in second language teaching tends to focus on learning outcomes rather than on learner perspectives, Allen and Goodspeed (2018) conducted a study within an advanced French course that examined both. The focal genre in their study was a letter-manifesto. Students first read a six-page excerpt of former French President Nicolas Sarkozy's (2007) "Lettre aux éducateurs," a public open letter arguing the need for major educational reform. Students were then asked to compose a letter to a current French government official with a call to action relating to one of four social issues: immigration, politics, religion, and the educational system. They then also completed a reflection describing their stylistic choices, how the process of analyzing the model text influenced their letter, and any aspects of their writing with which they were particularly satisfied or by which they had felt particularly challenged. Like Maxim (2009), they found that learners borrowed a wide range of micro- and macro-features and techniques from the model text but did not necessarily rely on the exact word choices or expressions of the source. Allen and Goodspeed (2018) cite the diversity of these design choices to argue that learners were not merely appropriating available designs but were weaving together borrowed resources and individual expressions, infusing their texts "with creative perspectives, ideas, and expression" (102). Learner reflections revealed an additional aspect of the designing process; although the majority of the participants (18 of 19) cited their work with the model text as beneficial, several mentioned difficulties they had encountered formulating a well-reasoned argument for social changes in a society, with which they had limited familiarity, and three referenced tensions they had experienced between their identities and the perspective they took up in the letter. This poses questions about not only what learners are being asked to write in design-oriented multiliteracies pedagogies, but who they are potentially being asked to be (i.e., what kind of designers) in the midst of the literacy practices of the classroom.

Designers

The New London Group organized their treatise on multiliteracies around three key questions: the why, the social changes in public and private life and work taking shape at the turn of millennium when they wrote; the what, i.e., the designs; and the how, the pedagogy of designing and the metalanguage that informs it. Given the scope of contexts within which the authors lived and worked, it is perhaps unsurprising but nevertheless striking that they did not pose the question *who*?

Multiliteracies pedagogies require a shift in the balance of agency; the notion of language use as an active process of meaning designs implies new positionalities for language learners (see Paesani 2016; Swaffar and Arens 2005, Swaffar, Arens, and Byrnes 1991). Kern and Schultz (2005) describe this as an ethical dimension of multiliteracies pedagogies because it put the accent on learners' capacity to deal—sometimes more, sometimes less successfully—with complex situations using the repertoire of resources available to them, rather than focusing on their potential deficiencies vis-a-vis prescriptive standards (388–9). And yet, in discussions of multiliteracies in second language studies, overwhelmingly the identities of the designers in the classroom are reduced to their position as learners (comp. Firth and Wagner 1997). Writing from the purview of linguistic anthropology, Duranti has noted that a deliberate focus on participation rather than context can encourage perspective, wherein social actors are viewed as not simply embedded, but as actively involved in linguistic practices (2001, 173). Because the linguistic practices of the second language classroom are often de facto positioned as contextually *othered*, i.e., as foreign, there is a tendency for context to take center stage, leaving designers and their active participation in meaning design in the wings.

While the artifacts of literacy practices, i.e., texts, are shaped through the cultural and situational contexts of their production, they also have a material nature that allows them to move across space and time in a relatively consistent shape or design; literacy is thus also *transcontextual* (Kell 2015; see also Risager 2006). Scholars in language and culture teaching have emphasized that literacy in a second language is thus not only about "what texts mean in an absolute sense, [but] what people mean by texts" and also "what texts mean to people who belong to different discourse communities" (Kern 2000, 2). Because literacy is transcontextual, it is necessarily dynamic—that is, what a text can mean shifts as it comes into contact with new readers.

Literacy involves a multiplicity of meanings—ambivalences, ambiguities, intertextualities, and complexities—that emerge as texts and practices move across social lives. Building upon Bakhtin's (1981) much-cited characterization of language as dialogic, we could say that not only every word, but every genre, every text has a history of usage which it echoes and to which it responds and at the same time is highly contingent. This means that even the most well-designed text is, in the midst of literacy activity, un(der)determined outside of its interaction with human designers of meaning. Across a series of publications, my colleague David Gramling and I have theorized the complex readerly positions of second language learners (Gramling and Warner 2011; Warner and Gramling 2013, 2014; Warner 2014). We argue that the most powerful potential of transcontextuality of texts, especially those read aesthetically such as literature, lies not in their reading as artifacts asking to be fixed back into their origin stories but in the multilayered semiotic worlds, with which they have come into contact and whose traces they carry. Relatedly, we propose a distinction between *nationalist readings* and *imperial readings* (Warner and Gramling 2013). Whereas the former are oriented toward historical and cultural appropriateness as located in nationally rooted speech communities, *imperial readings* are concerned with the value and valorization of certain messages, with the ways in which they are transmitted, and the kinds of social traffic they tend to encounter along the way. In other words, imperial reading asks students to reflect on their reading alongside other ways of reading as part of a larger conversation about available designs and acts of designing as they are situated in relations of power, within which some readings have been deemed more legitimate or authorized than others—and then to reflect on how they wish to position themselves as multilingual language users, i.e., as designers of meaning through and with literary texts, within this constellation of multilayered semiotic worlds.

When language learners are positioned as active designers of meaning rather than as cultural decoders or mediators, it quickly becomes clear that their positioning as flat, static, tourist-like personas, as found in many textbooks and materials, is an inadequate representation (Ros i Solé 2016, 56). An understanding of language learners as designers thus must acknowledge the unique subjectivities and lived experiences of second language users as more than simply representatives of or mediators for the given cultures with which they are identified (see Blyth 2018; Kramsch and Nolden 1994; Michelson and Dupuy 2014; Warner 2014; Warner and Gramling 2013), but as thinking, feeling languagers. To borrow from Ros i Solé's call for attention to the personal dimensions of language learning, "[L]anguage learners become not only performers and 'actors' of languaculture scripts, but they infuse it with new meanings and new voices …" (2016, 24). In the parlance of multiliteracies, they are the (re-)designers of new designs, and this by virtue of not in spite of positions as learners.

Learners' subjectivities and their identities as designers have received attention in some of the more recent publications on literacy and second language learning. Many of these studies emphasize the potential of aesthetics and fiction in creating opportunities for learners to explore this dimension of multiliteracy practice. For example, Blyth (2018) uses two case studies of French language learners and their engagements with poetry to show how students' opportunity to take up the position of multilingual subject contributed to an emergent sense of themselves as authentic speakers. Michelson and Petit (2017) and Michelson (2018) report on the integration of multiliteracies pedagogies with global simulation, wherein students acted as fictitious characters and interacted with others in the class within the simulated version of a Parisian neighborhood, and show how this created opportunities for learners to take up roles as social actors within culture, and in so doing to engage with positions and subjectivities other than their own in the act of designing meaning. Similarly, Timlin et al. (2021) developed a small-scale global simulation for a content-based German language-culture course on fairy tales, creating a space in which students could take up new perspectives and engage in worldbuilding, as they made connections between the imagined worlds of literature and film and the everyday lifeworlds of a simulated contemporary German town. Notably, subjectivity in these studies was not synonymous with personalization, but rather with something like what Krueger (2001) characterized as *creative personalization*, activities in which imagined perspectives or contexts provide a creative lens through which learners can engage meaningfully with communication or interpretation.

Several publications focus on the specific experiences of heritage language learners (e.g., Choi 2015; Colombi and Achugar 2008; Suh and Jung 2020; Zapata and Lacorte 2017). Like the already cited studies from "foreign" or "second" language classrooms, these studies suggest the opportunity to engage as active designers of meaning enables learners to construct emergent identities as multilingual speakers beyond the learner positionalities that are most foregrounded in many classroom practices. Scholars focusing on heritage Spanish learners in the United States also see learning by design as a much-needed alternative to deficit-models informed by idealized notions of communicative competence, which have contributed to the minoritization of Hispanic Americans (e.g., Colombi and Achugar 2008; Parra, Otero, Flores, and Lavallée 2017; Zapata and Lacort 2017; Zapata 2022). In comparison, multiliteracies pedagogies offer a framework for theorizing biliteracy "that embraces the multiplicity and polysemy of language use rather than conceiving of communication as the manifest singularity of expression and intent" (Samaniego and Warner 2016, 192). Zapata's book *Learning by Design and Language Teaching* (2002) expands the scope of her earlier work (i.e., Zapata and Lacort 2017), and brings lessons she learned from the Spanish as a heritage language classroom to bear on the broader framework of multiliteracies in language education. A key aspect of this is an emphasis on social justice pedagogies as a necessary principle for her model of learning-by-design, which invites learners to reflect on their own identities in relation to the diverse perspectives and experiences that shape how others make meaning, as well as the ideologies and systems of power within which they participate as designers and their responsibility to act in resistance to exclusion, prejudice, and injustice (Zapata 2022, 28).

A model of multiliteracies that attends to available designs and designing but not those doing the designing, as Allen and Goodspeed (2018) intimated, risks reducing literacy to the realization of often idealized text-based learning outcomes. Learners' perspectives and identities are sidelined—but so are complexity, care, and compassion (Levine and Phipps 2011). When designing happens in ways that are glib, unreflective, prejudicial, or narrowly self-centered and damaging, what is being promoted is not design, Cope and Kalantzis (2011) argue, but "undesign," "something less than design" (55). Undesign is the result of what Freire described as "naive thinking" in contrast to critical thinking. "For the naive thinker, the important thing is accommodation to this normalized 'today'. For the critic the important thing is the continuing humanization of people" (Freire 2007[1970], 92). The transformative potential of multiliteracies theory thus relies on not only the ability to reflectively reproduce designs but on a recognition—on the part of learners and educators—that designs and acts of designing have an ethical dimension vis-a-vis others and themselves. In the process of expanding one's repertoire for meaning making, learning a new language is, perhaps most importantly, an opportunity to reflect on what kind of designer one wants to be.

From the Designs to the Redesigners

A core premise of this chapter has been that design is a helpful heuristic for conceptualizing and realizing pedagogies that recognize the dynamic, creative, socially situated nature of all language use and that locate language learning in cultures of use that are inherently linguistic but also not exclusively so. At the same time, in the last section I expressed concerns about idealized models of design that do not take into account the complex subjectivities of designers (i.e., the human agents involved in the various processes of meaning making through which literacy takes on life). Without attention to learner's multilingual subjectivities, the notion of design risks becoming merely a new bottle within which the old wine of idealized communication might be poured (compare Warner 2020). What is potentially transformed in multiliteracies pedagogies is not only or even most importantly texts, but those who engage with them. The pedagogical heuristics and analytical metalanguages that have been developed under the rubric of multiliteracies have made important strides in realizing more meaning-oriented frameworks in second language and culture teaching. There is, however, a persistent tendency to position language learners in the role of interlopers and to idealize the complex semiotic worlds into which they are stepping as they learn new languages as targets that can be met through appropriateness.[5] Designs and designing lose much of their transformative potential, as they are rendered ways of realizing that which was already there.

Expounding on the notion of designing social futures from the New London Group's original manifesto, Cope and Kalantzis (2000) suggest that not all acts of designing meaning are equally transformative or creative; "there is agency and agency, designing and designing" (205). Designing is always transformative, but some acts of designing are, they note, more transformative than others. The distinction, they explain, can be understood in relation to Husserl's phenomenology and specifically the concept of the lifeworld, the world of everyday lived experience. It "is always already there, existing in advance of us" and yet we have the potential to be "wakingly alive in it ... somehow interested subjects" (206). This requires a reflecting back on what interests us, what is taken for granted, a suspension of belief (208). Cope and Kalantzis's emphasis on literacy as transformation rather than transmission aligns with views of language learning that emphasize not appropriateness but the "[r]eflection that accompanies interpretation and explores the diversity of interpretations, assumptions, perspectives, positions, expectations, and judgments, and includes reflexivity that turns one's own experience into an object of critical examination" (Leung and Scarino 2016, 90).

Viewing students as interested multilingual subjects, thus, compels us to acknowledge the unique subjectivities and lived experiences of second language users as more than simply representatives of or mediators for the given cultures with which they are identified (see Kramsch and Nolden 1994; Michelson and Dupuy 2014; Warner 2014; Warner and Gramling 2013). Kramsch's theorization of symbolic competence moves in this direction by defining it as the capability to make sense of the cultural memories evoked by symbolic systems, but also to create alternate realities and to shape and even reframe the multilingual game in which one invests (Kramsch and Whiteside 2008, 667; Kramsch 2011, 359). Kramsch's references to the "multilingual game" point to the influence of Bourdieu's practice theory, wherein "a feel for the game" is one of the favored metaphors for the interrelation between a field of social and symbolic activity and the habitus, or *sens practique* (practical sense) (e.g., Bourdieu 1980). Like Cope and Kalantzis's use of Husserl's lifeworld, Kramsch's Bourdeusian notion of the multilingual game[6] serves to simultaneously remind us that languaging, and most poignantly taking up a new language, involves stepping into a social terrain that has already been contoured with well-traveled paths and positions that have already been worn into comfortable ways of moving and being; but there are always sideways and byways to discover or stumble into.

Writing of the ecological theories that ungird her concept of symbolic competence, Kramsch notes, "[t]oday language users have to navigate much less predictable exchanges ... [t]hey are asked to mediate inordinately more complex encounters among interlocutors with multiple language capacities and cultural imaginations, and different social and political memories" (Kramsch 2008, 390). Literacy scholars Stornaiulolo, Hull, and Nelson (2009) have relatedly advocated for a multiliteracies perspective rooted in diversity "that understands literacy as a negotiation of multiple linguistic and cultural differences through the design and redesign processes" (382). Learning in these theories is not located in the destination but in the navigation and negotiation, that is, in the movement (see also Leader and Boldt 2018, 35–6). The movement of the learner, in the sense of the potential for self-creation that is captured in Cope and Kalantzis's (2009) insistence that the "process of designing redesigns the designer" (184); but learning is also connected to movement in the sense of worldmaking, "a process of constructing shared worlds through symbolic practices that intertwine the creative, ethical, and intellectual" through acts of meaning making (Stornaiuolo 2015, 561). To put it more succinctly: in the potential for changing themselves, learners also tap into their potential for changing the world. Kern suggested that this was indeed one of the most important affordances of engaging with texts in the second language classroom, because unlike speaking, written texts can allow "learners' language use to go beyond 'functional' [read: instrumental] communication, making it possible to create imagined worlds of their own design" (Kern 2000, 172).

This way of framing literacy and language development then also asks us to consider what moves our language learners. This orientation suggests some topics that are likely familiar to most second language education scholars and practitioners related to motivation and engagement but also a wider scope of experiences and dispositions, of pushes and pulls that come into play during learners' encounters with new meaning designs. In the next chapter, we will take up the question of how multiliteracy in second language and culture education not only involves the structuring potential of designs but also the destabilizing potential of desires.

2

Desires

Affect and Aesthetics in Literacy and Language Learning

Literacy as a Felt Experience: A Tale of Two Multiliteracies Lessons

Two first-year graduate student instructors are collaboratively designing a lesson plan for their beginning German language-culture courses at a university in the American southwest. The goal is to connect the textbook material to principles of multiliteracies pedagogies, and the provocation to do so comes from a graduate seminar on literacy and language teaching, within which they are both enrolled. This all just happens to align with the 25th anniversary of the fall of the Berlin Wall, and the two instructors—Liam, who is American, and Michael, who grew up in Eastern Germany—want to somehow connect these events to the textbook unit at hand; the overt objective is communicative, namely *talking about what one has and what one likes to do,* but the underlying focus is structural: students are learning about the verbs *haben (to have)* and *sein (to be)* and accordingly about the nominative and accusative cases. Inspired by the readings for the seminar, the two instructors, Michael and Liam,[1] have centered multimodality in their lesson. For the first activities students will be writing captions for photographs and in the second part of the lesson, they will watch a historical video clip. According to their lesson proposal for the seminar, they understand a "multiliteral" approach to not only encompass "socio-cultural contexts of different countries ... but also different cultures and their implications within the same country." In this case the different cultures are those that developed in the two Germanies, between the construction of the Berlin Wall in 1961 and its eventual fall followed by the German reunification starting in November of 1989.

In their co-authored lesson plan, the two instructors propose "descriptive and interpretive tasks" working with photographs that depict everyday objects and experiences that are likely to be commonly shared, e.g., cars, apartments, vacation spots; while one set of images depicted typical variations of these things that people might have had and done in West Germany in the 1970s and 1980s, the second set features those that would have been familiar to someone living in East Germany at that time. Students will be asked to imagine that these objects belong to them and to co-author short texts for each picture, stating what it is that they *have* or *do* (as represented in the image) and expressing positive feelings they might associate with this, using the simple set of adjectives they have learned in the first six weeks of class. Through this activity, the two instructors are very deliberately trying to bridge between communicative and multiliteracies pedagogies, as they write in their proposal:

> Due to the communicative nature of the basic language course and acknowledging the limited vocabulary of the first-semester FL learner, the student will be provided a vocabulary list to assist them in creating simple sentences to help scaffold the conveyance of meaning, including descriptions and elaboration on communicative topics, and the emotional state these 'texts' create.

While the theme *possessions and pleasures* (*Besitz und Vergnügen*) from their communicative-oriented textbook is central to their lesson, Michael and Liam's plans also express an emergent awareness of how meaning is designed in the images. The two instructors do not treat the photos as neutral illustrations, but as texts with the potential to be emotionally evocative. For the second part of the lesson, the instructors plan to bring in a documentary clip from a pivotal moment in the fall of the Berlin Wall—a press conference where Günter Schabowski, acting as a spokesperson for the East German Socialist Unity Party, improvised an answer to a question about a forthcoming policy change allowing East German citizens to travel more freely outside of the country. Pressed to say when the borders would begin to open, he declared that it would take effect "sofort, unverzüglich" (immediately, without delay). This prompted throngs of Germans on both sides to rush to border crossings along the Berlin Wall, who then pressed upon the rather unprepared border guards to let them through, hastening the opening of the wall and by many accounts the reunification of the divided nation-state. Liam and Michael's attempts to combine communicative and knowledge-focused learning objectives with multiliteracies pedagogical principles resulted in the following set of what they described as "language goals":

- The student can be able to give the date of the *Mauerfall* (fall of the wall).
- The student can describe the events that lead to the *Mauerfall* and can describe the people, and their emotions, affected by the event.
- The student will get an idea about the German division in east and west and the (still existent) differences.

In Liam and Michael's plan, we can see some tension between culture as facts and as meanings (Kern 2000, 31), with discrete information such as the dates on the one hand and the reference to the "people, their emotions" and how they were "affected" on the other hand. Within the proposal description itself, there are further connections made between language choice and meaning in the explanation of why this specific moment of history was chosen, as they hope to demonstrate "how just one sentence, one little mistake in wording can change the world."

The proposal and lesson plan co-created by these two instructors is an interesting artifact of how novice teachers' conceptual understanding of multiliteracies pedagogical principles might develop in dialogue with other frameworks. In this sense, Liam and Michael's lesson proposal illustrates the negotiation between teachers' already held beliefs about language and language learning and emergent understandings of new pedagogical concepts and frameworks, in ways that have also been documented by some of the scholars discussed in the previous chapter (e.g., Allen 2011; Allen and Dupuy 2013; Paesani and Allen 2020); but the diverging choices they made while actually teaching the shared lesson plan are revealing in their own ways.

At the start of the lesson, Michael greets the students as they enter the classroom, directing them either to the left side, where the desks had been arranged to face toward the center of the room, or the right side, where the desks were facing out a row of windows on an external wall. A line of tape running down the middle of the room and up the white board at the front of the classroom delineated these two sides. At the front of the classroom, the screen shows an image of the Berlin Wall. Once students are settled in, they are told that the left side of the classroom is East Germany and the right side is West Germany. Each group is then given their set of photographs along with the instructions for the first activity. Students work in their groups to craft short descriptions for each image, using simple sentences such as "Wir haben ein Auto. Das Auto ist klein und praktisch." (We have a car. The car is small and practical.) Although the instructor initially provided them with a list of vocabulary, students quickly ask if they can expand beyond this, and Michael responds in the affirmative and helps them to search for the words they want to use. A few minutes into the lesson, a woman arrives late to class and is assigned to the left side of the classroom, which is directly adjacent to the entrance. After pausing to take in the activity and the divided classroom, the student notices that her friends are on the other side of the tape "wall," and so she jumps with a theatrical leap across the wall into the West to work with that group. The instructor pretends not to notice this, but a smirk on his face betrays him. After they have worked for a while in their groups, students are asked to face forward. Michael opens a digital presentation, in which each slide features the two corresponding images, for example, a photo of a VW Beetle for the West German group next to an image of a *Trabi*, a car from Trabant, the most common automobile manufacturer in East Germany. The groups are asked to share their sentences, and their associations, and to compare with their counterparts, which results in a chorus of sentences in the first-person plural and the third-person plural orchestrated by the instructor. Even after seeing the contrasts between the different possessions and opportunities, many of the students on both sides insist vocally on the positive attributes they had used to describe the images, and some students from the East German side even grow competitive when asked to compare, arguing that theirs were the better cars, vacation spots, shopping centers, clothes, etc., and citing the attributes they had worked into their descriptions to support their case. The instructor encourages this by asking follow-up questions, always addressing the groups as West Germans and East Germans, thereby keeping the role-play premise of the activity salient. Students regularly, jovially talk over one another, creating a cacophony of voices around the photographic artifacts. The class then watches the clip of the press conference. When it becomes clear that the context and language of the video prove difficult for the students, Michael switches to English to briefly explain what had happened, as he does so, he also removes the tape line from the middle of the room. He then plays a short clip of the celebrations on and around the Berlin Wall on November 9, 1989. He finishes class by explaining that although the fall of the wall was a great celebration for many people, the process of reunification was more complex and ambivalent, and noting that many people in the East, where he himself grew up, felt loss and later nostalgia for everyday items and practices from East Germany.

Liam's class begins similarly. Like Michael, he had divided the room with a line of tape, displayed a photo of the Berlin Wall, and written East Germany and West Germany on the respective sides of the white board. He also directs students into their groups as they enter the classroom and indicates that they should talk only with other students in their group, but the desks remain facing the front of the classroom. Students are given the same images and asked to describe them using resources from the vocabulary list, but there is less deviation than in Michael's class. As Liam moves around the classroom, he, like Michael, supports students with designing their texts but the emphasis is on accuracy of expression rather than the role-play. The students are generally engaged and seem to take the activity seriously as language practice but pay little attention to the simulative framing. When the students are invited to share their sentences, the flow of talk largely follows what Cazden (1988) dubbed an IRE (initiation-response-evaluation) format, with Liam initiating student talk by calling on them to read their sentence and then following their contributions with an affirmative "gut" (good) or "Sehr gut" (very good). As the class settles into this pattern, the role-play scenario is abandoned completely. When Liam asks the students to compare their relative situations, students immediately deem the products and practices of the West better and state that life in East Germany was "unfair." As was the case in Michael's class, Liam switches to English to discuss the clip of the press conference where Günter Schabowski declared that the borders were open, but the feelings of ambivalence that surfaced in Michael's class are absent in their discussion. The object lesson of the images dovetails readily with narratives of Eastern Germany that are often assumed in US-based discourses around this historical context, and the resulting implication is that East Germany was unambiguously inferior, and the reunification was unequivocally good for Germans on both sides of the wall.

Michael and Liam's lesson studies were conducted as part of a graduate seminar, which I have had the opportunity to teach almost every other year since 2010. The course explores the relationship between multiliteracies and literariness in second language teaching research and practice.[2] The assigned readings have evolved over the last nearly a decade, but the lesson study has become a staple component, both because it gives the course participants an opportunity to engage reflectively with concepts and theories from our readings by working to realize them in practice (see also Paesani and Allen 2020), and because it gives me chance to observe the graduate students, who are all either in- or pre-service language instructors completing master's and Ph.D degrees in a range of language, literature, and linguistics programs and departments, within their diverse teaching contexts. The ability to compare co-written lesson plans brought to life in different classrooms has on multiple occasions served as a reminder of the ontological difference between task and activity (Thorne 2005, 399). Often, for the graduate student instructors, the reflective activities associated with the assignment and subsequent in-class discussion have brought to light the reality that there is no such thing as a perfectly designed lesson. Among the nearly 100 lesson studies I have observed as part of this seminar, the contrasting class sessions of Michael and Liam have stuck with me for the ways in which they brought into sharp relief that languaging and literacy activities are vitally felt experiences that cannot be captured or harnessed by even the best designed lesson plans.

The felt experience of Michael and Liam's classes can certainly, in part, be analyzed using the notion of design (discussed in the previous chapter). Through the lens of multiliteracies, we might note the role of spatial and gestural designs; the placement of the desks, orientation of students' gazes, kinesthetic choices of the students and instructors shaped the activities in these two classrooms every bit as much as the linguistic resources designed into the tasks, such as vocabulary lists, model sentences, and discourse structures adopted by Michael and Liam as they guided class discussion. However, bringing the joint lesson plan to life in Michael and Liam's respective classrooms offers multiple examples of the reality that language and our linguistic repertoires are not detached from our bodies, but manifest materially and spatially in ways which the designs alone cannot account for.

In both classes, students were using similar sets of linguistic resources—although Michael's students had opted to go beyond those provided—and they were responding to the same multimodal designs; and yet, the enactment of literacy was palpably different. Although students in both classes demonstrated evidence of being "engaged," in that they were attentive and responsive, Michael's class, through laughter and the buzz of talk, seemed alive with "the joy of being and doing things together" (Nordström, Kumpulainen, and Potter 2019). The convergence of semiotic resources, bodies, voices, space, and emotions also seemed to create different potentials for collective engagement and, in the case of Michael's class, for a more "open textured" literacy event (Barton and Baguley 2014), where some of the predefined stories and morals of East Germany became at least a little unstuck. Through their expressions of emotions of joy, love, pride, and pleasure in relation to the objects from East Germany, the students created an alternate space for the discussion of German reunification that followed. They were, to borrow from Leander and Boldt's arguments for affective literacy theory, not engaging in ways that were overtly critical or political, but which nevertheless held the potential for creativity, indeterminacy, and transformation (see Leander and Boldt 2013, 44).

While the metalanguage of design and semiotics can be immensely valuable for analyzing and conceptualizing the elements of meaning making that contribute to the lived experience of being a human subject who is bodily and emotional interacting with other subjects, it does not quite account for "the affective intensities" of languaging "and their effects produced across texts, bodies, and interaction" (Leander & Boldt 2013, 38). A growing body of work in literacy studies, applied linguistics, and second language studies in language teaching and learning considers these affective dimensions of language and teaching and learning. The current chapter takes up a question running through these studies: how can our pedagogies respond to students' desire to move and be moved through language learning? In order to engage with this line of inquiry and to consider how desire might relate to the model of designs discussed in Chapter 1, we must first develop a framework for affect in second language learning and teaching contexts.

Affect in Second Language and Literacy Studies: Emotions, Motivations, Desires

Within fields of the humanities and social sciences, it has become common to speak of an "affective turn" and its effects on scholarship in recent years (Athanasiou, Hantzaroula, and Yannakopolous 2008; Clough and Halley 2007; Gregg and Seigworth 2010). As previously noted in relation to the "multi-turn" in applied linguistics and second language studies (see Introduction), academic turns are more often than not a twisty mix of turning back and reframing a current moment, rather than a turn away or departure from a paradigm and the "affective turn" as it has taken root in applied linguistics and second language studies is no exception. In a 2019 contribution to a *Modern Language Journal* forum on the topic of emotions in second language learning and teaching, Prior notes that emotions and affect have long been present in discussions of second language learning, especially in relation to effective pedagogies that might support it; and yet, they have often remained the "elephants in the room—poorly studied, poorly understood, seen as inferior to rational thought" (Swain 2013, 11; also cited by Prior 2019, 516). What has shifted in recent years is both the place of emotions, as a legitimate and central object of study in second language studies and applied linguistics (Dewaele 2005; Dewaele and Li 2020; Douglas Fir Group 2016, 36), as well as the scope of research on the affective dimensions of language teaching and learning and the theories and concepts that inform that work (Benesch 2012; Pavlenko 2013; Prior 2019).

The Affective Filter: Cognitive Models

One of the most pervasive and persistent concepts in second language acquisition theories has been Krashen's "affective filter hypothesis." Drawing from Dulay and Burtt's (1977) essay on creativity in language acquisition,

Krashen (1982) proposed that three "attitudinal factors" (31) have a significant influence on successful language acquisition: high motivation, strong self-confidence, and low anxiety. As an innatist, whose model of second language acquisition was heavily influenced by the work of Chomsky, Krashen's attention to affect was directly connected to its potential impact on natural language acquisition, understood here in opposition to language learning, which for Krashen involves a conscious knowledge of a second language and the ability to articulate its rules and conventions (1982, 10). The "affective filter hypothesis" was in effect an elaboration on his core idea of the "input hypothesis," the idea that language acquisition happens through the understanding of language that contains structures just a bit beyond an individual's current level of competence (which Krashen dubbed i + 1) (1982, 21). Positive affect, i.e., motivation and self-confidence, predicts whether a person will seek out new comprehensible input, and negative affect, i.e., anxiety, can create a situation in which "even if they understand the message, the input will not reach the part of the brain responsible for acquisition" (31).

Krashen's ideas continue to be both highly influential and heavily debated. Critics have pointed out that the "affective filter hypothesis" is difficult to test and not supported well by empirical research (see Benesch 2012, 7); and yet, the underlying belief that affect has an impact on second language development and that there are positive and negative forms of affect has informed much of the scholarship on affect in this field until quite recently. The overwhelmingly cognitive focus of the field of applied linguistics in the 1980s and into the 1990s has helped to sustain Krashen's conjecture that affect is of interest exclusively because it can either facilitate or impair cognitive processes involved in learning and/or acquisition (depending on the preferred terms if a given scholar or model). This trend can be seen in the volume *Affect in Language Teaching* (Arnold 1999). The collection takes a self-described "holistic" or "cognitive humanistic" approach; the eighteen chapters all strongly emphasize cognitive dimensions such as memory, but there are also discussions of sociocultural theory and sociolinguistics, as well as what Arnold and Brown—in the first chapter of the volume—describe as "relational factors" (18), such as intergroup dynamics and collaboration. Despite this more interdisciplinary orientation, a focus in this volume, which is reiterated in Arnold's more recent work on the intersection between cognition and affect and shares assumptions with Krashen, is that an "affectively positive environment puts the brain in the optimal state for learning" (146). The instructor's role is accordingly, in such a view, to foster the good kinds of affect, while diminishing the negative kinds of affect, so that learners can "move beyond" emotions that might get in the way of learning.

Affect as Lived Experience: Sociocultural Models

Sociocultural models of learning and development see cognition and affect as not only related, as Arnold (1999) and others advocated, but as inextricably interconnected, and this can serve as a valuable counterpoint to cognitivist and psychological models. Inspired and informed by Vygotsky's development theories, sociocultural approaches conceptualize both cognition and affect as part of what Vygotsky in Russian referred to as *perezhivanie*, a word that has typically been translated as *experience* or *lived experience* (Lantolf and Swain 2019, 528). The concept of *perezhivanie* was first discussed by Vygotsky in *The Psychology of Art* (1971[1925]), where it was used more or less to refer to aesthetic experience, the ways in which one might respond to a work of art. In later work, however, the concept developed as part of his model of consciousness (e.g., Vygotksy 1997; see also Lantolf, 2021) into a broader claim that thinking always implicates an emotional response in relation to other individuals, objects, and events (see Lantolf and Swain 2019, 529). Furthermore, in sociocultural theory, neither knowledge nor emotions are located in individuals; instead, they are socially distributed, created within cultural systems of activity. "We internalize emotional meaning from our interactions with others" (Swain 2013, 204), and language is one of the primary tools we use for mediating this knowledge. Emotions are thus not seen as a strictly physiological process that exists almost independently or willfully in opposition to cognition and higher-order thinking. Emotional meanings are themselves internalized from our sociocultural world; they carry long histories but are also dynamic. An important implication of this is that the very categorization of emotions as positive or negative is itself culturally imbued.

It is striking how much of the work that delves deeply into sociocultural approaches to emotions and affect has focused not on language learning or acquisition but on teacher education (e.g., Golombek and Johnson 2004; Johnson and Golombek 2003). The intersubjective model of emotions and cognition that is promoted through sociocultural theory necessarily implies a recognition that not only language learners but also language teachers are thinking and *feeling* beings, and this in turn calls for second language research that considers the role that aesthetic experience and emotional meanings play in pedagogical practice.

Motivation as a Key Form of Affect in Second Language-Culture Learning

Motivation has been one of the, if not the, most researched and theorized kinds of affect in second language teaching and learning (see Dörnyei 2001). In discourses around language teaching, the assumption is both that motivation falls into the good kinds of affect, as suggested by Krashen, and that other affective factors can impact motivation. While early models of motivation and language learning were likewise cognitively focused, parallel discussions about the interconnectedness of cognition and affect in motivational studies since the 2000s have resulted in an increasing emphasis on the social and contextual dimensions of motivation (see Dörnyei and Ushioda 2021, 7). It is widely accepted that a particular context in the sense of a classroom or instructional setting can contribute to feelings of stress and anxiety on the one hand or comfort and collaboration on the other hand, which might impact someone's motivation—an aspect of this research that seems quite compatible with the affective filter hypothesis. However, more socially oriented theories of motivation also recognize that the cluster of feelings and relationships we associate with motivation are shaped by longer histories of social, cultural, personal, and emotional experiences that a person carries with them (macro-contexts), as well as local environments within which motivation is emergent and contingent (micro-contexts). Ushioda (2009) has theorized this more relational view of motivation in connection with an emphasis on what she calls "person-in-context." For Ushioda this entails,

> a focus on real persons, rather than on learners as theoretical abstractions; a focus on the agency of the individual person as a thinking, feeling human being, with an identity, a personality, a unique history and background, a person with goals, motives and intentions; a focus on the interaction between this self-reflective intentional agent, and the fluid and complex system of social relations, activities, experiences and multiple micro—and macro-contexts in which the person is embedded, moves, and is inherently part of.
>
> (220)

Dörnyei's (2005, 2009) model of the "L2 Motivational Self System" focuses attention on another vital dimension of motivation, the relationship between a given activity and one's imagined future selves, who we desire to be. As Dörnyei and Ushioda (2021) describe it, "The notion of possible selves concerns how people conceptualise their as-yet unrealised potential, and as such, it also draws on hopes, wishes and fantasies" (60). We orient ourselves toward who we want to become, and this in itself is closely tied to the emotional meanings we scribe to different identities and roles in our social worlds. Dörnyei (2005, 2009) theorized three different dimensions of the motivational self-system as it relates to second language learning: (1) the Ideal L2 Self, a specific facet of one's idea self that incorporates speaking the language(s) we are learning; (2) the Ought-to L2 Self, which relates to the characteristics one believes one ought to have to meet others' expectations and avoid negative consequences; and (3) the L2 Learning Experience, which concerns the situated motives that arise in relation to the learning environment, curriculum, peer group, teacher interactions, etc.

Norton's model of investment also theorizes desire for an imagined future self as a vital part of the experience of learning a new language. Drawing from Anderson's notion of *imagined communities*, Norton and other scholars have theorized one's investment in a language and/or a particular opportunity for language learning as inextricably bound to one's identity (Norton Peirce 1995; Norton 2000, 2013; Norton and Darvin 2015), defined as "how a person understands [their] relationship to the world, how that relationship is structured across time and space, and how the person understands possibilities for the future" (Norton 2013, 45). Motivation in Dörnyei's model of the self-system and investment in Norton's theories share in common a recognition that one's relationship to language learning can be ambivalent, complex, and fluid; however, Norton more deliberately centers power and struggle (Norton 2013; Norton and Darvin 2015), and consequently also raises questions of how the environment of the classroom and pedagogical practice intersects with socially inculcated structures of feeling and emotions (see Darvin and Norton 2015, 26).

By emphasizing not only learners' sense of themselves and their imagined, ideal future selves, Norton's model of investment emphasizes their engaged relationships with the sociocultural environments within which they use language, including the classroom, and treats motivation not as primarily psychological but relational. There are some notable parallels between this view and sociocultural theories of motivation and development, inspired by Vygotsky's theories. Motivation arises in what Vygotsky (1994) called the "social situation of development" (SSD), a dialectical relationship between an individual and their social surroundings, which mediate their experience. This in turn is shaped or refracted through *perezhivanie*, that emotionally charged lived experience of the situation. As Lantolf (2021), one of the preeminent scholars of sociocultural theory in applied linguistics, describes it, "Only those aspects of the environment that emotionally impact and intellectually challenge the individual in the process of developing (i.e., becoming what they not yet are) are refracted through the mental prism of that individual" (3). Emotional experience motivates thinking by creating a relationship between one's consciousness and an object, which can be a text or image or even an event, like classroom group work and discussion. Motivation as theorized by Vygotsky is neither positive nor negative, but it is caught up in one's emotional entanglement in the world around them. We learn exactly because we are motivated to engage with and act upon the world within which we live.

In the theoretical models discussed in this section, motivation comes to refer to what moves students to learn a new language in two senses—(1) in relation to their sense of self and their imagined and ideal potential future selves, including their multilingual subjectivities, and (2) in relation to their moment-to-moment engagement within their social environments, including the linguistic dimensions thereof. Across this body of research run two strands, which are helpful for understanding current discussions of affect and language learning more broadly. First, these models focus attention not on individual cognitive states or attitudes but on relationships between socially engaged human beings and the complex environments within which they live and learn. Second, although motivation is still a concern for educators, it is not positioned as operating like an on/off switch; the question is not only whether one is motivated (good affect) or unmotivated (bad affect) but what various factors and influences shape the sometimes ambiguous, nuanced experience of being motivated. Both of these dimensions come to play in the next two sub-sections, where we will continue to build from these social views of affect toward a theory of affect as desire.

Critical Affect Theories in Literacy Studies and Applied Linguistics: Theorizing Affect as Desire

While early discussions of motivation, emotions, and language learning are often psychologically grounded and share assumptions that feelings are either positive nor negative and accordingly can impact cognition and attitudes toward learning in more or less discretely measurable ways, the more contemporary discussions of motivation and investment cited in the previous section shift from viewing affect as discernible psychological dispositions to an interest in imagination, experientiality, and desire. This opens up a space for more nuanced, ambivalent understandings of affect, as situated, relational, and dynamic. Affect and desire in such accounts are conceptualized in conjunction with what are often labeled as post-structuralist or phenomenological views of subjectivity (e.g., Creese and Blackledge 2015; Busch 2017; Kramsch 2009; Penycook 2018; Ros i Solé 2016), which include an increased care for the "lived experiences of multiple language users" (Kramsch 2009, 2). These experiences are shaped by the environments in which languages are used and learned—as emphasized within sociocultural theory—and through the people's sense of who they are and who they might be—as described by the theories of self, identity, and investment. Desire in these theories does not just stand in for intentionality or want but is conceptualized as dynamic, embodied, and multisensorial (e.g., Blackledge and Creese 2019; Busch 2017; Kramsch 2009; Pennycook 2018; Ros i Solé 2016; Ros i Solé, Fenoulhet, and Quist 2020).

A dimension of these discussions, which extends beyond the particular focus on motivation, is the movement away from the conceptualization of emotions as individual learner variables and the related notion that they can be treated as discrete objects of inquiry and toward a much broader, more amorphous concept of affect. The collaborative and individual contributions of Guattari and Deleuze (e.g., Deleuze 1987[1980], 1997; Deleuze and Guattari 1994; Guattari 1996), whose works serve as one of the dominant theoretical inspirations within the larger affective turn, have also had an impact in second language studies. Guattari and Deleuze base their initial understandings of affect in a re-reading of the philosophies of Spinoza. In his *Ethics*, Spinoza used the term affectation to describe bodily (which for him include mental) states that are related to but not reducible to feelings and emotions, during which the powers of the body to act are increased or constrained.[3] For Spinoza, affect is transitional and transitory. Deleuze and Guattari share this understanding, leading them to define affect as "becoming" (1987[1980], 256) or in a more extended version offered by Guattari as "a process of existential appropriation through the continual creation of heterogeneous durations of being" (1996, 159). Acknowledging that much of Deleuze and Guattari's writings can feel somewhat opaque to those new to their ideas, Murphie (2010) offers a perhaps more accessible "translation" of their definition of affect: "Affects make up the relations within the temporary worlds we are constantly creating, and by which we are constantly being created. Affect involves the moment-to-moment question of being in the world, in all its constant change" (n.p.). Zournazi (2003), one of the leading scholars in this field, describes affect similarly: "When we navigate our way through the world, there are different pulls, constraints and freedoms that move us forward and propel us into life" (210). Affect in this sense is unstructured, pre-linguistic, and affect theory is positioned as part of a critique of poststructuralism, which is viewed as overly deterministic (e.g., Clough 2007; Massumi 2002; see also Benesch 2012, 40). Massumi (2002), a key translator of Deleuze and Guattari and an affect theorist in his own right, makes such a claim when he equates affect with "intensity," which he argues is not "semantically or semiotically ordered," but which "is embodied in purely autonomic reactions most directly manifested in the skin—at the surface of the body, at its interface with things" (24–5). Massumi challenges notions of meaning making that see every possible signifying move as "a selection from a repertoire of possible permutations on a limited set of predetermined terms" (2002, 3). Recasting his argument in relation to multiliteracy theory, Massumi would likely attune our attention less to the designs (the structures) of meaning and more to their movement, the unpredictable coming together of elements that are experienced.

Deleuzian/Guattarian understandings of affect have likewise been formative for a growing body of work on affect in literacy (e.g., Leander and Ehret 2019; Cole 2013). One of the seminal publications in these discussions is a critical re-reading of the 1994 New London Group, written by Leander and Boldt (2013), in which they take issue with what they describe as the "hyperrationality" of the multiliteracies framework. While the notion of design can help to conceptualize the complexity of language and literacy, it often suggests a directionality of purpose and intent, thereby overemphasizing the rationality behind design choices and underemphasizing the fluidity, creativity, and playfulness inherent in meaning making. Leander and Boldt argue that "[l]iteracy-related activity is often not projected toward some textual end point, but as living its life in the ongoing present, forming relations and connections across signs, objects, and bodies in often unexpected ways" (2013, 26) and it is therefore "is saturated with affect and emotion … it creates and is fed by an ongoing series of affective intensities that are different from the rational control of meanings and forms" (2013, 26).

A vital group of literacy scholars have shared in Leander and Boldt's critique and the implied interest in the "felt force" (Hollet 2020), and their work often appears as "affective literacy studies" (e.g., Ehret and Rowsell 2021; Leander and Boldt 2013; Leander and Ehret 2019; Pahl and Rowsell 2020). A parallel set of arguments has also been made by scholars Masny and Cole (2007, 2009) in their proposal for what they dub "multiple literacies theory" (MLT), sometimes referred to as "affective literacies," a model that they deliberately contrast with multiliteracies; whereas the former, they argue, conceptualizes experience in more phenomenological terms, privileging relatively stable categories, the latter they base in the same Deleuzian/Guattarian philosophies as Leander and Boldt's discussions, thus prioritizing connection, relationality, and affect (2007, 195–6; 2009, 14).

Whatever label it bears, the scholarship on literacy and affect referenced in this section recognizes that the multiliteracies framework does indeed make space for unintended meanings, creativity, and transformation in the notion of the redesigned; however, they argue, it also privileges organization and directionality over coincidence and relationality, and in doing so, locks our understandings of language and literacy in "freeze frames" while removing movement (Leander and Ehret 2019, 31). Both pedagogical practice and analysis in literacy and language studies thus need frameworks that will make space for the unpredictability of literacy and language as they are experienced in the flow of life. Drawing an additional contrast between their Deleuzian/Guattarian approach and sociocultural theories of literacy, Leander and Ehret (2019) describe their work as moving from a focus on the *with*, that is, what resources do individuals take up in order to engage in certain forms of activity, to an attention to the *and*, moments of collision and contingency that arise in the experience of literacy. Desire, in their understanding, arises as the potential "both more of the same along with the inevitability of something new" (37) in moments of what we might describe as inspiration, impulse, or improvisation.

The theoretical work of Deleuze and Guattari has also been influential in some recent scholarship in applied linguistics. For example, Pennycook (2017) and Ros i Solé, Fenoulhet, and Quist (2020) draw upon Deleuzian/Guattarian affect theory to propose approaches to translingual and intercultural encounters that focus on the "assemblage of bodies, of actions and passions, an intermingling of bodies reacting to one another" and the "collective assemblage of enunciation, of acts and statements of incorporeal transformations attributed to bodies" (Deleuze and Guattari 1987[1980], 88; cited by Pennycook 2017, 277). The notion of assemblage allows Ros i Solé, Fenoulhet, and Quist (2020) to theorize what they describe as the *vibrant identities* at play in intercultural encounters, of the kind facilitated in second language and culture teaching. In movement, the "slight misalignment of purposes, frictions, and rupture" that arises in encounters between intercultural agents, objects, and identities, "other realities and other possibilities" are created (397), thus opening up a space for indeterminacy. Similarly, Pennycook sees the idea of assemblage as a way to capture both the movement and indeterminacy already discussed in conjunction with Deleuzian/Guattarian strands of affect theory, but also human tendencies toward repetition and stability. Pennycook writes that while "we may appear to live in a world of fluidity ... fixity is always at play" (2017, 277). Pennycook (2017) and Ros i Solé, Fenoulhet, and Quist (2020) are concerned with how we can articulate and meaningfully analyze the complexity and the messiness of living across languages and culture, but also the potential joy that can be found in "new ways of seeing, interpreting, and thinking about ourselves" (Ros i Solé, Fenoulhet, and Quist 2020, 400).

Phenomenological frameworks (e.g., Merleau-Ponty 2012[1945]) including the affect theories of Ahmed (2004 and 2010) have also had a significant influence on recent scholarship on emotions and affect in second language teaching and learning (e.g., Benesch 2012; Song 2016). While sharing an understanding of affect as the intensities and resonances that circulate between (human and non-human) bodies, phenomenological approaches are interested in the ways in which these are pre-structured as emotional responses vis-a-vis recurring objects, circumstances, or relationships. In contrast to the emphasis on movement emphasized in the theories discussed above, Ahmed's work is concerned with the ways in which affect is socially shaped and shaping; although our experiences may not be wholly predetermined and presignified, there is an "already in place" dimension of affect that helps us to explain why we are "affected in some way more than others" (Ahmed 2010, 230).[4] Emotions and feelings are, as Ahmed describes it, "sticky"; they are always already attributed as good or bad, happy or unhappy (Ahmed 2010), and this itself is an effect "of the histories of contact between bodies, objects, and signs" through which these become sticky in the sense of stuck with certain kinds of affect (Ahmed 2004, 90). For Ahmed, emotions are not held by individuals, but circulate through objects and others, and through repetition sometimes result is an "accumulation of affective value" (Ahmed 2004, 92). Ahmed shares Massumi's driving question about how affect moves us, but likewise wishes to consider how it gets us stuck. This is of particular importance given Ahmed's interest in questions of racism, white nationalism, xenophobia (e.g., Ahmed 2004), and homophobia (e.g., Ahmed 2010), which also poses the question of how emotions in some moments might get unstuck (see also Ahmed 2010). Benesch (2012) shows how even more innocuous objects in the language classroom, like dictionaries and cellphones, can be sticky objects, with different affective values for students and teachers, and which contribute to classrooms getting stuck in practices that inadvertently entrench positions of inequity and power (57–75).

While the theories of affect inspired by Deleuze/Guattari and Ahmed differ in their respective and relative focus on the movement or stickiness of feelings, these ways of thinking about language learning and desires are not mutually exclusive. Languaging and literacy are both iterative and creative, generative and emergent, stabilizing and transformative. How we as learners, teachers, and researchers perceive languaging activities within the flow of experience (i.e., through *perezhivanie*) is shaped by what we understand to be at play in a given moment—which in turn takes us back to the role of second language users as multilingual subjects, as designers who are redesigned, which concluded the previous chapter and which will be the focus of the next sub-section.

Multilingual Subjectivities, Aesthetics, and Desire

In her conceptualization of multilingual subjectivities and desire, Kramsch (2009) includes both the predeterminate and the socially shaped dimensions of affect and language learning, albeit citing somewhat different theoretical inspirations. To theorize desire, Kramsch first draws heavily from Kristeva's (1980) psychoanalytical-feminist theory of humans as subjects-in-process who are continually being (re)made on the cusp of two realms: the semiotic, which for Kristeva is a pre-verbal, ahistorical, psychosomatic realm of emotions and feelings (see Kramsch 2009, 97), and the symbolic, which is mediated by linguistic and stylistic choices and meaning designs. Using Kristeva's theories, Kramsch highlights the aesthetic, affective dimensions of language learning that are not wholly outside of but are also in excess of rational assessments of material and symbolic capital, in ways that, while not wholly commensurate with the Deleuzian/Guattarian theories of affect, share some of the same concerns about the potential for transformation and change. For Kramsch desire is not necessarily directional; that is, it is not always a purposeful, intentional "desire to." She cites, for example, the many language memoirs in which language learning is associated with the desire for escape or for simply being *other* (14–15, 82–5). Kramsch's discussion of subjectivity and desire reminds us that language learning is not only shaped by actuarial decisions related to potential losses and gains, but also by often more affective pushes and pulls that are in excess of language and semiotic systems, even when they find their way into those modes of expression.

At the same time, Kramsch emphasizes, language is not only something we experience, but something we do with others, in social contexts. In this role of "social actor" (Kramsch 2009, 103; see also Liddicoat and Kern 2011), we develop a sense for how certain ways of speaking and engaging with language and other semiotic systems will be received, what kinds of "symbolic capital" they carry, and even what kinds of moral feelings are associated with them (Kramsch 2009, 112–13). Citing both the social praxis theory of Bourdieu and Damasio's neuroscientific model of emotion, Kramsch puts forth a model of social action as, to borrow Ahmed's verbiage, sticky with emotions.

The affective is thus a vital dimension of Kramsch's model of symbolic competence (see Chapter 1). In subsequent work, Kramsch continues to stress the centrality of emotions, memories, subjective resonances, and aesthetics in the development of this capacity (e.g., Kramsch 2009, 2011). Symbolic competence can be understood as a way of engaging with symbolic power, in its both social and affective dimensions. Although she does not say so directly, from Kramsch's writings (2009, 2011), we can extrapolate that symbolic competence can be wielded both in ways that subvert and are complicit in symbolic power (compare with discussion of design and undesign in Chapter 1). Putting Ahmed and Kramsch's theories in dialogue with one another, we can also consider to what extent symbolic competence creates the potential for unsticking some of the affective value accumulated by an object or activity.

Multilingual subjectivity has a dual nature, in that it is shaped by simultaneously acting upon (being the subject of/affecting) and being acted upon (being subjected to/being affected) the meanings and sensations of languages and languaging. Kramsch's repeated emphasis on aesthetics is also directly linked to a model of language learning that embraces this duality. In her seminal work on aesthetic ways of reading, which also influenced Kramsch's work, Rosenblatt (1986, 1982, 1994[1978], 1994) treated language not as "a self-contained, ungrounded, ready-made code of signifier and signifieds, but as embodied in transactions between individuals and their social and natural context" (Rosenblatt 1986, 123). In the act of reading, the reader consciously or unconsciously chooses a stance, a *selective attitude*, "bringing certain aspects into the center of attention and pushing others into the fringes" (Rosenblatt 1994, 5).

Rosenblatt conceptualized this push and pull of attention along a dynamic continuum of efferent and aesthetic, depending on whether attention is more focused on what is to be done when the reading ends (efferent) or whether she welcomes into awareness the sensations, images, feelings, and ideas evoked through reading (aesthetic). Aesthetic languaging is open to "the nature of experience as apprehended through perceptions, senses, and emotions, [...] the expressive and imaginative potential in the self and the primacy of the individual's ascription of meaning to experience," borrowing here from Leung and Scarino's more recent discussion of the role of the aesthetic in contemporary language education (2016, 89). In the sense used previously in connection with Vygotsky's notion of *perezhivanie*, language and literacy activities are for

Rosenblatt motivated; how they are motivated and what kinds of sensations they evoke reveal something to us about ourselves.

> In order to shape the work, we draw on our reservoir of past experiences with people and the world, our past inner linkage of words and things, our past encounters with spoken or written texts. We listen to the sound of words in the inner ear; we lend our sensations, our emotions, our sense of being alive, to the new experience which, we feel, corresponds to the text. We participate in the story, we identify with characters, we share their conflicts and their feelings. At the same time there is a stream of responses being generated. There may be a sense of pleasure in our own creative activity, an awareness of pleasant or awkward sound and movement in the words, a feeling of approval or disapproval of the characters and their behavior. We may be aware of a contrast between the assumptions or expectations about life that we brought to the reading and the attitudes, moral codes, social situations we are living through in the world created in transaction with the text.
>
> (1982, 270)

Rosenblatt's overarching argument is that aesthetic ways of engaging with language and literacy enable us to hold space for affect and desires, which in turn can create the potential for the development of the kinds of awareness Kramsch associated with symbolic competence. The contrast Rosenblatt describes between what we live through the text and our own assumptions and expectations calls to mind Spivak's theorization of the role of double-subjectivities in aesthetic education (see Introduction) and a comparable notion appears in Kramsch's concept of *third space* (1993), which is a conceptual predecessor to her thinking on the multilingual subject.

As a languaging activity that stands apart from other endeavors and experiences, learning a new language is necessarily an affective and aesthetic experience. This raises questions about how affective values accumulate around not only particular ways of languaging (as emphasized by Rosenblatt) but also particular languages as something to be learned. Scholars working in English language teaching including Pennycook (2020), Motha and Lin (2014), Takahashi (2013), and Kubota (2011) have explored the "economies of desire" within which relations to English language learning are shaped. Within the context of Japanese learners, the studies by Takahashi (2013) and Kubota (2011) both show how the desire to learn English has a range of entangled associations, including liberation, feminism, wealth, Whiteness, coloniality, and sexuality. Motha and Lin (2014) use Ahmed's idea of happy objects, that is, those that become sticky with desirability and good, to show how English speaker identity becomes heavily associated with a prosperous life and those "correlations are read as casualties, which then become the basis of promotion" (Ahmed 2010; 6; cited in Motha and Lin 2014, 334). English becomes a *happy object* even as its presence or absence is inevitably shaped by the English language's racialized and imperial history, every bit as much as the symbolic power it carries globally in today's world. It is noteworthy that many of these discussions of language learning and economies of desire are based on the experiences of English as a second language learners for whom the market value of the new language is a given. It stands to reason that in other contexts, such as the learning of languages other than English (LOTEs) in anglophone contexts, the choice to learn a second language is likely shaped by different economies of desire (see Anya 2020; Warner, Gaspar, and Diao 2021) with different affective values and entanglements.

At the beginning of this section, emotions and affect were treated as psychological states that needed to be regulated for the real cognitive labor of learning or acquisition to occur; through a cluster of approaches including sociocultural theory, poststructuralist applied linguistics, affective literacy studies, and lastly symbolic competence, we have been moving toward models that see affect as a vital aspect of languages and languaging. The lived emotional experience of language learning, what Vygotsky conceptualized as *perezhivanie*, includes both the undirected and undetermined intensities of experience, what we can think of as *affect as movement* theorized by Deleuze and Guattari and the emotional stickiness at the center of Ahmed's theories. Kramsch's conceptualization of the potential role of symbolic competence in the development of multilingual subjectivities and the attention to aesthetic language and literacy activities she suggests offer a way to connect affective experiences more deliberately with pedagogical practices and the space of the classroom.

Literacy as a Felt Experience (Reprise)

Re-examining the two classrooms at the start of this chapter through the lens of affect theory, we can both acknowledge the role that particular choices made in designing these two iterations of the lesson might have had **and** that the human experience of those class sessions can never be fully accounted for through a causal analysis of those designs. The different *feels* of the two classes emerged in the assemblage of designs, histories, emotions, bodies, and diverse ways of "responding to the energy of the moment" (Leander and Boldt 2013, 37). The experiential qualities of these two lessons were shaped not merely by premeditated designs but through affective intensities, "the relationships they buil[t], and the ways in which they create[d] unpredictable movements of texts and identities" (Leader and Rowe 2006, 432).

This is by no means a case against lesson planning. On the contrary, the collaborative work designing classroom activities and selecting texts and images was cited by both Michael and Liam as valuable to their professional learning in their post-lesson reflections. The process of planning the lesson also allowed the two instructors to engage more deeply with concepts from our seminar, and this was this clear in their written reflections after the class, where both Michael and Liam noticed that the activity with the images had somehow felt different in the two classrooms. They both noted the role that the positioning of the desks, i.e., the spatial design, might have played. For Liam this was indeed the key difference. Michael pointed to additional elements of meaning making that were relevant to the lesson, citing multiliteracies theories directly, to try to analyze how certain choices in language might have changed the flow of the in-class activity, e.g., the vocabulary that they had chosen for the image descriptions. It would be possible to stop here and attribute the contrast between these lessons to different conceptual understandings that two instructors had developed. However, Michael himself, in trying to make sense out of how the activity in his classroom had departed from the lesson plan, saw the planning as not *better* designed but rather *over*designed. As he described it: "What my overly caring preparation created was a too narrow field of actions for my students. I underestimated their creativity and their abilities vastly and have been shown that by this very task." Citing Bialystok (2001), whose work in applied linguistics he has consulted outside of the core course readings in the development of the lesson, Michael pointed to another dimension at play in the realization of the lesson as human activity: "As an aspect of human knowledge, language use includes also a social context, pragmatic applications [...], variation, motivational and other individual differences, conceptual content, experience and history, and many other nonlinguistic factors" (Bialystok 2001, 49; cited by Michael in his reflection). For Michael, the service he did for his students in the act of teaching the lesson was to make space for some of these "nonlinguistic factors."

Although his chosen metalanguage was different, Michael's reflection appears to me to respond to affective dimensions of the class session that I had also noted in my observation; dimensions which were testing the limits of the metalanguage offered by the seminar readings, which were focused on multiliteracies pedagogical concepts and ways of conceptualizing different elements of design. Leander and Ehret (2019) refer to this as "the surplus" and position it as the focus of affective literacy studies: "We wish to acknowledge the surplus; we wish to tell out loud the secret that teachers seem to know—that most of what happens on our best days, cannot be explained in rational frames. We are moved, and our students are moved, and we cannot explain how or why" (2).

Centering affect in discussions of language teaching and learning is not a case against lesson planning, nor is it a case against the kinds of metalanguage, reflection, conceptualization, and analysis that pedagogies of design enable; but it is decidedly for an acknowledgment of literacy as it is lived, namely as not only ways of knowing or acting in the world but as felt sensory experiences (see Pahl and Rowsell 2020). In the second half of this chapter, we turn to two student vignettes from an intermediate/advanced German language/culture class co-taught by myself and another instructor. In both cases, emotions and other expressions of affect were salient in the student's engagements with the core literacy practices at hand during a part of the course. In discussing the two cases, I rely on the students' written reflections, compositions, and other assignments, as well as my own notes, reflections, and memories. Following scholarship in affective literacy studies (e.g., Leander and Ehret, 2019), the stories of these two students are not presented as objective accounts of what happened and certainly are not intended as best practices, but rather as self-conscious *reassemblings* that point to different ways of feeling and knowing in connection with multiliteracy designs.

Desire and Affective Literacy in the Language-Culture Classroom: Two Vignettes

In this section, I will look at the cases of Klara and Jaden, two undergraduate students enrolled in the same intermediate/advanced-level German language/culture class. The curriculum for this this course was deliberately and systematically grounded in multiliteracies frameworks and notions of design. Like the opening vignettes from Liam and Michael's classrooms, these two stories serve to illustrate how different aspects of affect can shape the felt experience of literacy-based language pedagogies; however, the focus will now shift to the students. Although I cannot claim to capture the moment as it was felt by Klara or Jaden, through their literacy artifacts, post-activity reflections, and my teacher field notes from in-class discussions, I will attempt to reassemble (Burnett 2019, 209) some of the intensities of a series of in- and out-of-class experiences. These manifested as a range of expressed emotions, including happiness, depression, and fear. For readers who, like the author of this book, have been socialized to promote only the most positive of emotions in language teaching, it will likely not go unnoticed that two of the three in this list are what might commonly be categorized as negative feelings. My argument is not that we should promote *bad* feelings in our language classrooms but that we as teachers perhaps do not need to immediately regulate any form of discomfort. In the subsequent sections, I will continue to explore the question running through this chapter, namely, what kinds of learning experiences we might be missing when we shortcut the "not yet" of lived literacy (see Pahl and Rowsell 2020, 6) through a preoccupation with design.

Course Context

"Gateway to German Studies: Encounters in Language" was a third-year German and language course taught at a large public university in the US American Southwest. The course was typically described as intermediate/advanced because it included both students who had come directly from the so-called basic language sequence, i.e., the first two years of instruction, and those who had tested in from high school and students who had spent the summer before in an intensive study abroad program. Many of the academic programs on campus had a one-or two-year language requirement and therefore the third-year language course was the first in the curricular sequence to predominantly include students who had declared German as their major or minor area of study.

The multiliteracies-based curriculum of the course was organized around three topics, which were each linked to a particular genre family (see Table 4). The readings for each unit related to the theme, but also were selected as models of the genre or for specific aspects they exhibited thereof. For example, the

Table 4 Curriculum overview for "Gateway to German Studies: Encounters in Language".

Thematic focus	Featured genre families
The Individual in Society (Das Individuum in der Gesellschaft)	Description
Stories from German History (Geschichten aus der deutschen Geschichte)	Narrative
Digital Communities (Digitale Gemeinschaften)	Exposition/editorial

second unit, "Stories from German History," included examples of narratives in multiple modalities and in a variety of forms including poetry, prose, film, and recorded testimony. The core genre for the third unit on digital communities was an editorial and in addition to looking at models of this genre, students were guided to look in the online forums and websites, which they were exploring, to find examples of position-taking and evaluative language.

The primary assessments were three literacy-based tasks completed across multiple drafts: a description, a narrative, and an exposition (i.e., an editorial). The readings from each corresponding unit served as models for designing these compositions. There was openness in the tasks, but the genres introduced some deliberate constraints, which also created opportunities for reflecting on the kinds of available designs that might be relevant, e.g., past tense verbs, causal adverbs, and temporal expressions in a narrative or evaluative and attitudinal language in an exposition (see also Rose and Martin 2012). Additionally, students were asked to write a more informal response to each text read or viewed for the class in a journal, which was assessed based on completion every two weeks. Suggested writing prompts were sometimes given for a specific entry, but the journals were generally envisioned as a space where students could respond more freely to the readings, while also giving the instructors a chance to dialogue a little with each student's thoughts—since this was otherwise not easily afforded by the size of the class (22 students).

The stated objectives of the course were organized around specific available designs, i.e., those related to the three genre families associated with each unit, but both my co-teacher and I had extensive discussions throughout the semester about how to also make space for student responses to the texts. Rather than foregrounding the historical context or dominant readings, as is often done in second language-culture textbooks (see Warner 2014; Gramling and Warner 2011), we promoted an iterative process of reading, where discussions of the students' first responses and evocations were guided toward questions that allowed the students to revisit texts with new forms of awareness—of linguistic or visual choices, genre patterns, cultural discourses, and historical references. By oscillating between moments of experiencing the texts and guided practices conceptualizing and analyzing elements thereof, the aim was to weave students' readerly responses together with their emergent linguistic and cultural/historical knowledge, giving them space to redesign rather than correct their interpretations. At the same time, by creating opportunities where learners could experience literacy practices separate, at least momentarily, from any pedagogical agenda, we tried to leave space for the flow of affect and aesthetic response.

Example 1: Klara and the "Break"

The first student example for this section is situated in the second unit of the curriculum and features Klara, an undergraduate student, who had, at the time of this class, declared German as her minor area of study.[5] Klara was outspoken and generally engaged, when she was in class, but had suffered from frequent absences through the semester. She had participated in a short-term study abroad program the summer before our class and cited that as a formative experience for learning German and developing "cultural awareness." In her responses to a survey question about her reasons for studying German, she ranked positive affective reasons most highlight, i.e., finding it "interesting," the courses "comfortable," and her "love of German"; however, she also stated that she hoped to someday study medicine in Germany.

The second course unit, "Stories from German History," included four thematic sub-modules, each representing a different moment of twentieth- or twenty-first-century German history: post-war Germany, the student movements, contemporary German society, and the Berlin Wall and everyday life in East Germany. The intention was not that the students should master the historical contexts—although the texts, media, and supplemental materials offered them a sense of key events, figures, and discourses; instead the mini modules were connected by a set of questions related to the ways in which personal narratives can stand in for broader experiences and learner's awareness of how these were designed was the pedagogical focus. Students' core assessment for this unit involved the composition of a personal recount, which they were told could be fictional or non-fictional.

For our purposes here, I consider Klara's engagement with texts in the last of these mini modules. The primary readings included the poem "Naturschutzgebiet" (1982; Nature Preserve) by Sarah Kirsch, which is a first-person description of the space surrounding the Berlin Wall, an excerpt from the novel *Helden wie wir* (1995; *Heroes Like Us*) by Thomas Brussig, which is a parody memoir about growing up and being socialized into East German society and specifically into the youth group *Die junge Pioniere* (the Young Pioneers), and two autobiographical vignettes from the collection *Meine freie deutsche Jugend* (2003; My Free German Youth) by Claudia Rusch, which depict her experiences as the child of political dissidents in East Germany. The latter three texts all partake in a cultural phenomenon during the 1990s and early 2000s that is often described as *Ostalgie,* a portmanteau of the German words for "east" (Ost) and "nostalgia" (*Nostalgie*). A defining feature of literary works associated with *Ostalgie* is a thematic focus on making sense of what it meant to grow up in East Germany and humor is often evoked to express the related feelings of ambivalence that this conjured up for many authors.

Generally, student responses to the personal recounts from East Germany were mixed. While some enjoyed the opportunity to learn about a time in German history that they felt they knew little about, others felt frustrated by the insiderliness of the narratives, which included many cultural references related to childhood and adolescence in the 1980s in East Germany. Several members of the class reported that they felt excluded by this way of writing. In many instances, students' feelings of dissonance with this set of readings echoed the tensions Byram and Kramsch (2008) describe in connection with another group of US-based students of German language and culture who similarly struggled to make sense of narrators who did not actively oppose but held more contradictory or unequivocal views about East German social practices and politics (27).

Both during in-class discussions and in her reading journal entries, Klara was vocal that she did not like this mini module. She wrote in one entry that she found Brussig's and Rusch's stories "silly and boring," while she preferred "romantic" stories. I was thus surprised to find that although almost all of the other students had chosen to tell a story from their own lives for the final composition in the narrative unit, Klara submitted a narrative, which was directly inspired by the course readings about East Germany. Klara's story, titled "Ich laufe …" (I run …), opened with the following:

> Ich laufe gerade, so schnell, aber es ist nicht schnell genug. Wo sollte meine Geschichte beginnen? Ich war ein Kind, ich war? Nein, das ist nicht meine Geschichte. Es war der 14. August 1961 und ich war in das Haus meines Freundes.[6]
>
> *I am running now, so fast, but is it not fast enough. Where should my story begin? I was a child, I was? No, that is not my story. It was the 14th of August 1961 and I was in the house of my friend.*

In the next few lines, it becomes clear that the young, male narrator was visiting a friend in East Germany, when the wall went up and he was stuck there. He approached an "officer" and asked for assistance but was turned away.

> Ich hatte kein Pass, keine Mutter, kein Vater, und keine Schwester. Ich war ein Kind hinter dem eisernen Vorhang.
>
> *I had no passport, no mother, no father, and no sister. I was behind the iron curtain.*

The narrator then describes how he was accepted into the home of his friend where he attended school there Monday through Saturday, where he is learning Russian—all details about everyday life in East Germany that Klara had encountered in the course readings; however, he still missed his family and sunk deeper and deeper into depression, as life became a boring cycle, "Schule, junge Pioneers … und dann?" (School, Young Pioneers … and then?). Finally, in an act of desperation, he decides to jump.

> Es war der 13. August 1964, ich bin nun 15 Jahre alt. Ich stand, ich wartete, ich dachte über meine Mutter und meinen Vater und meine Schwester, ich hatte für nichts zu leben. Ich lief. Jetzt laufe ich gerade, Ich springe über die erste Wand. Ich sehe die zweite Wand. Ich springe und ich höre einen Schuss und ich kann meine Beine fühlen nicht. Ich vermisse meine Eltern und meine Schwester. Ich habe für nichts zu leben.
>
> *It was the 13th of August 1964, I am now 15 years old. I stood, I waited, I thought about my mother and my father and my sister, I had nothing to love for. I ran. Now I am running. I jump over the first wall. I see the second wall. I jump and I hear a shot and I cannot feel my legs. I miss my parents and my sister. I have nothing to live for.*

When I first read Klara's composition, it struck me in a few different ways. First, and this bears noting, Klara had clearly fulfilled the assignment and met the learning objectives, based on the metalanguage related to genres and available designs associated with personal recounts that we had used to articulate this unit. Her composition shows substantial awareness of the lexico-grammatical forms found in narratives, which had been the primary focus of this part of the course. She also demonstrated cultural-historical knowledge in her description of school and recognition that the narrator would have to jump not once but twice to cross the Berlin Wall (which was in actuality two walls with a strip of land down the middle). Knowing Klara's frustration with the *Ostalgie* literature on the basis that it felt too unserious, I found it intriguing that she had chosen to write a tragedy, and one that allowed her to incorporate her expanding repertoire of linguistic and cultural knowledge into a likely more familiar narrative of the Berlin Wall as a mechanism for imprisonment constructed by a malevolent state. The premise of Klara's story, that a teenager who is a citizen of West Germany would be held captive by the Berlin Wall, was historically implausible, but this narrative choice created an opportunity for Klara to reconcile her aesthetic frustrations with the readings from the class.

A little more than a year after the course had ended, I re-encountered Klara's composition, when sorting through various learning artifacts from this course as part of a research study. Although Klara had not been a student in my class again, we had stayed in touch enough for me to know that she moved back to the city an hour away from our campus to live with her family. I reached out to ask if she remembered writing this story and why she had chosen to write what she did. She responded in an email, in which she affirmed that she remembered this assignment quite clearly and went on to share the following:

> This time in my life was particularly hard, my mom had cancer and that put a kind of depressing overtone to a lot of my writing ... I re-read the one you sent, and I have half a mind to correct it, lol.
>
> German helped me get out of my depression [...] I had really not known anything about the Berlin Wall, but thinking about that period of time, I had wondered what I would do if I was separated from my family for good instead of me just being a city away from them; not knowing how they were doing, not knowing if I'd ever see them again. And I think that's what prompted the story. If I was young and I wanted it that badly for that many years, would I try to do it; no matter what the costs?

This was a dimension of Klara's experiences with the readings that I had not been privy to during the class. Despite giving an impression of being outspoken and forthcoming, Klara had not shared anything of what was happening with her family life with me or in class. But this had also been a part of her affective experience of the readings from the class including the *Ostalgie* texts. The narratives seemed to create an affective space of imagination within which she was able to experience feelings that were both familiar and defamiliarized.

In his work on literacy and affect, Ehret suggests that literacy events have major and minor keys; whereas the former relates to "the structural tendency that organizes itself according to predetermined definitions of value" (Souto-Manning 2016, 1; cited in Ehret 2018, 567)—the sorts of stickiness described by Ahmed, while the latter "produces transformations that are primarily felt" (Ehret 2018, 571), i.e., the intensities emphasized by Leander and Boldt through their reading of Deleuze and Guattari. Both relate to the human capacity to affect and be affected; however, they each also draw attention to different layers of language teaching and learning experiences. This idea of keying can be a helpful heuristic for recognizing the push and pull between feelings and affects and the structures of value shaped by our social histories of reading described previously by Rosenblatt, including those of the classroom.

Based on her reflections, writing the story "Ich laufe ..." enabled for Klara something like what Ehret (2018) describes as a relational transformation, a break "where the major's tendency is broken through a minor gesture" (571). In this case, a clash in aesthetic attunement across two different scales perhaps contributed to this rupture. *Ostalgie*, the literature Klara characterized as "silly and boring," with its bemused and laconic tone broke with prevailing emotional evaluations of childhood in East Germany as tragic. At the same time, the symbol of the wall and the feelings of ambivalence expressed in the texts about the experience of borders and limited movement gave Klara a set of narrative designs where she could displace her feelings of separation, fear, and sorrow in relation to herself and her family. The affective intensities of these experiences are only indexed through Klara's expressions of dislike and through her narrative choices, as well as her re-storying of the experience in her email to me; at the same time, Klara's affective and aesthetic experience with the texts she had read and the story she wrote was both in relation to and in excess of their designs. Desire, as Ehret notes, often "escapes such grand notions of what constitutes development, change, or outcome" (570). It creates relational transformations not through intentions and goals—the purpose of Klara's writing was not to get her out of depression, for instance. But by forging connections between affective tonalities in and through her engagements with the German texts, Klara was exploring a minor key of her own identity, an undercurrent to the major representation of herself (Ehret 2018, 573).

Example 2: Jaden and the Stickiness of Designs

Like Klara, Jaden was an undergraduate at the time of our course, and she had also participated in the short-term study abroad program in the previous summer. In the surveys administered at the start of the term, Jaden cited positive associations, i.e., "seems like fun" and "love of German," as primary reasons for studying German, but she also hoped to someday study and work abroad. "I will likely go to Grad school for neuroscience then I hope to do neuroscience research in a lab in Germany." She shared in her reflections that she liked studying literature, especially texts about German history. In contrast to Klara, Jaden reported really enjoying the *Ostalgie* readings and her favorite material from the class had been a short story related to the Holocaust. In the perceptions of both instructors, Jaden was one of the most academically conscientious students in the class; her assignments were always handed in on time and she followed directions with precision. In the third and final unit of the curriculum, however, Jaden's relationship with the course shifted somewhat.[7]

An overarching goal of the "Digital Communities" unit was to give students an opportunity to apply what they had been learning to compare and apply what they were learning about particular genres and styles within an active community of users. On the first day of the new unit, students were asked to reflect on their associations with the word "community" and to brainstorm (1) in what types of digital communities they or their peers regularly participate and (2) topics of interest to them that are discussed in these forums. After I had gathered these ideas onto the board and we had discussed them, we were left with a short list of possible topics. Students then self-selected one that they would be willing to continue to explore within German-speaking online communities, and they were grouped accordingly. In this way, the class of twenty-two students was divided into four groups—one focusing on music, one on literature and film, and two on politics. For much of the remainder of the unit, the students met in these small groups during class time, as they completed a series of guided tasks, which first reviewed the genres already encountered in the class. For example, they were asked to observe and describe both the language used in these forums and the visual composition of the online sites and platforms, in other words, the designs. They were asked to take note of a couple of critical moments they had observed in these digital communities and to recount (i.e., narrate) them. An additional activity asked students to select a couple of moments, in which someone expressed a point or view or opinion and someone else responses and then to examine how the participants interacted with one another. These mini ethnographic and sociolinguistic tasks served as a foundation for group presentations, which were held toward the end of the semester. In the presentations, students were asked to focus on the following elements, which all connected back to previous class activities:

- Composition of the internet sites: How do they look? What functions do they include (e.g., chat, discussion, liking)?
- The participants/intended audience: What values/beliefs/interests/positions are represented and how? Can you identify a particular social milieu? Where does that appear? Is it directly on the "About Us" page or in the user profiles? Or is it more indirectly expressed through the selection of themes, word choice, or speech styles?
- Critical or exemplary moments and interactions: Choose 2–3 moments that you found typical or interesting. Analyze these interactions. What does this moment reveal about the community, the participants, and the topic?
- Your impressions: What did you like or not like about this digital community?

The final composition for the unit was an editorial for *Deutsch Perfekt*, a magazine from the newspaper *Die Zeit* published specifically for learners of German. Students were asked to offer an opinion as to whether this particular digital community was a worthwhile space for readers to visit if they want to learn more and/or interact with German speakers.

Jaden had opted to join one of the two groups focusing on German politics, perhaps because the other members of this group were the classmates with whom she most often worked. Early into the project, both instructors noticed that Jaden seemed uneasy during the digital communities activities in class. She seemed more withdrawn from discussions than she had in the past. In a journal reflection from about a month into the unit, Jaden expressed her discomfort as a response to the medium:

> Yeah, sometimes I forget that I am in the internet and I ask myself "Is every German person completely crazy …?" And then I breathe deep and remind myself, that the internet is to blame. The internet is not a good representation of people.

In a later reflection, submitted between the presentation of the project and the completion of the editorial, Jaden elaborated on her feelings:

> Ja ich mag Deutsch und ja ich mag digitale Gemeinschaften aber wenn ich Interessen in Weltpolitik habe, dann werde ich bei internationellen Zeitungen stellen. Ich fürchtete mich vor diesem Kurs, als wir die digitale Gemeinschaften forschten. […] Ich hasse dieses Projekt. Meiner Meinung nach, habe ich nichts gelernt, als wir das Projeckt machten. Ich hätte lieber ein ganzes deutsches Büch gelesen haben – wie in kleinen literarischen Gruppe. Dann hätte ich mich freuen – und auch mehr gelernt.
>
> *Yes I like German and yes I like digital communities but if I were interested in world politics then I would go to international newspapers. I feared this course, when we were doing the digital communities. I hate this project. In my opinion, I learned nothing when we were doing this project. I would have rather read an entire German book - like in little literary groups. Then I would have enjoyed it and learned more.*

Although we had picked up on the shift in Jaden's mood in class, my co-teacher and I were caught off guard by the intensity of her negative emotions, expressed through the words "feared" and "hate." Equally surprising to us was her sense that she felt she had learned nothing, in particular because she had excelled in all of the activities and assignments thus far.

Jaden's group had initially started with the online version of a well-respected newspaper, *Der Spiegel*. For the first task, they analyzed the layout and composition of an article and related forum focusing on the political situations surrounding a rise in asylum seekers to Germany and other European countries. At some point shortly thereafter, the group shifted their focus to two online discussion forums—*Politik sind wir*, a platform for "critical discussions on political topics," and the threads devoted to German politics on the social news aggregator Reddit. In their presentation, they were particularly attuned to the differences in register between these two sites. One group members presented examples from a discussion of Israel in *Politik sind wir* and commented how surprised they were to see such a civil discussion about such a controversial topic, citing examples of polite speech from the excerpt. Jaden and a fellow student then co-presented on Reddit for their part of the presentation, noting that German users only seemed to get mean (schlecht) when someone said something racist or made jokes about "the ugly part of German history," i.e., the Holocaust and other events of the Second World War.

The same attention to discourse, perspective, and ways of speaking, which Jaden and their group had analyzed so thoroughly for the in-class presentation, was also the focus of Jaden's opinion piece. For the final composition, Jaden focused on a political topic that she had encountered during the project, yet which was not included in her group's presentation—German discussions of the terrorist attacks in the United States on September 11, 2001. Jaden enacted the imagined context of a magazine for German language learners through her design of her document, which she formatted like an online article, complete with a section header, *Kultur* (Culture), a headline "Internationalen Außenperspektive von 9/11" (International Outside Perspectives of 9/11), and a lead photo of the New York skyline with the twin towers smoking. The subtitle, "Wie die Deutsche Leute diskutieren 9/11 in der Kontexte der Amerikanischen Politik und Krise" (How the German people discuss 9/11 in the context of American politics and crisis), is indicative of the distanced, journalistic tone of the rest of the article. Jaden's stated preference for academic discourse is also thematized in the article itself:

> Diese Thema ist so heikel in den USA, dass sie sehr schlecht diskutiert ist – manchmal scheitert die ganze Diskussion wegen starken Emotionen und Perspektiven. Also ist es leichter, wenn Leute von anderen Länder diese Ereignis diskutieren, weil sie ein emotionelle Distanz—und auch so einen größeren und kläreren Ausblick—haben können.

> *This topic is so controversial in the USA, that it is difficult to discuss—sometimes the entire discussion fails due to strong emotions and perspectives. Thus it is easier, when people from other countries discuss this event, because they can have an emotional distance—and thus also a larger and clearer view.*

Jaden further noted that while most participants in the German political forums agreed that 9/11 was a terrorist attack, a minority believe otherwise. Despite these differences in opinion, which Jaden noted, she stated that people were "meistens höflich und akademisch" (mostly polite and academic). The subsequent two paragraphs describe a moment when one user suggested that the US government orchestrated the attacks to start a war.

> Niemand nannte die Skeptiker "verrückte Verschwörungstheoretiker", wie Amerikaner bei einem amerikanischen Forum wohl sie nennen würden. Sogar hatte diese Theorie zu viel Zustimmung und nicht genug Gegner. Aber wenn man eine Meinung nicht zustimmt, richtet sich nicht an die Person-—das Ethos-—sondern an ihre Berechtigung-—das Logos. Die Antwort ist manche sarkastisch und es ist richtig, dass die Users gemein und erniedrigend sein können, aber meistens sind die Users kulant.

> *No one calls the skeptics "crazy conspiracy theorist," as Americans would certainly call them in an American forum. Indeed this theory has too much support and not enough opponents. But when one does not agree with an opinion, they direct themselves not at the person—the ethos—but the justification-—the logos. The answer is some [sic] sarcastic and it is right, that users can be mean and insulting, but mostly the users are fair.*

Jaden concludes her essay with the opinion:

> Jede Person soll an diesen Foren kommen, um die Deutschen besser zu verstehen. Man wird doch sehen, dass Deutschen bei dem Internet höflich sich betragen.

> *Every person should come to these forums, to better understand the Germans. They would then see that the Germans behave politely in the internet.*

It might be tempting, especially as an instructor, to want to read this as a pedagogically inspired perspective shift, i.e., to invest in the belief that Jaden through the attention to design choices came to see the discussion forums not as a deficient representation but as "as a social practice of meaning making and interpretation" (Álvarez Valencia and Michelson 2022, 9). In her final course reflection, Jaden's comments about the project were more muted. When reflecting on what she had found least helpful this semester, she noted: "Perhaps the digital communities were good for other students, but for me they were not so good."

In a previous study, Richardson and I have (Warner and Richardson, 2017) examined Jaden's participation in the digital communities unit as an example of what we called "symbolic struggles," that is, moments in which social positions an individual wishes to claim for themselves seemed at odds or incommensurate with those available to them in a given literacy activity. We argued that Jaden's comfort with more traditionally academic practices, such as discussions of literary texts representing pivotal moments of German history, and her intense discomfort (her lack of investment) with classroom activities that asked her to step into the digital wild (Sauro 2022), posed questions about what counts as success in a multiliteracies curriculum. Jaden's ability to analyze, conceptualize, and transfer linguistic and visual designs in the process of composition was clearly evident. But how could we make sense of her "resistant positioning" (Warner and Richardson 2017) vis-a-vis contemporary political discussions, especially those where the United States was an object of scrutiny and even critique. Bringing in the lens of affect theory, I want to shift this question slightly and consider the affective entanglements within which Jaden's ambivalent and even resistant responses to the digital communities unit and the related project manifested.

My primary access to Jaden's affective experience of the class is of course through her own accounts, but running through these are multiple references to different forms of literacy activities and the kinds of feeling words she associated with them. In addition to her emotional responses to the digital forums and the project captured in words such as "feared" and "hate" and described in physical responses, e.g., the need to "breathe deep," Jaden characterizes these literacy practices as "not good." This stood in contrast to literary texts, which she suggests are better representations for the language classroom and associates with her own happiness—even though she simultaneously associates them with sadness. In her final reflection, in answer to the question what most surprised her this semester, Jaden mentioned the sadness of German stories and went on to say, "Die Geschichten haben mir gefallen … aber sie waren sehr sehr traurig" (I liked the stories … but they were very sad.). This is in line with what she shared in the earlier reflection, where she cited Holocaust literature as an area of interest in German cultural history.

Jaden's case points to another facet of collective affective entanglements with historical events. In an essay on the role of emotions in political life entitled "Beyond empathy and compassion," Ross (2018) argues that the emotional stickiness theorized by Ahmed can also help to explain how the Holocaust can work "as a pivoting point for the redirection of emotion" (201). "As a 'sticky' concept, 'genocide' functions as a conduit of moral energy that spills over onto the various events and objects with which it develops recognizable attachments" (202). While the Holocaust is often included in curricula as a means of introducing human rights and social justice issues (e.g., Porto and Zembylas 2022), Ross's argument suggests that transformative potential can get stuck on topics and concepts like genocide, exactly because the structures of feeling we associate with them are preconceived and defined. This may help to explain why *sadness*, a seemingly negative emotion, was for Jaden in relation to Holocaust literature desirable; this stood in contrast to the kinds of discomfort she experienced when reading debates around 9/11, where her aesthetic relationship with the texts positioned her as what Ahmed has called an "affective alien" (2010, 42), someone who feels out of place in a given affect community.

Making Space for Desires: A Critical-Aesthetic Approach to Second Language Literacy

The classroom-based examples in this chapter show students creatively engaged in the design of meaning in relation to genres, stories and discourses, vocabulary, grammar, images, layouts, and other available design resources. At the same time, there are multiple moments across these reassembled learning and teaching experiences that point to affective and aesthetic intensities that are in excess of those designs but were very much a part of what made them meaningful. In some moments, these intensities are represented as emotions, for example, in the reflections from Klara and Jaden; at moments I had also noted a changing feeling in the classroom or in a given interaction in my observation or teaching notes, indicating that had affectively shifted. And to an extent the affective dimensions of languaging resist being captured completely through my or the students' attempts to narrativize their experiences—which has methodological implications for both research and teaching practices. As a concept to work with, desires require a more humble orientation than many others might, a simultaneous attention to feelings in the classroom and acceptance that they cannot be easily pinned down.

The lens of affect theory provides a way out of the binary between "good" and "bad" feelings in the classroom and an opportunity to instead consider the range of different intensities that enter in when learners and teachers enter into new relations with other humans, objects, ideas, and materials in the flow of language and literacy activities (see Leander and Boldt 2018, 35). In the initial examples from the start of this chapter, one difference between Michael and Liam's classrooms was arguably that Michael's class felt more *fun*, there was more laughter, more banter, but that adjective does not hold the assemblage of elements that transformed the lesson into more than the sum of the designs. Klara and Jaden were, by their accord, not having fun during the units described in the previous section; but it would be an oversimplification to relegate their experiences to the category of learning activities that students disliked, as student self-report data often does. If anything, their assessment of the experience, as a whole, ended up being ambivalent, with moments of intensity woven in where the pushes and pulls of the texts, designs, activities, memories, and ideas collided in ways that were unpredictably transformative.

In the classroom, students' reading stance—whether they read efferently or aesthetically and how they position themselves in relation to the world of the text—is, at least to an extent, shaped by the learning activities introduced by the teachers. It is not incidental that the examples in this section arose in creative writing tasks that asked learners to integrate into their aesthetic responses to other texts into their own compositions (see Warner 2023). It is likely also not a coincidence that these responses manifested most clearly in the vignettes from Klara and Jaden, in moments where something about the readings provoked *resistant positioning* (Warner and Richardson 2017) vis-a-vis the structures of affect offered by the texts. It was in connection with these moments that emotional words such as *hate* and *fear* appeared.

An underlying argument running through my discussion of the classroom examples in this chapter is that for languaging and literacy to be meaningful, they must be felt, and to do so they must provoke a response. In her expansion of Rosenblatt's theories, Smith (2012) proposed a third reading stance to stand along efferent and aesthetic, *deferent reading;* in deferent reading the focus is on meaning, but on meaning finding rather than on meaning making. Deferent reading thus often takes on the form of a kind of didactic game of hide and seek (see also Phipps and Gonzales 2004, 135, on the potential of resonant reading). Deferent reading practices in the classroom do often include descriptions of affective or emotive responses, Smith notes; however, these are less aesthetic and more accurately anesthetic, in that reading becomes an emotionally numbing process. The emphasis is on performing an accepted reading that reproduces a predetermined meaning and aesthetic responses that have already been attributed to the text. Returning to a concept from the previous chapter, we can say that the result of deferent reading and deferent writing is not redesign but *undesign*—a performance of meaning design that shuts down the kinds of meaningful feelings of surprise, joy, discomfort, uncertainty, and even fear that emerge when assemblages of historical and cultural and educational worlds come together and learners are asked to try to make sense of themselves within these multilayered spaces.

For Rosenblatt, aesthetic reading is not wholly separate from critical ways of engaging with language. On the contrary, aesthetic reading holds the potential for ethical reflection. By working out why they respond to a text or other semiotic object in the way that they do, she argued, readers can clarify their values and share in the values of others. Writing in the immediate aftermath of post-Second World War, this ethical dimension of aesthetic reading was for Rosenblatt a basis for a democratic and anti-authoritarian education (comp. Vytniorgu 2018). By making space for affect and then for the critical reflection on how one's feelings and desires may be at odds with those of others, aesthetic engagement in a new language becomes an opportunity for negotiating the emotional responses and affective structures through which we define ourselves (see also Kramsch 2006, 55). Making space for desires thus becomes the basis of something more than critical thinking, critical feeling.

Attending to desires asks educators to infuse the activities through which students are asked to design and redesign meanings with space for movement, for learners and ourselves to be moved through thoughts, feelings, and relations that are shared and unshared, and for meaning making to be as much in the moment-to-moment experiences of living in relation to texts as in the destination. In conjunction with these critical-aesthetic engagements with language, learners need a chance to explore and expand their repertoires of available designs—to play with new ways of making meaning offered by new languages and cultures, new ways of being, thinking, and feeling in the world, and even new possible worlds, new social futures they may wish to design. In the next section of the book, I propose that play can be a core pedagogical principle for fostering a multiliteracy pedagogy that attends to both designs and desires and then develop this proposition through three classroom-based mini studies. Before moving into Section 2, the Intermezzo chapter, which follows next, offers opportunities for reflecting on the concepts introduced thus far.

Intermezzo: Second Language Literacy as Designs and Desires

The previous two chapters have explored the notions of designs and desires, as they have been theorized in education, second language studies, and applied linguistics, and have sought to connect them as part of a framework for second language and culture education that centers not only meaning, but meaningfulness.

Thinking with these core concepts, designs, and desires enables us to embrace more fully the promise of a paradigm shift that multiliteracies pedagogies have held for many language educators and scholars of second language studies in recent years. Borrowing a metaphor from education scholar Maxine Greene's work on curriculum and consciousness (1971), we can think of designs as maps. The maps used in foreign language teaching help learners to orient themselves within a given text or text-type by enabling them to trace processes of production and reception through the linguistic and stylistic "landmarks" that lead their way; however, as Green cautions us, our urgency to get students from point A to point B, to ensure their linguistic and cultural competence, all too often neglects to account for learners' feelings of disorientation and discomfort at having to discern what stances, footing, and positions are available to them in a new terrain. Walking around with a map is one viable way to maneuver a city, but it is one that is markedly foreign; the question at hand here is how we can not only map the texts that students encounter in the language classroom onto the culture, within which they were produced, but also enable students to map the field of reading positions they might occupy as learners of but also participants in these literacy practices (see also Warner 2014).

Design focuses our attention on the *possibilities* for making meaning and the effects of the choices we make as we navigate systems of available designs in multiple languages and cultures. Design is a principle of selection. **Desires**, on the other hand, attune us to the *potentials* that exist in the flow and fissures of meaningful languaging activities. Desire is thus an acknowledgment of the emergent quality of meaning making, the *not-yet become*, but also of the ways in which affect sediments into familiar patterns that are, in Ahmed's sense, emotionally sticky. As pedagogical precepts, **design** is a foundation for critical thinking, while **desire** can enable critical feeling. These two dimensions of literacy operate on somewhat different time scales and as different modes of being and sense-making. Both are key to learning to language and live within new systems of meaning, as one aspires to do in the second language-culture classroom.

Viewing second language literacy development as shaped through designs and desires is a reminder that language learning is most importantly about new ways of existing in and making sense of one's lifeworlds. This comes with a recognition that engaging with new literacy practices is not as neutral or *an*aesthetic as taking up new available designs as if they were tools.

As we move into a more deliberate discussion of pedagogy in the subsequent section of the book, this intermezzo is an invitation to reflect on ideas that you have encountered in your own teaching and learning contexts.

1. Reflect on the role of designs and desires in your own multilingual life:
   - In a poem titled "Intermezzo," Lithuanian poet Janina Degutyte describes the experience of being "opened bare to the farthest nerve …" "At the source, at the very source are live streams/Through my body trickles air like birch sap/And the buzz of bees, the midsummer sun/Ripple inside me and ripple above."[1] Can you remember a moment with a language that you were learning or that was otherwise new to you where you felt "open wide" in the way described by Janina Degutyte in the poetic excerpt that opens this intermezzo chapter? What was that like? What was happening at the time? What associations do you have with that experience?
   - Using the language figure below as a model (Figure 3), visually depict your own language portrait. Which languages and others forms of speech, communication, or expression play a role in your life? How can you portray all this repertoire? Which colors relate to which languages or forms of expression? And where could these languages and forms of expression find a place in the body silhouette? (See also Busch 2018 for a discussion of the use of language portraits in qualitative research.)
   - Now go back and look at what you have drawn. What designs are most important to different aspects of your language portrait? Where do desires come in? You can also add to your visualization if you wish or just jot down some thoughts.

Figure 3 Language figure.

- To what extent would you expect these to be shared with the students in your classes? Keep in mind here that it may be difficult to generalize or conjecture about your students, so the intention here is to reflect on the possible differences and diversities rather than to make assumptions.
2. Think about your classroom or language-culture classrooms you have been in—what designs and what kinds of designing activities have been more salient? What positions have learners occupied as designers?
3. Can you remember any class session you were teaching where the energy in the room felt particularly intensified? What did this feel like? What was happening at the time?
4. Based on what you know from the examples featuring Klara and Jaden, how might you redesign the lessons described in Chapter 2 to be more attentive to desires and affect? This is intended not as a critical provocation

but rather as an invitation into a stance of inquiry, "a continual process of making current arrangements problematic; questioning the ways knowledge and practice are constructed, evaluated, and used; and assuming that part of the work of practitioners individually and collectively is to participate in social and educational change" (Cochran-Smith and Lytle 2009, 121). Given that this type of reflective positioning can at times be difficult to wholly embrace in the flow of teaching, deliberating on classroom vignettes can be a helpful way to foster a stance of inquiry. If other examples from your own teaching or classrooms you have observed come to mind (e.g., when answering questions 2, 3, and 4) you may want to think on these instead.

Part Two

Play and Poetics: Toward a Critical-Affective Approach to Multiliteracies

3

Learning by Designs and Desires

Toward a Playful Pedagogy of Multiliteracies

Across the previous two chapters, I have laid the theoretical foundation for a humanistic approach to second language literacy that deliberately recognizes the linguistic and sociocultural aspects of language and learning, while also embracing the affective and aesthetic dimensions of stepping into new symbolic systems—as one necessarily does when developing literacy in a new language. In Chapter 1, I argued that the metaphor of design, this core concept in multiliteracies frameworks, enables attention to the dynamic, creative nature of languaging as well as the resources, the richly multilingual and multimodal repertoires that we draw upon in the act of designing. Alongside this claim, which is shared across the range of literacy-oriented pedagogical models for language and culture teaching, Chapter 2 advocated for greater attention to the affective dimensions of languaging—and more specifically languaging in a new language—which are not captured in the notion of *designs*. I proposed *desires* as a shorthand for these intensities that often take the shape of emotional or aesthetic effects aroused through our engagement with and through language. The first section of this book has thus left us with an unresolved question: how are we to foster literacy in our language and culture classrooms in such a way that we are cognizant of and even nurturing of both designs and desires?

In the second section of the book, I propose the notion of play—understood as a stance vis-a-vis teaching and learning activities, as an orientation for engaging with designs in the language classroom, and as a relationship to social systems—as a pedagogical principle for a view of multiliteracies that attends to both designs and desires. The first part of this chapter introduces theories of play as they relate to contexts of second language and culture learning. I draw from scholarly discussions of play and its close semantic cousin, creativity. Like literature, creativity has never been far removed from discussions of language teaching and learning, but it has moved in and out of a more central position over time (see Tin 2022). Much of the recent renewed interest in creativity and language learning is closely linked to other contemporary discourses in second language teaching and applied linguistics, discussed already at various moments in this book (see Introduction). For example, in expanding understandings of language use beyond rule-based, generative models, the notion of linguistic and semiotic repertoires, which provides conceptual support for both the concept of translanguaging and meaning design, also emphasized creative and imaginative dimensions of languaging (e.g., Allen 2018; Pennycook 2007; Phipps and Gonzalez 2004). Social justice-minded approaches to language education have also contributed to an interest in creative and playful uses of language as part of a larger critique of the normative tendencies of many frameworks for language teaching and learning (e.g., Pahl and Rowsell 2020; Schufflebarger 2022).

Scholarship on creativity and language learning informs and inspires the pedagogical framework proposed in this chapter; however, my preference for play as a critical term instead of creativity has two main motivations. First, creativity continues to hold an individual connotation, which means that it too often conjures up the implication that it emanates from a special kind of person, who can be deemed *creative*. In her study of adult second language learners of English, Schufflebarger (2022) found that while most of the participants did not perceive themselves as creative, they all engaged in languaging activities in which they creatively played with available designs to express a wide range of meanings in relation to their thoughts, experiences, and hopes. Similarly, I have observed university students, who—when asked to engage in creative literacy activities—insist that they are simply not creative people, despite evidence to the contrary. In contemporary discourses, creativity is bound to identity in a way that play is not. Everyone plays, even if the ways in which they do so vary widely. Secondly, play immediately implies the question *with what*, which is helpful for the context of language and culture teaching, where teaching and learning goals often encourage an awareness of specific available designs—whether lexical, grammatical, discursive, visual, intertextual, etc. In our work with the *Foreign Languages and the Literary in the Everyday Project*, Carl Blyth and Joanna, Luks and I found that play as a core concept enabled a metalanguage for conceptualizing and analyzing the various kinds of available designs, which come together in the creation of poetic effects (see Blyth, Warner, and Luks 2021). This made the literary dimensions of language and thus the notion of design more accessible to both teachers and learners.

In theorizing play as a way of doing language pedagogy within a multiliteracies framework, a central question is of course what kinds of learning play affords. The first section of this chapter considers research on play and language learning that addresses exactly this question. Then, building upon the conceptual thinking around play that emerges from that foundational scholarship, I will propose a framework for multiliteracy play with three interconnecting dimensions: bricolage, or creative assemblage; the modulation of affect; and potentially subversion meaning-making activities. Running through this chapter is an argument that play—as an awareness of and relationship with modes of meaning making—can allow teachers to attend to both linguistic designs and to the affective and aesthetic experiences of learning a new language.

Play and (Language) Learning

Within fields of applied linguistics and second language education, play is most frequently and most acutely associated with positive affect. To know if an activity is play, the key question is—to quote the title of a seminal article by Broner and Tarone on the topic—often a matter of "is it fun?" (Broner and Tarone 2001; see also Bell 2005; Crystal 2001). However, just as integral to work on play and language learning is the underlying argument that the amusement, aesthetic pleasure, and joy of language play are not merely fun for fun's sake. Cook's seminal volume on the subject, *Language Play, Language Learning* (2000), opens with a focus on the playful languaging activities of young children, exactly to make the case that while language play "appears superfluous, it is not actually so," that playful languaging is "… there to be exploited to our advantage in many areas of human activity, including language learning" (5). How play supports language learning is another line of questioning running through this body of research.

In scholarship on play and language development, "is it fun?" is a central but not the singular question; in their work, Broner and Tarone (2001) distinguished between ludic views of language play, for which Cook (1997, 2000) is their primary inspiration, and play as rehearsal as theorized in Lantolf's (1997) Vygotsky-inspired model of play. Writing at the peak of communicative and proficiency-based language teaching, Broner and Tarone's purpose is to reconcile two seemingly contradictory models of language play—play as fun and play as rehearsal—by arguing that they are connected by the lack of obvious communicative intent and distinguished through the positive affect associated with the former. Both types of play, they argue, have "separate and distinct" functions in language development (376), and consequently different potential roles in language pedagogy.

As discussed in Chapter 2, Vygotsky's theories of learning and development are the theoretical foundation of contemporary sociocultural theory. Within this framework, cognitive development is understood as mediated through social interactions, including face-to-face interactions between people, as well as communication mediated and enabled through technologies, ranging from the paper and pen to mobile phones. In his discussion of play, Lantolf (1997) is primarily interested in Vygotsky's work on private speech. In a survey that was administered to students as part of the study, his examples of play include the following: talking loud to yourself in Spanish, repeating phrases to yourself silently, making up sentences or words in Spanish, imitating to yourself sounds in Spanish, and having random snatches of Spanish pop into your head (Lantolf 1997, 11). According to Lantolf, these kinds of play as rehearsal may have a noticing function for language learners, in that they allow them to compare what they are learning with what they know in a relatively low-stakes context.

Because of his focus on linguistic development, Lantolf (1997) characterizes language play in the form of private speech as "rather sophisticated pattern drill activities" (8), which is what leads Broner and Tarone (2001) to emphasize the rehearsal aspects of this activity. The question of what actually renders moments of private speech *play* is relegated to the sidelines. Lantolf's examples of play as rehearsal focus on what is visible linguistically and not on the experience of or relationship to that activity, even though it is difficult to argue that every instance of private speech would be experienced by students as playful.

In a later co-authored article (Lantolf and Yáñez 2003), Lantolf's understanding of the relationship between play and private speech seems to have shifted, such that there is greater attention to "symbolic play," as a form of private speech. Borrowing from Lightbrown and Spada's (1993) study, Lantolf and Yáñez (2003) cite the following example:

David (3 years, 11 months)
Mother get undressed (after many repetitions)
David I'm getting undressed
    I'm getting on dressed.
    I'm getting on dressed.
    I'm getting off dressed.
        (Lightbrown and Spade 1993, 7; cited in Lantolf and Yáñez 2003, 99)

Imagining what this excerpt would have sounded like, we can hear the rhythm in the mother's instructions flowing into the child's response—an example of what Cook (2000) called play on the formal levels of language. Arguably, what makes this exchange playful is not simply the repetition or rehearsal, but the feelings aroused as David disassociates "the intentional affordances from their associated objects and artifacts," quoting Lantolf and Yáñez's citation of Tomasello's definition of symbolic play (Lantolf and Yáñez 2003, 99; Tomasello 1999, 85). Of note is that this is not strictly speaking an example of private speech, even if David appears to be talking to himself. Indeed, the symbolic play here is every bit as much about the undoing of the imperative command issued by the mother as it is the sound play of *un-* and *on*, which leads from *on dressed* to the creative expression *off dressed*. It is the mother's (conceivably unplayful and even frustrated) repetition and her voice that are being played with, or we could say redesigned, here, and this likely has very *inter*personal, phatic effects. At the same time, her power as the parental figure is toyed with, as David perhaps satisfies his own desires, subverting his mother's commands by getting *off* dressed instead of undressed. Examples like this seem to suggest that play as rehearsal is not a distinct form of language play—and that *fun* alone may not capture the affective complexity of playfulness.

Play, for Vygotsky, functions as an integral part of not only linguistic and intellectual, but also social, emotional, and symbolic development, all of which are bound up in one another; and private speech is not the only or even the most quintessential form of play. Much of Vygotsky's work looks instead at sociodramatic play, including activities like playing pretend and fantasy. Based on his study of how children engage in these kinds of imaginative activities, Vygotsky posits that play is ultimately about desires. When our desires cannot be immediately resolved, we enter into imaginary, illusory worlds of play where these can be realized (Vygotksy 1978; 2016[1966]). Vygotsky goes on to clarify that play does not result directly as a consequence of each unsatisfied desire, but often rather manifests in a more undirected way:

> [A] child wants to ride in a cab, the wish is not immediately gratified, so the child goes into his room and begins to play cabs. It never happens just this way. Here we are concerned with the fact that the child not only has individual, affective reactions to separate phenomena but also generalized unspecified affective tendencies.
>
> (Vygotsky 2016[1966], 8)

The two forms of affective intensity referenced by Vygotsky have some parallels to the ways of thinking about affect theorized in Chapter 2, both as an emotional relationship with an object (or person or event) as theorized by Ahmed and as an experience of not-yet-structured intensities as theorized by Deleuze and Guattari. In both cases, play is not instrumentally oriented toward gratifying a wish or resolving a feeling but rather desires for something *other than what is* flow through the playful activities.

While fantastical, fictional realities are important in his work, one of Vygotsky's much-cited examples of sociodramatic play features two young sisters (ages five and seven) who say to each other "let's play sisters"—they are, in other words, playing at reality. In Vygotsky's analysis, instances like this, in which we *play* at being ourselves, create an opportunity to step outside of our already internalized ways of behaving: "What passes unnoticed by the child in real life becomes a rule of behaviour in play," (2016[1966], 10)—and in this way, through play, meanings get separated from events. In Vygotsky's anecdote of the sisters, they "are dressed alike, they walk about holding hands—in short, they enact whatever emphasizes their relationship as sisters vis-a-vis adults and strangers" (2016[1966], 10). In this scenario, play is not about *being* sisters, which these two children do unthinkingly all the time, but about exploring what it *means* to be sisters and through what kinds of symbolic action we enact (we might say design) those meanings.

In ways that parallel some of Vygotsky's work on play in childhood, research on adult language learners has suggested that play with language can help learners to develop a sense of themselves as multicompetent languagers, that is, to explore what it *means* to be a speaker of multiple languages. Pomerantz and Bell (2007) draw upon a study of an advanced-level university Spanish course to show how moments of spontaneous play with word meanings and sounds, dramatic roles and different ways of speaking, and even classroom norms arose during stretches of relatively serious, non-playful interaction. Based on their data, they posit that playful language use can help learners to not only develop a stronger and broader communicative repertoire, but also to express a range of meaning beyond utilitarian ones. In her study of German language learners in the United States, Belz (2002) shows how instances of multilingual language play can act as "textual indication of changes in learner's self-conceptualizations" (15) as they discover new ways of understanding themselves and interacting with the world. Belz concludes with the following quote from Cook (1996): "Not only does play with language demonstrate that [language] is *within* our control, but it is also a celebration of an infinite potential and unexpected creative power which, though *beyond* our control, is key to change and freedom *from* control" (Cook 1996, 266; cited in Belz 2002, 35–6). In contexts where learning a new language is a choice (as opposed to an inevitability, e.g., in cases of forced migration), play can be both a means and an end, aiding in the acquisition of new forms and offering a chance to explore through what forms of expression we design ourselves.

Within second language/culture teaching and learning, there emerges a set of connected but distinct arguments for how play influences and interacts with the kinds of development that are considered within the purview of this field, ranging from play as a form of noticing (as in rehearsal and repetition), play as a means of decoupling linguistic expressions from their meanings (as in sociodramatic activities), and play as the actualization of multilingual subjectivities (with expanded repertoires for engaging with and making sense of the world). What is needed is an understanding of play that can help us to attend to all these elements within the context of the second language classroom.

In the next section, I consider three interconnecting dimensions of play in the context of second language literacy education as a bricolage (a creative assemblage) of meaning-making resources, as an affective modulation in relation to an activity and its everyday meanings, and finally as a form of subversive action. These three intersecting aspects are inspired by work in play theory, and they also correspond to the three parts of the design model proposed by the New London Group: designs, designing, and the redesigned—which allows me to begin to weave together theories of multiliteracy and play. Taken as a whole, they form the basis for a play-based pedagogy of multiliteracies that works to both attend to the new linguistic and other semiotic designs learners take up when they learn a new language and the intensely affective experience of stepping into new expressive landscapes.

Dimensions of Multiliteracy Play

Bricolage: Play with Available Designs

Writing about the place of creativity in his human ecological model of language education, Levine (2020) notes, "the basic materials of creativity are widely available and almost anything might be turned into a tool for creative play" (54). Levine is drawing attention to the fact that the same transferable and recontextualizable qualities of available designs that allow them to be taken up in a range of novel moments of languaging also leave them malleable and repurposeable. Within humanistic fields of study, the improvisational creation of something from a diverse range of things that happen to be available is sometimes described using the French loanword *bricolage*. As a critical concept, *bricolage* comes into English through the work of anthropologist Levi-Strauss (1966[1962]), who contrasted the *bricoleur* (i.e., the person who engages in bricolage) with the *engineer*; whereas the latter is concerned with structural well-craftedness of their product, the former is adept in the art of making do, putting pre-existing things together in new ways and repurposing things for new functions. While much more can and has been said about Levi-Strauss's use of *bricolage* and *bricoleur* within the context of his anthropological work, it is the distinction in dispositions here that most interests me for the discussion at hand; while the engineer enters into design with scientific projection and planning, the bricoleur's work is more ad hoc and it is in the creative combination of elements that design emerges. Connecting bricolage to play theory, we might think of the bricoleur as someone who engages what Zimmerman (2008), a game studies scholar, describes as *play literacy*, the capacity to see "the world's structures as opportunities for playful engagement" (27).

In her research on the play and creativity of adult language learners, Schufflebarger Snell (2016) draws a connection between bricolage and symbolic competence. The latter is understood in Kramsch and Whiteside's (2008) sense of the "ability to shape the multilingual game in which one invests" (667). Kramsch and Whiteside (2008) observe that multilingual speakers "seem to display a particularly acute ability to play with various linguistic codes" (664). Schufflebarger Snell's (2016) use of the term bricolage similarly highlights the ways in which, through their acts of meaning design, individuals are not only creating something but are also solving complex problems in new ways, drawing upon their diverse multilingual repertoires (81). Schufflebarger Snell sees symbolic play as part of the potential of bricolage, noting that there is a "reflective detachment" (81) involved through which linguistic forms and practices are temporarily disassociated from their real-world consequences, even as those consequences do not cease to exist. For example, students in Schufflebarger Snell's (2016) study were invited to visually represent an English language idiom. One student, working with the expression "you're wasting time," depicted a wastebasket surrounded by a cross out circle on one side and a clock with a check mark next to it on the other. The visual symbol for something prohibited (here waste) and something that is sanctioned or approved (time keeping) support the phrasing of the idiom as it is written at the top of the image as a directive addressed in the second person. Another student created a poem in Spanish, which she later translated into English, for the expression "better late than never."

> It's better late than never
> when you have a dream
> because to fight is worth the victory
> and fight until you can reach
> you can achieve anything with effort
> it's better late
> than never
> Sincerely, Time.

The poem is also a letter, from Time itself. In the original version, the text was surrounded by small hearts, giving the impression of a love note. As in the first example ("you're wasting time"), second person address is used here, rendering the clichéd expression more personal, even intimate. These were idioms that the students had likely encountered in their lives outside of the classroom, but the opportunity to play with them and to bricolage around them created alternate relationships with the directive acts implied by these colloquialisms.

Schufflebarger's understanding of bricolage also shares some conceptual commonalities with Derrida's (2007[1967]) critical re-reading of Levi-Strauss, wherein he sees the distinction between the engineer and the bricoleur as less absolute. For Derrida all language use is bricolage; we are always left to make do with the set of meaning-making resources available to us. The bricoleur and the engineer then describe not two distinct types of people, but two modes of engaging with the necessity of making do with inherited texts and meanings. The question is where our attention is focused along the continuum between play and stability, creativity and convention. By re-contextualizing, remixing, and translating lines and phrases from texts introduced into the class, the participants in Schufflebarger's language class are engaging in a form of bricolage marked not by innovation but by repetition and mimicry, by creativity in convention (see also Pennycook 2007). The iterative nature of play points to the capacity of redesigning that is always inherent in design.

Play and creativity are often positioned within a binary opposition between freedom and constraint. Callois (2001[1958]), one of the early theorists of play and game theory, categorized play along a continuum between these two poles, with free form, improvisational activity on the one end and goal-oriented, rule-guided activity on the other. The former he called *paidia*, from the Greek word for child, because the quintessential examples were children's make-believe play (although, as we have seen, Vygotsky might have questioned how free form such play actually is); the latter Callois dubbed *ludus*, from the Greek word for game. For Callois, paidia and ludus are not two separate genres or categories of game but rather two forces that exert themselves on human activity. Although some games or activities are more associated with or afford themselves more readily to a paidic or ludic orientation, play emerges in the activity itself, as part of the interaction between human and material participants (including the semiotic resources of the game designs).

As Tin notes in her work on creativity and language teaching, constraints are often assumed to be impediments to creativity (2022, 71); however, research has suggested that the reality is more nuanced and that certain kinds of constraints may actually help foster creative engagement both with reference to activities that are more aesthetic and those geared toward problem-solving (Tin 2022, 71–71; see also Budach, Sharoyan, and Loghin 2022). Tin's research (2011, 2012, 2013) with second language learners demonstrates how certain constraints on creative tasks can encourage greater linguistic complexity and creative thinking styles. For example, in Tin (2011) students were asked to write acrostic poems, a literary genre that imposes a formal constraint, every line must begin with a letter provided by the keyword, and a semantic constraint, the poem as a whole must relate back to the concept expressed by the keyword. Tin's analysis shows how the form of the acrostic encouraged both syntagmatic and paradigmatic language play, as the student-poets played with sentence structures and word choice, but also that it promoted moments of "chaotic thinking" (Finke 1996), creative thinking that is more spontaneous, responsive, and divergent "focusing mainly on momentary occurrences and exploring novel alternatives without specific plans or goals" (Tin 2011, 224).

Tin's finding that tasks emphasizing play with form can result in semantic play is echoed in Cook's claim that linguistic play can serve as a catalyst for imaginary worlds. Take the following moment of interaction from a meeting between myself and a cohort of German language teachers. One of the instructors was commenting on a reading strategies activity that students had completed as homework, in which they had been asked to list words they understood. Reading aloud from one submission, she said "I like this one. Words you understood—'wir, fliefen … '" This was met with laughter from the group because although the first word is in the second person plural in German, the second sounds like a plausible German word but was likely a misspelling of the word "to fly" or "fliegen." The amusement arose from the sound of the word, which at least from my perspective has a little something of the English word "fluff." We began to speculate about what the word "fliefen" might mean. One suggestion was that it described the movement of a particularly feathery bird at flight. I could imagine in my head a shaggy fantasy bird with long, shaggy plumage billowing in the breeze.

Cook provides numerous examples from poems, children's literature, and folktales to underscore his point that this kind of semantic play is an intrinsic form of human activity. Instances of imaginary play based in formal creativity show neatly how the dissociation of meaning from language's usual referent creates the potential for bricolage in the form of worldbuilding. For Cook it is then just a leap in complexity to understand the kinds of rich worldbuilding that happens in fantasy, make believe, and works of fiction. Since Cook's book was published, a rich body of work on creative world building has emerged from scholars in stylistics and cognitive poetics (e.g., Gavins 2016; Gavins and Lahey 2016) and in education (e.g., Stornaiuolo 2015; Stornaiuolo and Whitney 2018; Pahl and Pool 2020). McRae (1991), one of the long-term advocates of creativity and play in foreign language teaching, has argued that the imaginary is also a core part of what it means to learn a new language. In addition to the kinds of referential texts that are the mainstays of communicative curricula, McRae has argued for the inclusion of *representational texts*, which engage readers in world building, by requiring them to make connections between the text, their personal experiences, and what they believe they know about the world. Representational texts "stimulate and use areas of the mind, from imagination to emotion, from pleasure to pain, which referential language does not reach" (McRae 1991, 3).

In addition to the formal and representational elements of meaning design, types of behavior or activity can be resources for play. Bateson (1972), in his study of humans and other animals, noticed the close relationship between play and other types of behavior such as threats and deceit. Bateson (1972) is generally interested in those interactions that make use of premises not overtly connected to the language itself to render the primary meaning of an action or set of actions non-literal. In such interactions, the meta-communicative premise acts like a frame, which enables an utterance such as an insult to denote an insult, but not the denotation of the insult. Cook (2000), drawing on Bateson's work along with other social theories, identified this as pragmatic play. His central example for this was verbal dueling, a form of competitive language play, in which participants engage in a linguistic battle of wits. Notably, the main function or effect of verbal dueling is not amusement, that is, fun, and there is rather a thin line between play and the threat of violence in such interactions.

As part of his social interaction theory, Goffman (1974) took up Bateson's notion of the frame to get at the question of how we organize experience, that is, how we form a sense of what is going on at any given moment. Goffman argues that we often manage quite readily with our primary frameworks, those socioculturally shared frames that we have internalized as the meaning of a set of circumstances; at the same time, humans (and many other animals) also operate within frames of interaction that require a return to components in the primary frame and a transcription of this meaning. Goffman calls this process, by which an already meaningful event is transformed into something modeled after it, but to be understood quite differently, a *keying*. What Goffman calls a *key* is then "the set of conventions by which a given activity, one already meaningful in terms of primary framework, is transformed into something patterned on this activity, but seen by the participants to be something quite else" (1974, 43–4). By playing with the frames, participants point back to the expectations that often tacitly design our interactions. For example, thinking back to Chapter 2, Liam's class maintained the frame of *instructional activity* while completing the task, but Michael's class modulated the frame to something more like simulation or play pretend, which re-assembled the relationships between elements including the classroom space and linguistic resources.

In this section thus far, I have suggested three types of language play, which arise through bricolage with available designs: play with form, representation, and frame (see Figure 4; see also Warner 2004, 2022). *Play with form* involves those instances where it is the materiality of language or another semiotic system

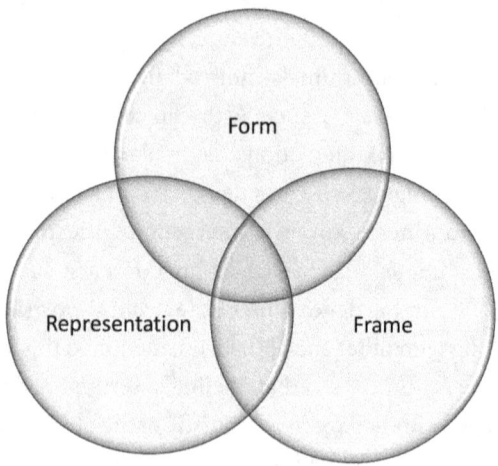

Figure 4 Types of design play.

that is being creatively manipulated. This includes many aspects of play that Cook dubbed linguistic, such as rhyming and punning, as well as poetic devices such as alliteration, parallelism, and repetition. In *play with representation*, creative uses of language afford new possibilities for conceptualizing and representing the world. This includes more familiar forms of figurative language like metaphor and metonymy, as well as acts of world-making, through which language users can imagine new realities and roles for themselves within them. Finally, *play with frame* draws attention to the performance of the text as a social act and the roles of the participants (i.e., speakers/listeners, composers/readers) therewithin. This includes, for example, shifts in narrative perspective, which frame the story in a different key, as well as other types of play at this level of discourse, such as creative uses of genre, register, and modality.

To give a sense of what these types of play look like in practice, I will turn now to a short creative text from a German learner named Zeng[1], who at the time of writing was enrolled in a content-based language and culture class at an American university. Students had been asked to author an imagined first page of their own autobiographies—followed the reading and discussion of excerpts from three literary autobiographies (see also Warner 2023).

Jetzt bin ich in Tucson, 15 Stunde von Singapur, 12.5 Stunde von Indien. Es riecht nach Fische zu Hause; leckere Fische, die meine Mutter für uns immer kocht. Vielleicht essen sie jetzt Fische in Singapur, wie die Fische, die ich gerade gekocht habe hier. Ich habe meinen Lunch genau gegessen und jetzt muss ich die erste Seite meine Autobiographie schreiben.

Wie soll ich das tun? Mein Leben jetzt ist so unwichtig wie meine Geburt. Soll ich mit meiner Geburt anfangen. Nein, ich achte auf traditionelle Stile. Ich habe zu viele postmodernische Literatur gelesen, und ich habe gelernt, dass wir jetzt in einer postmodernischen Epoche sind. Man schreibt heute anders.

Ich habe mich von mir distanziert. Jeder Tag gehe ich zu Klasse, schreibe ich gerne die Notizen, lerne ich gerne neue Ideen. Denken andere Leute an mich, diese normale Frau? Wenn ich ein Mädchen war, schaffte ich die gleichen Dinge. Ich habe zu Klasse gegangen, ich habe Notizen gerne geschrieben, ich habe auch neue Ideen gelernt. Kein wichtiger Unterschied. Was für ein Leben ist das! Will jemand mich von meinem Leben retten vielleicht?

Now I am in Tucson, 15 hours from Singapore., 12.5 hours from India. It smells like fish at home; delicious fish, which my mother cooks for us. Perhaps they are eating fish now in Singapore, like the fish that I have just cooked here. I have exactly eaten my lunch and now I must write the first page of my autobiography.

> *How should I do that? My life is as unimportant as my birth. Should I begin with my birth? No, I attend to traditional styles. I have read too much postmodern literature, and I have learned, that we are now in a postmodern epoch. Today one writes differently.*
>
> *I have distanced myself from me. Every day I go to class, happily write notes, happily learn new ideas. Do other people think of me, this normal woman? When I was a girl, I did the same things. I went to class, I happily wrote notes, I also learned new ideas. No important difference. What a life is this! Would someone like to save me from my life perhaps?*

Zeng's text opens with some examples of formal play, the repetition of phrases like "15 Stunde (15 hour)," "12.5 Stunde (12.4 hour)" and the multiple appearances of the word "Fische (fish)." Again in the final paragraph, there is similar repetition between the phrases in the present tense "Jeder Tag gehe ich zu Klasse, schreibe ich gerne die Notizen, lerne ich gerne neue Ideen. (Every day I go to class, happily write notes, happily learn new ideas.)" and in the past tense "Ich habe zu Klasse gegangen, ich habe Notizen gerne geschrieben, ich habe auch neue Ideen gelernt. (I went to class, I happily wrote notes, I also learned new ideas.)." These instances of formal play also initiate two parallel moments of representational play. In the opening they set up a relationship between three places, Tucson where Zeng was studying and the two countries with which she has familial ties; in the final paragraph, the contrast is temporal, between the current moment, where she is a student at the university, and her childhood experiences as a schoolgirl. In the middle of the text, Zeng plays with the frame, the premise of writing the first page of her autobiography. Referencing examples that we had seen in class, Zeng rejects the idea of beginning with her birth, noting that she has learned that we live in a "postmodern epoch" and that "today one writes differently." By playing with the available designs for what an autobiography looks like, Zeng, like the participants in Schufflebarger Snell's 2016 study, is engaging in a multilingual language game of her own. The resulting bricolage creates relationships between past and present, homeland and current house, while also calling into question the genre's tendency toward tidy coherence with her desire to be "saved" from the monotony of her life.

Sensation and Orientation: Designing Meaning Playfully

In the previous sections of this chapter, the notion that play is straightforwardly or even necessarily fun has been complicated, most overtly through the notion of play as rehearsal; but the relatively anesthetic notion of rehearsal continues to sidestep important questions about the broader range of affective experiences that can converge when playing in and with a second language, which this section will return to. Across the range of theorizations about what play is, there is a shared sense that our perceptions and feelings shape the experience of play as such. "[I]t is very often ... attitude which makes something play," to quote Cook's (2000) book on its role in language learning—which can lead to rather tautological definitions of play as what happens when we are playing. In an example like Zeng's, we can see a range of feelings that manifest through aesthetic reading and writing, which cannot be reduced to fun or amusement. So, if not fun, then what is this feeling we get when we know we are playing?

For as long as there have been theories on the subject, scholars have cautioned against equating play with fun or pleasure and have demonstrated the rather thin line between play and other emotional intensities including fear and anger (e.g., Bateson 1972; Cook 2000; Vygotksy 2016[1966]). To paraphrase Vygotsky, if it is pleasure that we seek, any number of non-playful activities will do. Furthermore, both children and adults engage in a range of feeling states during play, often overlapping with one another (Vygotsky 2016[1966]). Think of walking through a haunted house; assuming you are a person who likes this sort of thing, you might feel both terrified as you engage in the make-believe world in which vampires and zombies jump out at every turn, while also feeling happy as a horror aficionado because you are partaking in a favorite type of play. Play is quite frequently not unambiguously enjoyable but also a little risky, thrilling, and perhaps outside of one's comfort zone.

In my own study of university-level German learners' interactions in classroom-based computer-mediated communication, instances of language play were likewise often affectively ambivalent rather than straightforwardly fun (Warner 2004). The titular quote of the article "It's just a game, right?" refers to such a moment, when a student expressed self-doubt about whether the jovial teasing that they engaged in during a role-play activity was also being perceived as play by another student. In Cook's discussion of verbal dueling and Bateson's analysis of the relationships between play and threat, we can see that the line between the positive affect associated with play and negative experiences is often thin and gray. Even acknowledging that play is more complicated than "is it fun?" or "it's just a game, right?", the questions posed here point to a central problem in play research—how do we know it is play? The "right?" at the end of the student's question is a reminder that there is often some ambiguity or ambivalence, which results in those moments when we have to check in with others, claim in protest, "hey, I'm just playing," or offer some equivalent signal that what is happening right now is somewhat marked off from other forms of social activity.

Even as specific feelings or sensations alone do not make an activity play (see Upton 2015, 21), play does seem to be associated with an aesthetic that we can recognize as such, when we agree that something is play. In the theories of Vygotsky, Bateson, and Goffman discussed already in this chapter, a common theme has been that play involves above all a decoupling of meaning from ordinary events. Linguistic forms become separate from their familiar communicative uses, representations are loosened from referents, and the social understandings normally ascribed to certain behaviors are no longer given primacy. In the context of the kinds of semiotic activity of interest to the current discussion, play can thus perhaps best be understood as first and foremost a relationship with meaning—admittedly one that has often acute aesthetic and sometimes otherwise emotional effects.

Following the social theories of Bateson and Goffman introduced in the previous section, play can be understood as an example of the more general phenomenon of *keying*. Through *keying* an event frame becomes transformed, such that "the set of conventions by which a given activity, one already meaningful in terms of some primary framework, is transformed into something patterned on this activity but seen by the participants to be something quite else" (1974, 43–4). For Goffman, play is one of the several basic keys employed by our society, alongside make believe, contests, ceremonials, regroundings, and technical redoings. He also recognized that not every transformation is straightforwardly a key; for example, fabrications are transformations in which participants are deliberately deceived about the actual seriousness of events. A keyed event such as play requires that everyone is, so to speak, in on the game.

In moments of doubt, participants may check in overtly, as the student did in the computer-mediated communication example above. But more often than not participants are able to quite readily tacitly agree when play is at hand. Dutch cultural scholar Huizina, who was one of the first to theorize play and its role in human life, proposed the notion of the "magic circle" to try to account for this phenomenon (see also Salen and Zimmerman 2003 and Zimmerman 2012 for a critical discussion of the use of this term in game theory). Huizinga writes, "All play moves and has its being within a playground marked off beforehand either materially or ideally, deliberately or as a matter of course" (1955 [1938], 10). Play, like magic, like ritual, exists outside of ordinary life in ways that are clear to participants. Although Huizinga cites multiple physical spaces as examples, e.g., the playground, the stage, the arena, it is likewise clear that the magic circle here can be more virtual, a shared idea that the moment of play is somehow outside of normal life. Play thus often has a community effect, according to Huizinga, "Inside the circle of the game the laws and customs of ordinary life no longer count. We are different and do things differently." This sense of being togetherness, the creation of a "we," can also extend beyond the sphere of play and into the formation of affinity groups or even classroom communities.

Huizinga's emphasis on the spatial and temporal demarcation of the magic circle is a recognition that material elements often help to signal that an activity is in a different key—this can include formal linguistic play, laughter, smiling, and other forms of non—and paraverbal signals, or meta-communicative remarks such as "Let's play" or "It's just a game, right?" But as Callois (2001[1958]) noted, the experience of play is not tethered directly to the design of an activity—which is one of the reasons that attempts to bring extracurricular forms of play into the classroom can sometimes fail (see e.g., Reinhart, Warner, Lange 2014). Just as musical keys evoke different feelings, social activities that are keyed as play involve an affective modulation, which can be choreographed or provoked through different designs but does not stand in a directly causal relationship with them. Returning to terms from the previous chapter, play unfolds within assemblages that include (but are not reducible to) organized patterns of affect that can be crafted and designed—whether by artists, everyday languages, teachers, or learners (see also Hickey-Moody 2013).

While the academic context of the classroom can sometimes anaesthetize the experience of play, there are also reasons to believe that the second or *foreign* language itself can evoke a magic circle effect. Rampton's (1999) study of the use of German amongst a group of multilingual adolescents at an inner-city school in London shows how the introduction of a language marked as *foreign* (i.e., part of the educational system rather than the extracurricular lifeworlds of the students) was being used to "display heightened sensitivity to either actual or potential disruptions to the orderly flow of everyday social life and relations" (496). Rampton makes a compelling case that the students were playing with German from the classroom in these moments not to project a sense of themselves as German speakers per se, but to negotiate intersecting social relations including class, gender, ethnicity, and migration. The use of German words or phrases in the flow of talk seemed in many instances to inaugurate a rekeying, whereby students were about to frame an interaction playfully or perform self-dramatization.

In my own study of German language users and their interactions in classroom-based computer-mediated communication (e.g., Warner 2004), the combination of the online chat space (a so-called MOOC) and second language seemed to also create a magic circle effect in moments. Students frequently engaged in verbal dueling and sideplay, as in the excerpt below (Warner 2004, 77). For example, in the excerpt below the students Mir and steffigraf, two close friends in the class, were exchanging insults and friendly name-calling in German, testing out slang they otherwise would not use in a classroom setting.

> Mir says, "ja. jetzt gehen wir Schlampe ... ich werde dein Po kicken"
> Jieve says, "**im Arsch treten**"
> steffigraf says, "Das ist aber lacherlich"
> UC_Regents says, "Wir brauchen Geld!"
> UC_Regents says, "Wir brauchen Geld!"
> UC_Regents says, "Wir brauchen Geld!"
> UC_Regents says, "Wir brauchen Geld!"
> UC_Regents says, "Wir brauchen Geld!"
> UC_Regents says, "Wir brauchen Geld!"
> UC_Regents says, "Wir brauchen Geld!"
> UC_Regents says, "Wir brauchen Geld!"
> Jieve says, "steffigraph, ich hae (probably misspelled word for hate) dich"
> **arsch** says, "**nicht treten**"
> Mir says, "yeah. let's go then sleaze ... I am going to kick your butt (idiomatically incorrect)."
> Jieve says, "to kick butt (idiomatically correct)"
> steffigraf says, "That's just ridiculous"
> UC_Regents says, "We need money (repeated eight times consecutively)!"
> Jieve says, "steffigraph, I hae (probably misspelled word for hate) you"
> arsch (butt) says, "do not kick"

Another student, Jieve replied, correcting Mir's language use from "dein Po kicken" to the more idiomatic "im Arsch treten." This then prompted someone to quickly change their username to "Arsch" (butt) to beseech the others "nicht treten" (do not kick). Working with the playful affordances of the technology, the student had taken a typical moment of peer correction and transformed it into an alternate reality where lexical items speak back. In the midst of this verbal dueling, an additional participant appeared as UC Regents (the governing board of the University of California system) to declare (in German) "We need money." The computer-mediated language classroom, which was markedly different from *normal* instruction, seemed to encourage play with a wide range of available designs and positions, through which students negotiated social relations and identities, alongside the communicative language tasks, which they did indeed complete as well.

Like make-believe or art, second language learning allows us to connect with the world in new and different ways, and play may not only be helpful but inherent in the aesthetic experience of learning a new language (see also Leung and Scarino 2016; Ros i Solé 2016). Returning to the earlier discussion of bricolage, we can think of play as an affectively modulated activity that both recognizes the relative stability of the systems of meaning through which we normally operate within the world and points to the potential instabilities in that system. Play with new languages creates opportunities for expanding our "imaginative capital" (Embeywa 2023), not by granting freedom from the constraints of our other more familiar systems of meaning, but by drawing attention to the extent to which the conventions and norms of those systems are subject to play—they can be wiggled, new ideas can slide into their gaps, and they can be transposed and transformed. Scholars of language from Cook (2000) to Tin (2022) have argued that meaning often arises in the midst of creative play in unpredictable ways. At the same time that a playful orientation comes with a shiftiness, it also carries the ordinary world and its meanings and consequences right along with it; it is no wonder then that we come to associate play with emotional intensities, but it is the orientation to meaning and trusted ways in which it is designed that marks activity as play. And the capacity to develop this kind of orientation, this kind of play literacy, is arguably one of the valuable, and too often understated, outcomes of learning additional languages.

Subversive Literacy Activities: Redesigning through Literacy Play

"In play there is something 'at play' which transcends the immediate needs of life and imparts meaning to the action" (Huizinga 1955 [1938], 155). Huizinga's observation that play brackets out activity from ordinary life is coupled with his contention that play is meaningful. It is not incidental that Huizinga was writing his theories of play in the Netherlands in 1938, during the rise of radically violent National Socialist rhetoric. A resulting tension in his work is that even as Huizinga explicitly separates play from seriousness, treating the two as binary oppositions so that he can preserve a safe space for the imaginative freedom of play, he often undercuts his own argument and points instead to the reality that elements of play and seriousness are inextricable from one another (see Upton 2015, 14). Play is decoupled from ordinary life, but it does not exist outside of the real world; it carries everyday meanings along with it as a sort of substratum with which it is in constant contact.

Exactly because play is a way of engaging with ordinary life in a different key, there is a transformational dimension of play. Play can act as a form of creative disorder (Phipps and Gonzalez 2004, 78). By playing with and within language and literacy activities, we can explore the affective space of "not yet" and "what if?" (see Pahl and Rowsell 2020, 6), which has led Pahl and Poole (2020) to argue that literacy play is a hopeful activity, one that "requires an element of daydreaming, a distancing from the preconceptions and modes of thinking that keep us from seeing how we might build something better" (79). Through multiliteracy play in their second and additional languages, learners can consider what it would be like for meaning systems and the social realities within which they are at home to be *other than*. In this sense, redesigning takes on transformative as well as subversive potential.

In his writings on "the practice of everyday life," de Certeau (1984) recognized the subversive potential of ordinary literacy activities in late capitalist societies. De Certeau was generally concerned with how people, through quotidien acts of consumption, reassert themselves as active agents. Lacking access to the kinds of power maneuvers that shape institutions and the dominant discourses within them (what de Certeau called *strategies*), people creatively respond to situations through *tactics*—"making do" with readymade cultural practices as they "make with" those practices (i.e., though bricolage). Everyday practices of consumption (including activities like reading or even doing homework for one's language class) can be tactical in that they re-signify and disrupt the schematic ordering of reality produced through the strategic practices of the powerful. Through acts of what he dubs *reading-as-poaching* (and today we could add others such as *viewing-as-poaching* and *gaming-as-poaching*), readers step into others' spaces and make unauthorized use of semiotic materials (i.e., available designs that are not their own). Poacher-readers appropriate (redesign) others' words for their own uses; however, poaching as a metaphor also points to other aspects of the experience of designing meaning with others' texts, such as the double subjectivity involved in trespassing within losing oneself in the text

There are clear elements of de Certeau's *reading-as-poaching* in Kramsch and Nolden's (1994) discussion of second language literacy as oppositional practice. They write:

> Oppositional practice is not resistance, dissidence or contestation. It just claims the right of the readers to position themselves at equal par with, i.e., in (op)position to, the text, by virtue of the very linguistic and conceptual power that the text has given them. By becoming aware of their oppositional stance, readers can enter into dialogue with the text and with other readers and eventually, through this dialogue, experience "changes in desire" that potentially lead to social change.
>
> (29–30)

Oppositional practice is a deliberate way of responding to the kinds of difficulties and discomforts individuals may face when they try to position themselves within multilayered social spaces, such as those that emerge when fields of cultural production collide with educational spaces and historical moments collide with contemporaneous cultural practices and affect worlds. These *symbolic struggles* (Warner and Richardson 2017) are part and parcel of entering into new literacy landscapes of a second language and culture. In oppositional practice, language learners play with what they recognize as the deferent reading by positioning themselves at odds with it by questioning and negotiating accepted meanings (see also Ros i Solé 2016, 8). In this way aesthetic reading can afford readers the ability to step into "the actual, the imagined and the virtual worlds in which others live" (Kramsch 2011, 366; see also Chapter 2), and this kind of literary imagination fosters symbolically aware acts of designing meaning that become redesigned meanings. Kramsch, in her later work on the symbolic dimensions of language and culture learning, has specifically emphasized the role of "literary imagination," in enabling students to not only reflect on the design resources available to them, but also to experience alternate realities, including other possible selves (e.g., 2006, 251). Engaging with literary and other aesthetically oriented forms of cultural production in a second language can thus be understood as a form of multiliteracy play with particularly subversive potential.

Although de Certeau characterizes it as a playful and protesting form of activity, the word poaching carries a negative connotation that is more likely to conjure spirits of colonialism and plunder than oppositional practice. Finding de Certeau's metaphor of reading-as-poaching problematic from a twenty-first-century purview, Mandzunowski and Henningsen (2021) propose a series of alternative metaphors, many inspired by de Certeau's other writing. These include reading-as-wandering, reading-as-jaywalking, reading-as-trespassing, reading-as-remixing, and reading-as-commoning—all of which capture different dimensions of readerly tactics. At the same time, the poaching metaphor can potentially serve as a reminder that there is an ethical dimension to stepping into others' words and worlds. While she would likely agree with de Certeau's critique of the author's sovereign authority over meaning and accept that readers may assume a "right to roam" (Mandzunowski and Henningsen 2021), Rosenblatt's views of aesthetic reading also included a sense of care and respect for the author and the text (Rosenblatt 1994[1978]). Just as we recognize that some forms of play pretend or make-believe can cause symbolic violence (think for example of the wearing of Black face or childhood games of cowboys and Indians in US American society), we must also consider the ethical consequence of stepping into others' discourses and designs. The question of when to roam and how far and into whose territory to trespass and what can be poached is a question of positionality and ethics, which learners ought to be invited to deliberate as they play with others' words and meanings. Spivak offers a note of caution that is also helpful here, where she writes that "An aesthetic education teaches the humanities in such a way that all subjects are 'contaminated'" (2012, 9). To engage subversively in the sense of imagining new forms of meaning and life, a pedagogy of multiliteracy play must enable students to recognize that the playing field is never a free-for-all.

A parallel set of concerns has been voiced within discussions of intercultural learning in language education. In a critique of what she called *sympathetic imagination*, Carr (1999) argues that language pedagogy needs to push beyond the notion of intercultural transformative experiences directed toward immersing oneself in the feelings of others to foster empathy and tolerance. Instead of prioritizing this kind of *sympathetic imagination*, Carr advocated for attention to *dialogic imagination*, which invites learners to not only appreciate difference but to *do* difference. Carr's inspiration for the concept of *dialogic imagination* is Baktin (1981), who used the term to refer to the multiplicity of voices, discourses, and languages (the heteroglossia), in dialogue with which we develop our complex and multifaceted selves. In multiliteracies terms, Bakhtin's argument is that the only available designs of meaning are already imprinted with the uses and intentions of others, but at the same time, when we use these words, they are inevitably redesigned in our own voices.

For Quist (2013) transformative intercultural learning relies on elements of both sympathetic and dialogic imagination. Language-culture education must recognize both the struggles that individuals face making meaning out of the words of others, but also the responsibility born to those with whom one comes into dialogue. To capture both dimensions, Quist proposes the addition of *cosmopolitan imaginings* as a way "for students to imagine themselves in future roles where they have impact and effect on the world" through language learning (341).

> [I]magination, both dialogic and sympathetic, becomes a crucial tool. Through dialogic imagination we form and reform our multifaceted selves in a constantly shifting dialogue with others, appropriating their voices to differing extents. And through sympathetic imagination we imagine ourselves in the shoes of others with an understanding that we are part of a larger cosmopolitan project which compels us to take responsibility for others, work towards justice, equality, respect and even friendship.
>
> (336)

Quist specifically associates this pedagogical potential with playful, creative tasks, including reading literary texts and viewing films as well as opportunities for learners to "'author' themselves in creative and responsible ways" (341).

One possible example of what such cosmopolitan imaginings might look like in practice comes from a collaborative student project that took place in a course titled "The Task of the Translator," which my colleague and co-author David Gramling had developed as a fourth-year advanced German language course (Gramling and Warner 2016). Students in the course were asked to establish "translation agencies" in small groups, and then to decide on the ideals, goals, and priorities of their practice (i.e., on the aesthetic beauty of the translation, its accessibility, its fealty to the original, its precision of expression, or its sensitivity to cultural context). Groups also were able to review the mission statements of the other agencies, and in so doing the whole class engaged with their assumptions about translation practice as they also developed their own agencies, and contemplated their ethical responsibilities as language mediators.

Students then worked on a collaborative translation of a literary text across multiple phases. Looking at the case studies of three students who came to the class with diverse prior experiences with German and with multilingualism, our research shows how the opportunity to play as translators and with modes of translating enabled these students to subvert discourses of deficit and difficulties that so often haunt instructed language learning contexts. Instead, they opted for working principles of joy, rediscovery, and ambiguity as they were enabled to explore through translation "pleasurable problems with purposes other than being overcome that are all too often sidelined in foreign language curricula" (Gramling and Warner 2016, 95). Through their translation work, they were authoring themselves multilingual in creative and critical ways.

The imaginative potential of second language learning is potentially subversive because through our acts of everyday meaning making, we redesign the world and what languages and multilingualism mean and do within it. By orienting less toward predetermined outcomes and encouraging a suspension of what is and what has been taken for granted as having to be, we make space for the capacity to imagine what might be (see Stornaiuolo 2015, 568). Play is a mode of languaging that affords us with different ways of understanding the world and engaging with others. Through multiliteracy play learners can find opportunities to discover the relative roles available to them in mediating between languages and as potential creators of translanguaging spaces, where the symbolic and affective meanings attached to the world and ourselves and others acting within it are themselves understood to be *at play*.

A Model of Multiliteracy Play

Summarizing the previous three sections, we can think of multiliteracy play as having three intersecting dimensions:

1. Multiliteracy play as bricolage involves a recognition of available designs as semiotic elements that both function within systems of constraints in ways that are somewhat predictable and, which, at the same time, can be co-opted for new meanings. These elements include linguistic forms, the representations they convey, and understandings of the activity frame at hand.
2. Playfully designing meaning involves stepping outside of ordinary life while also making use of the activities of ordinary life. Activities and events marked as play are in a different key—they *mean* differently, and they also *feel* differently. Our sense of playfulness does not arise merely in going through the motions of gameplay but in being moved by and within the process of play. At the same time, certain design elements, configurations of elements, or contexts can cue play. Just as artistic and other aesthetically oriented designs can be crafted in attunement with feelings and emotions, however, playfulness cannot be causally designed into literacy or learning activities; because it comes into being as part of a sensorial assemblage that includes but cannot be reduced to elements of design.
3. Because what is being toyed with in multiliteracy play are the ways in which meaning is designed in our everyday activities, it is also always potentially transformational. Through multiliteracy play learners can develop an awareness of and the capacity to engage with what is (i.e., semiotic systems, positionalities, worlds) instead as it could otherwise be. Recognizing the need to familiarize learners with what have been conceptualized as available designs, McRae (2014) has argued that an emphasis on creativity in language learning does not mean that learners' knowledge of language systems and how they operate in use is no longer valued or prioritized; however, it does allow for the "rules" of language to be "questioned, played around with, and put to different uses" (17).

As we think about what multiliteracy play looks like in the language-culture classroom, it is important to keep in mind that play is rarely all or nothing. Play can often be found during long stretches of serious interaction (Pomerantz and Bell 2007, 562) and even in literacy activities, which one might not typically associate with playfulness, such as academic writing (Tardy 2021).

To understand the pedagogical choices that might enable a sense of play and exploration, McKee and Heydon (2020) examined one lesson cycle from a classroom from a multiple-case study of teachers' professional learning in literacy. Through narrative and ethnographic data collected in meetings of the professional learning group and the focal teacher's classroom, the authors identified two aspects that seemed to have the most impact: the introduction of flexible pedagogies, which integrated multimodal and digital literacies, coupled with the positioning of students as capable meaning-makers and as co-designers of not only their individual projects but the curriculum. The effect was a "co-decision to allocate classroom time, space, and materials to exploration, not just curricular outcomes" (793).

Based on their teacher research, McKee and Heydon suggest that there is an ethical imperative for such playful pedagogies as a means of realizing diverse forms of participation and reflective civic engagement, including decisions about which digital communications platforms and tools to use and why. Pomerantz and Bell (2007) have similarly argued that play itself may need to be not only enabled but actively fostered in the language classroom, given that practical and economic benefits of language study are often emphasized over social, emotional, and aesthetic reasons (see 575). These studies suggest that although play cannot be planned or coerced, it can and should be a pedagogical consideration in the design of classroom activities and curricula.

In Chapter 1, we looked at the framework multiliteracies pedagogy proposed by the New London Group (1996) and further developed by Cope and Kalantzis (2000). Recognizing the need for flexibility, these scholars focused on four pedagogical acts (New London Group) or knowledge processes (Cope and Kalantzis), which can be sequenced in different ways, to support active meaning making in the classroom. Returning to this framework, we can start to add in another layer of what kinds of pedagogical acts might encourage and enable multiliteracy play (see Table 5).

Working with this modified framework, we can think of multiliteracy play as a stance vis-a-vis design activities rather than as a new set of teaching and learning practices. And within this purview, learning is understood as only ever partially designed (through lesson plans and curriculum outcomes). A playful pedagogy is then about making space for the rest, the unplanned, the un-anticipatable, the undesigned.

Table 5 Learning activities in multiliteracy pedagogies/learning activities at play.

New London Group (1996)/ Cope and Kalantzis (2009)	Foundational aspects	Learning activities at play	Guiding questions
Situated practice/ experiencing	Emphasis is on knowledge activation and experiential learning	*Emphasis is on aesthetic aspects of experiencing and going with the flow*	*How does this text/literacy activity make me feel? How am I affected by it? How does it move me?*
Overt instruction/ conceptualizing	Emphasis is on guided attention to design elements	*Emphasis is on design elements as potential resources for bricolage*	*With which available designs (or elements thereof) do I want to experiment? Which attract me and why? How might I combine them together or with other design elements to different effects?*
Critical framing/ analyzing	Emphasis is on which meanings are enacted, whose perspectives are represented, and whose interests they serve	*Emphasis is on critical feeling as well as critical thinking*	*How might the feelings, sensations, and thoughts that I experience in relation to this text/literacy practice differ if I were engaging with it in a different moment/ place/positionality/perspective?*
Transformed practice/ applying	Emphasis is on the application of new knowledge through literacy practices that have been redesigned	*Emphasis is on the transformational potential of the redesigned*	*In what ways am I poaching, roaming, engaging in oppositional practice with the available designs and what are the ethical implications thereof?*

Introduction to the Classroom-Based Chapters

Multiliteracy at Play

In the first parts of this book, I have been building toward a pedagogy of multiliteracy play that intentionally integrates the kinds of deliberate attention to meaning design that multiliteracies pedagogies have proposed and an openness to desire, the unscriptable pushes and pulls of affect and aesthetics that infuse language and literacy activities with life. Play, as discussed in the previous chapter, points to a disposition vis-a-vis designing, in which the ordinary relationships between design elements and each other and the meanings one is likely to ascribe to them are suspended or at least palpably suspendable. Because multiliteracy play is relational—it is aesthetic and affective as much as it is designed—it can be fostered and encouraged through specific pedagogical activities but not designed into them.

Each of the chapters that follows focuses on a different classroom context, each taken from a large public university in the United States but from three different language programs—German, Spanish, and Italian. The student examples that are showcased originate from three different classroom-based research studies, and thus the level of detail and kinds of information presented varies somewhat between them; however, the curricular contexts within which they arose shared in common a commitment to multiliteracies pedagogies and a pedagogical openness to play. Both the pedagogical and scholarly work represented by these classroom-based sketches is the result of collaborations between myself and teacher-researchers, who were graduate students during at least the initial phases of our work together; thus, my sense-making around the students' literacy practices is interwoven with the reflections and observations of these teacher-scholar-curriculum designers.

As strategic sketches, in Boldt and Leander's (2013) sense, the classroom-based examples are offered as opportunities "to think and feel within the possibilities of the data" (26), and in so doing, to reflect on what a pedagogy of multiliteracy play that aims to balance designs and desires might look like in practice. In line with contemporary discussions of reflexivity and reflective practice in language education (e.g., Byrd Clark and Dervin 2014), these vignettes serve are models of multiliteracy play at play, but they are not intended to serve as exemplars of best practices that can be transposed to any context. They are rather reassemblages of teaching, learning, and inquiring through which we can reflect on an overarching question that guides this book—how can we foster a critical-affective approach to language and culture learning and teaching?

4

Poetic Play in a German Language-Culture Classroom

Introduction

This first set of classroom-based examples originates from a curriculum development project implemented across multiple levels of the German language-culture program, where I have served as Language Program Director—that is, as coordinator and curriculum developer, as well as the primary supervisor and mentor of the cohorts of graduate student instructors teaching these first- and second-year courses. Over the course of several years, I worked together with these instructors to augment and expand the existing communicative curriculum with multiliteracies activities and literacy-oriented assessments (including smaller compositions and larger projects).[1] The resulting curriculum was interwoven with a range of everyday genres, such as letters and roommate ads, as well as creative, new media, and literary texts. In this chapter, I will focus on one example of the latter, taken from first-semester courses.

The decision to focus on a poetry-based lesson is in part motivated by the overarching argument of this book. Given ongoing scholarly discussions around the role of literature and the literary in contemporary second language teaching and learning (e.g., Paran 2008; Scott and Tucker 2001; Carroli 2008), and the concerns about curricular divides between beginning and advanced language study raised by scholars writing about multiliteracies pedagogies in second language contexts (specifically those based in North America) (see also Chapter 1), I wanted to showcase students' play with canonical poetic texts and their aesthetic engagement in multiliteracy play in a beginning-level course. However, the focus of a poetry-based lesson also has some empirical support. As discussed in Warner (2022), the lessons that included texts that are traditionally categorized as literary, i.e., poems and short narratives, tended to be the most successful, measured in terms of the quantity of student responses (i.e., how many students submitted the assignment) and quality of student responses (i.e., how many of the compositions exhibited multiliteracy play).

Chapters 2 and 3 have already showcased examples of students transferring design elements from literary source texts that were part of collaborative reading practices in the classroom; here we will look more closely at how learners re-designed poetry, claiming some of the original author's designs for their own and in doing so, at least in some cases, found an affective connection with experiences very distant from their own.

Course Context

As part of a curriculum development project implemented between 2014 and 2020, a collection of literary and creative texts was piloted across the first three semesters of the curriculum. Each of these texts was paired with corresponding creative compositional activities that asked the students to respond to the model texts by redesigning them. Although the specific learning objectives associated with each text correlated with the course goals and the thematic and linguistic focus of the relevant unit, an overarching aim was to foster the kinds of design play conceptualized in the previous chapters. The composition activities associated with the texts were thus all examples of what Tin (2011) describes as "sanctioned play tasks," i.e., those deliberately introduced "for both playful language and pedagogical purposes" (216).

In a previous study (Warner 2022), I discussed the compositions that students created in dialogue with two of the literacy-based activities that were part of this study—one related to the poem "Die Lore-Ley" (originally published in 1824 as part of the poem "Heimkehr"; see Heine 1924) by Heinrich Heine and the other the story of Siegfried from the epic tale the *Nibelungenlied* (thirteenth century). In this chapter I will look at the classroom activities and student compositions related to another poem that was introduced as part of this curriculum development project—Gunther Eich's "Inventur" (Inventory) (1991[1945]). Like was the case with the other two poems, the teaching and learning activities associated with "Inventur" were well received by instructors and students, but the place of "Inventur" relatively early in a beginning-level curriculum and directly in dialogue with more traditionally communicative activities provides an opportunity to consider multiliteracy play within a broader curriculum and to begin to reflect on how learners can play with more than language when they engage with poetic texts.

"Inventur" was added to a unit on "Possessions and Pleasures" (Besitz und Vergnügen) as part of a first-semester German curriculum. At that time, the textbook for the course was the *Kontakte: Communicative Approach* (Tschirner, Nikolai, and Terrell 2013), which is widely used in North American secondary and tertiary German teaching; I had worked with "Inventur" in a curriculum using this same textbook at another institution and had originally included it as an optional, supplemental text for the German language program that I was newly directing. One of the instructors, Chelsea Timlin, later decided to solidify and develop a lesson plan around the poem and this eventually resulted in a set of OER materials, which were published as part of the *Foreign Languages and the Literary in the Everyday (FLLITE) Project*.[2] With these models and materials now available, "Inventur" became a core text, as we investigated how deliberately aesthetic experiences might expand the scope of existing curriculum.

In the textbook chapter on "Possessions and Pleasures," questions about what one has or does not have were used as a communicative excuse to teach the accusative case. For example, one activity, titled "Hast du einen Schlafsack?" (Do you have a sleeping bag?), featured a cluster of labeled images, including items such as a computer, an iPod, a motorcycle, a horse, and—as the title suggests—a sleeping bag (80). A model dialogue demonstrates for students how they might answer such questions, i.e., "Ja, ich habe einen Schlafsack" or "Nein, ich habe keinen Schlafsack" (Yes, I have a sleeping bag. No, I do not have a sleeping bag). The notes in the instructor edition point out that students are using the accusative and indefinite pronouns and that their attention should also be directed to the importance of grammatical gender categories in the German case system. In a follow-up activity labeled "Interview: Besitz" (Interview: Possessions), students are presented with a set of questions about what they have and what they want. One of the questions specifically zeroes in on their possible "wertvolle Sachen" or "valuable things" (82). DVD-player, laptop, cell phone, iPad, television, and car are offered as examples.

One of our primary motivations behind integrating the "Inventur" lesson into this unit was a desire to foster critical reflection about the notion of "wertvoll," what it is assumed to mean in the textbook activities, and how our very understandings about what is "wertvoll" are situated and relational. In Eich's poem, which was written while he was a prisoner of war during the Second World War, the value of possessions is shaped by scarcity and necessity. Most of the items mentioned in the inventory, which shaped the poem's content and form, are seemingly mundane necessities: eating utensils, clothes. As the second half of the poem reveals, the first-person voice in the text ascribes the greatest value to a small bit of pencil lead because he is able to use it to write verses at night. This is a far cry from the tech gadgets valued in the textbook interview task, which assumes that worth is primarily monetary and that listing out one's possessions is a neutral activity.

The poem's title, "Inventur" or "Inventory," and the genre play it implies, whereby its presence in a poem transforms the list of items, foregrounds the central irony of text; it is a tally of possessions from an individual who has almost nothing left.

Inventur	**Inventory**
Dies ist meine Mütze,	This is my cap,
dies ist mein Mantel,	this is my coat,
hier mein Rasierzeug	here my shaving kit
im Beutel aus Leinen.	in a bag of linen.
Konservenbüchse:	Tin can:
Mein Teller, mein Becher,	My plate, my cup,
ich hab in das Weißblech	in its metal plate I have
den Namen geritzt.	scratched my name.
Geritzt hier mit diesem	Scratched here with this
kostbaren Nagel,	Invaluable nail,
den vor begehrlichen	which I hide
Augen ich berge.	from covetous eyes.
Im Brotbeutel sind	In a bread bag are
ein Paar wollene Socken	a pair of woolen socks
und einiges, was ich	and something, which I
niemand verrate,	reveal to no one,
so dient er als Kissen	so it serves as a pillow
nachts meinem Kopf.	at night under my head.
Die Pappe hier liegt	The paperboard here lies
zwischen mir und der Erde.	between me and the earth.
Die Bleichstiftmine	The pencil lead
lieb ich am meisten:	I love the most:
Tags schreibt sie mir Verse,	In the day it writes verses for me,
die nachts ich erdacht.	which I think up at night.
Dies ist mein Notizbuch,	This is my notebook,
dies meine Zeltbahn,	this is my tent strip,
dies ist mein Handtuch,	this is my towel,
dies ist mein Zwirn.	this is my twine.

In the in-class activities, we wanted to encourage students to first respond to the style of the poem and to conceptualize the kinds of items cited by the lyrical subject, e.g., eating utensils, clothing items, and basic toiletries. The class participants could then work together to critically analyze how a list of possessions can reflect aspects of a person's identity and their priorities in a given cultural/historical moment. We also wanted to highlight the role of understatement and the unsaid in the poem. For example, the two items that connect to eating, the tin can and the bread bag, are both being re-utilized in ways that index lack—the lack of food and eating implements. To support these teaching and learning activities, we developed a set of guiding questions for the FLLITE lesson on "Inventur," which are listed below:

1. Was für einen Text ist das? Warum denken Sie so?
   What kind of text is this? Why do you think so?
2. Wie sieht der Text aus? z.B. lange Sätze, kurze Sätze, einfache Sätze, komplexe Sätze, viele Verben, viele Nomen, viele Adjektive.
   How does the text look? e.g., long sentences, short sentences, simple sentences, complex sentences, many verbs, many nouns, many adjectives.
3. Machen Sie eine Liste von Objekten aus dem Text und versuchen Sie diese Wörter zu kategorisieren. Welche Kategorien finden Sie? Was gehört zu keiner Kategorie?
   Make a list of the objects in the text and try to categorize these words. Which categories do you find? What does not belong to a category?
4. In welcher Strophe gibt es viele Besitze? In welcher Strophe gibt es weniger Besitze? Welchen Effekt hat das?

The final two questions—discussed in smaller groups and then as a class—were intended to draw students' attention to the relationships between objects and to the pencil's position—possibly semantically and within the structure of the poem—as separate from the other items.

As already indicated, the introduction of the poem, in some sense, is itself an act of redesigning, in that it offered an alternate approach to the question "what valuable things do you have?" For the final set of activities, we wanted to invite the students to express the personal values they attach to objects in their everyday lives by composing their own poems. Students were first asked to think about the items they bring to campus with them on a daily basis and to compare this list with those of other students in the class. As a stand-alone, an activity like this is quite similar to a typical communicative language task, but in the context of the literacy-based lesson it helped instructors to set up a reframed discussion of questions about what the items we carry with us say about our identity, our values, and our priorities. As a final discussion question, students were asked what items in their list they viewed as essential and why. As homework, students were asked to write a poem in the style of Eich's "Inventur" and to include a brief reflection on the choices they had made in their poems. The student compositions and reflections will be the primary focus of this chapter.

In Kramsch and Zhang's book on *The Multilingual Instructor* (2017), Kramsch discusses one iteration of this lesson, which had been shared with her by my collaborator, Chelsea Timlin. Kramsch notes that "at first sight, it [specifically the redesigning activity] did not strive to raise their [students] historical and political consciousness" (162). As we move into the students examples, it is worth remembering Leander and Boldt's caution that educators must attend not only to those forms of learning that are obviously critical or political (44). Indeed, Kramsch goes on to show how for some students the opportunity to engage in transformed practice in connection with the aesthetic reading of literary texts created a personal space within which they were able to develop their symbolic awareness (see Kramsch and Zhang 2017, 168–9); building on the framework for multiliteracy play proposed in this book, we can think of the relationship between learner texts and the original poem as being a "composition of desire" (Deleuze and Guattari 1987[1980], 399), an assemblage of materials, time/space, experiences, and emotion through which they form a relationship between themselves and other humans through a kind of emotional entanglement realized in and through the new language—rather than in spite of it. An underlying argument in this book, which is relevant in this chapter, is that forming these new relationships can be a critical act, even in some cases where there is no overt discussion of social and political implications.

In the remainder of this chapter, I share four examples from beginning-level German courses where the poem "Inventur" and the lessons prepared by Chelsea and me were piloted by our teaching colleagues to explore this idea of multiliteracy play as a way of designing poetic effects in relationship to everyday objects in their physical vicinity, such as those they carried in their bags or that surrounded them as they sat completing their German homework in their dorm rooms. Similar to the examples from Chapters 2 and 3, the student compositions here offer a sense of how lessons that are deliberately play-based can engage learners in poetic ways of designing meaning, while fostering critical-aesthetic perspectives.

The Poetic in the Everyday

The four focal poems in this section—composed by Oscar, Lia, Olivia, and Song—were chosen both because they are representative, in that they echo elements found in other poems from the class, and because they are exemplary, in terms of the deliberate use of poetic play and symbolism evidenced in their compositions and associated short reflections. To contextualize this selection of poems within the collective oeuvre of our first-year cohort, it is important to note that there were plenty of students who took a more literal approach to the assignment. For example, one student composition began with the following two stanzas:

Dies ist meine Lampe	This is my lamp
dies ist mein Handy	this my cell phone
hier mein Bleistift	here my pen
Mein Laptop	My laptop
ich habe in mein Rucksack;	I have in my backpack;
Mein Computer	My computer
ich habe auf mein Schreibtisch	I have on my desk

Like the original text from Eich and with the student poems I will discuss in more detail, this poem redesigned one genre—a list—into another—a poem; however, the use of play with frame does not seem to initiate any other forms of symbolic meaning. The poetic genre lends the structure here and that is all. In the concluding section of this chapter, I will discuss in more detail some of the ways in which these four examples were similar or different from those written by their classmates; but it is important to note from the offset that they were chosen because they were among those that engaged most clearly with other types of play that poetry affords.

"It Represented Other Stuff": Oscar's Poem

Oscar's poem does not follow Eich's structure closely, but he worked quite deliberately with the notion that objects can symbolize other aspects of one's life. At the same time, Oscar was motivated by language-learning goals that extended beyond this assignment, and he saw the composition as a chance to use vocabulary that had been a part of the unit.

> I wrote it [the poem] like this because it incorporated things that we had learned and new words. The poem is less serious and sad than the example but

it still talks about relatable things. I wrote it with an intention of being funny but I focused on one thing and said how it represented other stuff instead of literally talking about it.

(Reflection)

The "one thing" that was the focus of Oscar's poem was an item that was mentioned more than any other in the collection of student compositions—the cell phone. Phones were often featured in the more literal poems, such as the one excerpted at the start of this section—a symptom of their ubiquity in contemporary society—but they also often took on symbolic meanings, as was the case in Oscar's poem.

Mein Handy	My cell phone
Meine Atemschutzmaske	My face mask
Die Erde sind null	The earth are [sic] zero
neben das.	near that.
Dein Flash	Your flash
Ist meinen Sonnenschein	is my sunshine
Mein Handy ist	My cell phone is
jetzt mein Hand.	now my hand.
Das ist meine Hausaufgabe	That is my homework
Das ist meine Familie	That is my family
Das ist meine Erinnerungen	That is my memories
Das ist meine Träume	That is my dreams

In the German text, there is a clever bit of wordplay; the colloquial German word for mobile phones, *Handy*, which contains the word "Hand" symbolizes how the phone has become an extension of oneself. In the first stanza, Oscar equates his phone with a protective face mask, *eine Atemschutzmaske*, a term that evokes gas masks such as those used in times of war but also more recently the face coverings used in Covid-19 mitigation. The meaning of the final lines of that opening section of the poem is not clear to me, but they suggest that Oscar's phone stands for him above everything else on earth. The final stanza is a list of other aspects of student life, which all relate back to the cell phone.

In his reflection, Oscar expressed his desire to be "funny" instead of "serious," setting up an aesthetic distinction between his and Eich's poems. With the exception of the pun *Handy/Hand*, however, the poem does not strike me as a reader as particularly humorous. It is, however, quite playful. Oscar redesigned Eich's use of objects as symbolic for other aspects of a person's life to make a laconic statement about the pervasiveness of cell phones in modern life. This representational play connects to the play with form, for instance, the repetition in the final stanza. Although the play with frame from Eich's original text, through which a poem is also an inventory of possessions, is largely absent from Oscar's poem, this final section of the poem echoes this listing structure of the original. Oscar's poem is an exploration of how stuff can be "represented by other stuff," as he expresses it in his reflection.

"Unimportant, but Significant": The Poems of Lia and Olivia

Like Oscar, Lia and Olivia—the authors of the next two examples—played with Eich's use of everyday objects as symbols; however, they also experimented more with the poem's structure as an available design.

Dies ist mein Geldbeutel	This is my wallet
Die ist meine Stöckelschuhe	This is my high heels
Hier ist mein Lippenstift und Lidschatten	Here is my lipstick and my eye shadow
in eine Kosmetiktasche.	in a cosmetic bag.
Die Hausschlüssel:	The house key,
Mein Handy, mein Spiegel	My cell phone, my mirror
Hier auf das Hinterteil	Here on the back
Habe ich meine Name eingraviert	I have engraved my name
Graviert es hier ein	Engraved it here
Mit meinem kleinen Messer	With my small knife
Ich verstecke es	I hide it
Weltabgewandt	Away from the world
Ich halte in mein Rucksack	I hold in my backpack
Ein Paar Schuhe	A pair of shoes
Und ein Paar Dinge ich	And a couple of things I
Halte zu mich selbst.	Hold to myself
Und auf diese forme ich	And on these I form
Mein Tag bis Tage Leben	My day to day life
Die Grube, das ich mein Leben heiße	The pit, that I call my life
Von Haus zur Schule nach mein Beruf nach Hause	From home to school[3] after my job home
Meine Familie ist das Ding	My family is the thing
Das ich am meisten liebe:	That I love the most:
Sie halten mich auf nachts	They hold me up nights
Während halte ich die Welt auf Tag	While I hold the world up by day.

Dies ist mein Rucksack	This is my backpack
Dies ist mein Mäppchen,	This is my folder
Dies ist mein Laptop,	This is my laptop
Dies ist mein Leben.	This is my life.

At first the items Lia lists in her inventory may seem not only everyday, but quite superficial: wallet, high heels, and makeup. The second stanza introduces her cell phone, that favored item in the student texts, and it is also the first one to be associated with a function, namely serving as a mirror. Playing off Eich's tin can, Lia depicts her cell phone as having her name engraved on the back—a physical symbolization of possession. The next stanza elaborates on this, explaining that she had engraved her name with a small knife that she keeps hidden. This description echoes Eich's hidden nail, with which he engraved his name. In the next stanza, Lia also draws a parallel to Eich, when shoes are described as hiding in her backpack in a way that is similar to the hidden socks in the bread bag of "Inventur." At the same time as these moments connect with the model text, the imagery is very different; while the implication in Eich's poem is that these meager belongings must be hidden to prevent them from being stolen in a context of extreme scarcity; it is less clear why these items are hidden in Lia's poem other than that they are something the "I" keeps to themself. The fifth stanza deviates the most from Eich's poem. The second line points back to the ways in which these objects form the "day to day" (*Tag bis Tag*) of the poetic narrator's life, and then, in a moment of representational play, the everyday is rendered as not only mundane but as a kind of pit, in which one gets stuck. The word *Grube* in German, which I translated as "pit," denotes a hollow, usually in the ground, and might in the context of the poems seems to describe a track worn into the ground from moving repeatedly in the same path between house and school and job day in, day out; however, this same word can also refer to a grave, and this would have shown up as a possible translation for that word in most dictionary searches. The sixth stanza introduces another common theme in the student texts, which was already in Oscar's poem—the role of family. For many of the students, the most valuable thing in their lives was not an object but family, which draws attention to the loneliness in Eich's poem. Although the word has multiple meanings, Lia's use of *aufhalten* in the seventh stanza was likely the result of a dictionary search for "hold up" in the sense of support; thus, her family is what supports her at night, while she has to support the world during the day. The final stanza brings things back to the mundane with a list of everyday items, again playing off of Eich's model.

More so than any other student poem in this collection, Lia's followed Eich's structure. As in the original "Inventur" text, her untitled poem included seven stanzas, each consisting of four lines. Lia's reflection indicates that this was deliberate. She wrote:

> In the original poem, I saw that Eich had started off with things that seemed unimportant but significant in some case. As the poem progressed, he slowly started talking about still insignificant items that had momentous importance to him. For others these objects would mean nothing but to him, they're everything. His pencil, it writes his poetry, his tin, his identity. So in the beginning steps of writing my poem I wanted to think about the little things I couldn't live without.

Whereas the cellphone in Oscar's poem is depicted as part of a larger social phenomenon, Lia wanted to show how seemingly trivial items are imbued with meaning for individuals with a specific identity in contemporary American society. She then goes on to explain the choices made in the first stanza:

> My lipstick and the rest of my makeup creates the face and the person I want to see. It's how I invent myself.

The bulk of the objects in Eich's poems are significant primarily because they are key for his day-to-day survival as (presumably) a soldier on the front or even a prisoner of war; for Lia, as a female university student, *survival* is more euphemistic, perhaps; getting by is about projecting a carefully crafted social identity. The pencil lead in Eich's poem stands out because it is the one item that is not instrumental for the physical ordeal of surviving the war. Lia identified the introduction of the pencil as "the climax" of Eich's poem, where he "talks about what is most important to him." Respectively, for Lia, this part of the text was occupied by her family. Lia does not elaborate further on this section of her composition but she does conclude with an explanation of the inventory from her final stanza.

> Eich ends the poem with what he began with—unassuming objects that obviously have deep and sentimental meaning to him. The end of my poem is the seemingly unimportant objects from my life that not only identify me within the crowd but make my life doable and easy. My backpack, my laptop, I simply couldn't go to school without them.

Although Lia has tried to follow the overarching form of Eich's text, and to adapt the representational play that arises when everyday objects are symbolic of an individual's set of specific circumstances, she recognizes at the end of her reflection that these available designs mean differently in her context. "Since

I am not an object of war, my important objects in life reflect the current trend for my generation—education." Given Lia's poetic choices and other comments in the reflection, "education" here seems to stand in for life as a student rather than intellectual pursuits per se. Lia's final comments acknowledge that although she could borrow certain aspects of Eich's design, there are also crucial historical and experiential incommensurabilities between their lives. At the same time, the reflection completely neglects that there is an element of *survival* implied in the fifth and sixth stanzas of Lia's poem, and accordingly an attempt at an affective connection through the aesthetic activity of working through how Eich's poetic design might be meaningful in the context of her life.

Olivia's poem opens with two stanzas that are quite similar to Eich's and Lia's, in that they are ostensibly an inventory of objects: a notebook, ink, books, and stories. Unlike these other texts, however, the objects named are closely semantically related; rather than a diverse set of things, they all relate to writing. Each of these opening two stanzas ends by more overtly associating more personal, symbolic meaning with these items. The notebook and ink are her inspirations (*Eingebung*); the books and stories home (*Heimat*) to her imagination.

Dies ist mein Heft,	This is my notebook,
Dies ist meine Tinte	This is my ink
Hier meine Eingebung	Here my inspiration
im mein Umfeld	In my environment.
Hier sind meine Bücher	Here are my books
Und hier meine Erzählungen.	And here my stories.
Sie sind die Heimat	They are the home
von meiner Vorstellung.	Of my imagination.
Familie:	Family:
Meine Mutter, mein Vater.	My mother, my father.
Sie sind meine Lehrer.	They are my educators.
Geduld, Liebe, Güte.	Patience, love, goodness.
Ich schreibe,	I write,
Ich begreife,	I understand,
Ich schaffe.	I create.

The third stanza introduces the theme of family. The mother and father are described as "educators" of values that are listed in the last line: patience, love, goodness. The final stanza of the poem features another short inventory—a list not of objects or value this time but of actions: writing, creating, understanding. This set of creative activities connect the implements from the opening of the poem with the role of the parents; the objects and the values enable their accomplishment.

Similar to Lia, Olivia spoke in her reflection about the representational choices made by Eich and indicated that she worked with those as an available design for meaning.

> I wrote this poem the way I did because I began by looking at the original poem by Günter Eichs [sic]. The reason the original works so well is that the objects described are immensely important to the narrator. These aren't objects that are particularly special, but rather they are objects that are important because of the situation the narrator finds himself in.

Olivia then went on to say that she wanted to keep this same theme on objects and their significance but that she ended up "using things that were less tangible" than Eich's. Like Lia, she recognized that adopting the use of Eich's design was not an indication of equivalency.

> Hence, my poem differs from his because I am in a completely different situation than he was, and because he was trying to convey something intrinsically different. (IE how war reduces people down to the things they own, versus mine, where I write about my desire to write and the objects and people that help me to write.) However both are created from items the narrator uses to define themselves.

Both Olivia's and Eich's lyrical first-persons define themselves through their writing, and Olivia's redesign of the model poem creates a shared composition of desire vis-a-vis writing. At the same time, she is very aware through the choices in her text and in her reflection that the significance of this desire and what is needed to satisfy it are vastly dissimilar in their two contexts. The move from objects to actions in the final stanza is a linguistic departure from Eich's poem that also marks the tangential nature of their shared experiences; Olivia's lyrical subject has agency within the text and likely her context in a way that Eich's does not.

"Freedom to Play": Song's Poem

The movement from objects as essential for one's life and livelihood to activities, which was seen at the end of Olivia's poem, was a central aspect of Song's submission—which is the final example for this chapter.

Inventur	**Inventory**
Meinem Freiheit	For my freedom
Sprechen	Speaking
Erschaffen	Creating
Spielen	Playing
Gehen	Going
Sie sind unentbehrlich	They are indispensable
Ich spreche mit Winter	I speak with winter
Ich erschaff mit Frühling	I create with spring
Ich spiele mit Sommer und	I play with summer and
Ich gehe mit Herbst	I go with fall
Das ist wie ich bin	That is how I am
Ich bin frei	I am free
Das ist wie ich lebe	That is how I live
Ich bin frei	I am free

Although it bears the same title, Song's poem deviates structurally from Eich's more than Lia and Olivia's. Song's inventory is a set of verbs that are all framed by the first line "for my freedom."[4] In the second stanza, each of these activities is connected to a season. The poem ends with two declarations of "Ich bin frei" (I am free), returning to the opening of the poem.

Freedom was a recurring theme in the student poems, perhaps because of the phase of life US-American first- and second-year college students would find themselves in; many of the students will have left home for the first time that year and would be experiencing a greater sense of independence. As referenced in the reflection, Song's poem treated freedom as an individual personality trait, i.e., how he is and how he lives, rather than an experience he might share with other classmates. Song's reflection began:

> I chose these "things" because that's what's really important to me. More than anything else (nothing else is even a close second). I hate being restricted. I hate rules; all they do is prevent me from doing things in a better way. To me freedom is the most prized thing in life. Freedom to play, to walk, to speak, to create. But each thing in itself is unimportant.

The everyday activities in Song's poem take the place of the objects in Eich's, Oscar's, Lia's, and Olivia's poems, but there is a parallel type of representational play here. The introduction of a more abstract theme, freedom, subordinates the activities to this ideal. Whereas Eich's poem is laconic, relying on the unsaid,

Song's poem is explicit and this is underscored by the contrast to what he "hates" in the reflection, i.e., anything that hampers his freedom. There is perhaps even a little playful irony in Song's deviation from Eich's poetic structure given his disdain for "rules" and "restrictions."

In the second half of his reflection, Song explains the middle stanza of his poem, where the activities are connected to the seasons:

> So no matter what the season is, I can do these things, and as time passes by, I hope to be like the four seasons, something that no one can restrict. It just comes and goes no matter who is in the way.

The seasons thus represent both the passage of time and the forces of nature that define them, which cannot be impeded by human systems of control.

Song does not mention Eich or the original poem at all in his reflection; however, the focus on freedom and powers that are superordinate to human systems of constraint is perhaps not incidental given that the model text is about wartime captivity and confinement. In Eich's poem, everyday objects become significant because they represent the vestiges of humanity in an inhumane time; Song's poem takes everyday actions that are in themselves unimportant and uses them as symbols of human agency and free will.

Conclusion: Taking Inventory and Designing Relations of Affect

The four poems from Oscar, Lia, Olivia, and Song illustrate some elements that were shared across the collection of student texts. For example, there was a small number of items that appeared repeatedly—cell phones, laptops, writing implements. These seemed to be objects that are emotionally sticky, in Ahmed's (2004) sense (see also Chapter 2). For example, cell phones were often placed in relation to themes of family and friends, and the distances that lay between them now that the author/lyrical I was away studying at the university. Paper and pens were also referenced in many of the poems, as were laptops and computers. These functioned as indexes for student life while also pointing back to Eich's poem where the writing tools are the most prized possessions. Some students, like Olivia, saw an affinity here between themselves and Eich as a writer, and focusing on this rather than the differences between their situations was a way to seek a connection between the affective world of the poem and the students' everyday lives.

The final discussion questions in our set of activities related to "Inventur" had framed the compositional task as a mediation on how the items with the closest physical proximity also expressed something about their identities. This resulted in a set of poems and reflections where the reality of being a student was mentioned frequently; and yet, schooling and education were not central themes in the poems as a whole. The students' sense-making in relation to their own inventories was refracted through their reading of Eich's poem and the aesthetic experience of engaging with that text, and thus the thematic dimensions were perhaps less salient than the affective ones. Across many of the poems there emerged a shared tone of loss and longing. The former was often associated with the absence of family, friends, and in a few cases pets in their everyday lives. Longing was also often connected to another recurring theme, freedom, which can be seen in Song's poem.

Although the four poems here and the others written by students in the class were not overtly politically or historically conscious or critical, they do suggest that the students were grappling with the potential connections and incommensurabilities between the world of the first-person voice in Eich's poem and their own lyrical selves in critical ways. While the textbook activities were topically relatable, in assuming that value is measured monetarily, they glossed over the webs of emotional entanglements within which these objects take on value in the sense of significance. This was especially the case for the types of everyday technology that were both featured in the textbook and the students' poems—although, as we have seen, not all the students centered these objects. Eich's model text offered them available designs, models of multiliteracy play, through which they could take a critical aesthetic perspective vis-a-vis the question of what is valuable or even indispensable for your life, not by overwriting the experiential differences between their circumstances but by bringing them into contact in the play space of poetry.

5

Translation Play in a Spanish Language-Culture Classroom

Introduction

In play, activities and genres from everyday life are rekeyed (see Chapter 3); in multiliteracy play in the language-culture classroom, one's own relationship with language takes on new layers of meaning. While an underlying argument throughout this book has been that these moving relationships with how languages and related semiotic systems make sense of the world are the crux of language-culture education, there are some learning contexts in which the exigency of this shift feels even more acute. The instructional context for the examples in this chapter was an introductory course in a Spanish translation and interpretation program, which was taught with a revised curriculum as part of a dissertation study conducted by Sara Alcázar Silva in 2020[1]; the course, "Introduction to Translation and Interpretation: Social Justice and Practice," served both students who would continue along that track, moving into specialist courses on legal and medical translation, and others majoring in Spanish, who were seeking an additional elective. Furthermore, most of the students in the course and all the focal participants in Alcázar Silva's study were heritage Spanish speakers—a fact that is unsurprising given that the institutional setting was a city around sixty miles from the US-Mexico border and where 43.6 percent of the population identifies as Hispanic. With this body of students in mind, Alcázar Silva had conceptualized the course such that translation was as much about pedagogy and positionality as practice. She wrote of her motivations: "By engaging heritage learners as translators, the goal is to develop their identities as language mediators whether or not they ever choose to become professional translators" (2022, 10).

The course—and even more specifically the module I will highlight in this chapter—was already designed to enable the students to negotiate their relationships with Spanish and English as individuals identifying as Hispanic, Latina/o/e, and/or Mexican American; halfway through the semester, however, the onset of the Covid-19 pandemic introduced a whole new set of sociohistorical factors that are relevant to the student compositions presented in this chapter. Instruction moved rapidly online, as everyone struggled to make sense out of this new disease and its potential impact. Suddenly the questions of how to communicate and translate public medical information, which were already a part of the translation and interpretation curriculum, were ever present in public discourses and debates.

In her study, Alcázar Silva's (2022) analysis focused on translation competence as a form of symbolic competence, that is, the ways in which learners attended to aspects of language and visuals as forms of representation, social action, and symbolic power in their composition of bilingual texts. I will build upon her work, using the lens of multiliteracy play to emphasize rather the ways in which the students use translation activities and the mediation between languages and between text and image to respond to discourses around public health crises that impact their everyday lives. One of the student examples discussed in this chapter is a PSA related to health mitigations for the coronavirus; the second raises awareness about the importance of safe sex. Both PSA proposals respond directly to public health concerns that might directly impact students. My re-analysis of Alcázar Silva's study focuses on how, in a moment of heightened awareness around the individual choices that shape public safety and wellness, the activity of designing PSA proposals and engaging in translation play across languages and modalities allowed students to respond to and make sense of the sociocultural discourses about health and illness in connection to their own realities.

Course Context

For the purposes of this chapter, I borrow examples from just one module in a larger curriculum redesign project conceptualized, created, and taught by Alcázar Silva (2022). This unit is of interest not only because the core assignment, a medical PSA, encouraged multiliteracy play, but also because this was the first part of the class to be offered in an emergency remote format following the campus closures. This context created a heightened field of affect around this genre that was suddenly ubiquitous in everyday life, situated within a web of ideological debates around Covid mitigations, public and private responsibilities, and the role of governmental agencies like the Centers for Disease Control and Prevention (CDC) in influencing behaviors and attitudes. Before looking at how the PSA composition was set up, it is helpful to understand how this set of activities was positioned within the semester-long course.

The introductory course had always centered translation and language mediation as issues of social justice. The first learning objective cited on the syllabus was that learners would be able to "identify, describe, and reflect on issues and personal experiences related to human rights, populations with limited English proficiency (LEP), social justice and equal access, and relevant aspects of applied translation and interpreting in the United States." In redesigning the class, Alcázar Silva was inspired by multiliteracies pedagogies and wanted to work with them to more systematically integrate genre and multimodality into the texts and practices students would work with. This is reflected in the remainder of the learning objectives, which are listed below:

- identify text characteristics in written and oral texts in the medical, legal, and business contexts through genre analysis;
- go beyond words to render and analyze a translation considering social and contextual factors;
- use varied and appropriate meaning-making resources to describe, narrate, explain, and persuade, considering genre;
- expand their repertoire of formal and informal vocabulary in medical, legal, and business contexts;
- develop sociolinguistic awareness through which they identify linguistic variation and language powerplay;
- find, experiment, and assess translation resources.

(see Alcázar Silva 2022, 35)

Interwoven through these multiliteracies-oriented learning goals, Alcázar Silva wanted to create space to recognize the learners as "not just communicators and problem solvers, but whole persons with hearts, bodies, and minds, with memories, fantasies, loyalties, identities" (Kramsch 2006, 251, cited in Alcázar Silva 2022, 6). In conceptualizing this dimension of the curriculum, Alcázar Silva was inspired by Kramsch's notion of symbolic competence and her attention to how desire and power shape multilingual lives. "Heritage [Spanish] language learners, as multilinguals and members of a minoritized group, must learn to not only negotiate between language systems, but to navigate contradictory language ideologies and racial hierarchies in the United States" (Alcázar Silva 2022, 10; see also Negrón 2018, 129). This "powerplay," Alcázar Silva argues, is often tacitly reproduced in curricular structures, within which heritage speakers are positioned as deficiently bilingual rather than "multilingual, creative, and powerful" (28). Drawing on Kramsch and Whiteside's metaphor of the "multilingual game" (Kramsch and Whiteside 2008, 667), Alcázar Silva thus actively sought opportunities for learners to explore new ways of playing with the relationships between Spanish and English, between these languages and other semiotic systems (especially visual designs), and between themselves and these repertoires for meaning making and the various contexts of use within which they might draw upon them as language mediators.

Against this theoretical backdrop, genre was a core organizing principle for Alcázar Silva's introductory translation course (see Alcázar Silva 2022, 36). Genre served as a linchpin between multiliteracies pedagogies and translation studies (see also Colombi and Achugar 2008), and genre-based models of literacy provided a systematic way of sequencing the curriculum from the primary, conversational discourse types already familiar to many heritage learners to the increasingly complex texts from secondary discourses associated with advanced academic literacies. Table 6 provides an overview of the three genre families that

Table 6 Overview of Alcázar Silva's (2022) curriculum for "Introduction to Translation and Interpretation: Social Justice and Practice".

Genre family	Narrative	Explanation	Argumentation
Core Composition Activity	Digital Story	Medical PSA	Op-Ed (for newspaper or web site)
Thematic Focus	Migration/ Human Rights/ Language Access	Medical and Legal Translation as Subject Areas	Ethics/Language Brokering/ Translator Identity/ Language Policy
Language Features	• Point of view • Appraisals • Identifying setup, conflict, resolution • Temporal expressions	• Causal expressions • Passive voice • Timeless present tense, e.g., are, have, exists, and grows. • Action verbs e.g., run, hunts, erupts, breaks, flows, and changes. • Adjectives that are factual and precise such as, "5.6 megabytes", "sandy colored". • Linking words and phrases expressing sequence (after …; then …; next …; finally) • Technical terms	• Appraisals • Subordination • Intersentential cohesion • Transition words and phrases • Repetition: anaphora and tricolon • Overstatement and understatement • Rhetorical questions • Appeal forms: ethos, logos, pathos • Figurative language, e.g., similes and metaphors, metonymy, personification

shaped the resulting course structure along with the corresponding composition activities, thematic emphases, and some of the linguistic features highlighted.

For the discussion of translation play in this chapter, I will draw examples from the medical PSAs (public service announcements) designed as part of the middle unit here. As Alcázar Silva (2022) explains, PSAs were chosen as a culminating project for this module because they are an explanatory genre and their main function is to raise awareness about an issue of general interest. At the same time, there is typically a persuasive element to a PSA, a specific behavior or way of approaching the issue that is implicitly or explicitly endorsed. One frequent way of communicating the importance of an issue and of persuading the public to regard it in a certain way is through narrative. In the context of the curriculum, PSAs thus provided a bridge between the first, second, and third parts of the course by incorporating aspects of all three genre families.

As a form of literacy practice, PSAs are typically multimodal because of how they are disseminated, that is, through public media like television, internet, and radio, or as posters displayed in well-trafficked areas. Visual and audio elements also help PSA to realize their chief purpose, i.e., to capture widespread attention. Pedagogically, the assignment was intended to challenge students to be deliberate about their language choice in both Spanish and English as well as the overall multimodal design of a real-world explanatory genre. Because, as Alcázar Silva notes, PSAs often involve an emotional elicitation, often one based in fear or empathy (2022, 97), they are highly aesthetic informational genres.

The core project in the second module was a pitch for a short-form video PSA on a medical issue of current interest, imagining that they were trying to get funding to support this campaign. In the pitch students were asked to include justifications for the musical genre and to emphasize why the PSA is relevant. The main content was the PSA itself. Students were asked to include a storyboard, lyrics for a song, and a translation of those lyrics.

> For the song, students were given the following format:
> Verse 4 lines
> Chorus 4 lines
> Verse 4 lines
> Chorus 4 lines
> Verse/Bridge 3 or 4 lines
> Chorus 4 lines

It was not specified whether they should write first in English or Spanish. In a written reflection submitted after the main assignment, students were also given a chance to explain their choices, specifically how they had addressed the target audience and sought to communicate the PSA's intended message.

Because the class had moved online, students shared their PSAs with the rest of the class using the collaborative tool VoiceThread and were asked to comment on two of their classmates' pitches. This not only created an opportunity for peer feedback, but also created a chance for interaction and community-building, during remote learning and social distancing. The peer review process was set up to promote metacompositional awareness; students were encouraged to address one or more of the following elements in their comments on others' PSAs:

- effectiveness of the PSA
- use of images
- choice of musical genre
- lyrics
- suggestions for improvements

Students' first introduction to the PSA genre was a series of short-form animated videos raising awareness of the common signs of a stroke, which were distributed on the Massachusetts Department of Public Health YouTube channel.[2] The series includes videos in a range of languages including Spanish, English, Cambodian, Portuguese, and Thai—each with different graphics and musical styles accompanying the song texts, which are translated versions of the same song. Students first watched the Spanish-language video and used this to conceptualize some of the elements of PSA as a genre. They then compared this video with one of the others in a different language and were asked to reflect on principles of *domestication* and *foreignization*, which they had already been introduced to as part of their discussions of translation studies; the former denotes a translation strategy that favors modifying any cultural aspects, which might be unfamiliar to the intended audience, while the latter promotes retaining such elements and allowing the text to point back to the context of production.

When analyzing the videos from the Massachusetts Department of Public Health, students noted that domestication seemed to be the preferred guiding principle in the stroke PSA, and that this was realized across different multimodal dimensions of a text: in the music genres, physical appearances of characters in the videos, and in the activities they were seen undertaking. Three of the students raised concerns about the potential dangers of domestication, and the ways in which it could reinforce and propagate stereotypes.

These questions of *domestication* and *foreignization* also entered into the students' choices in designing their PSAs, both in terms of scope and design. For example, Alcázar Silva notes that one student chose to focus on diabetes because Hispanics are at higher risk for developing this disease. Another set her target audience as people living in or visiting the southwest, and opted for a country music sound, which she felt like viewers would associate with that region (see 107-108). For a group of students living in a city near the US-Mexico border, a region that has been shaped by Spanish and English-speaking residents, as well as the indigenous peoples who inhabited these spaces long before they were colonized by either of these groups, the questions of *domestication* and *foreignization* also raised questions about what it means to design something for a particular culture or linguistic community without essentializing the identities of the audience or the bilingual designer themself.

Living Literacy in Translation: Making Sense of Public Health Crises through Multiliteracy Play

"It Reaches the Heart More": Yazmin's PSA

In April of 2020, when students were submitting their PSAs, schools and universities in the United States had been closed for a matter of weeks. It is thus likely unsurprising that the corona virus showed up in two of the proposals. One of those two belonged to Yazmin. At the time of the class, Yazmin was a major in health sciences, with plans to continue to nursing school after completing her bachelor's degree. On a survey distributed at the start of the term to get to know students in the class, Yazmin had identified herself as Hispanic, Latino/a/e, American, Mexican American, Mexican; notably, she was the only student in the class to select all the options provided. Yazmin had also shared with Alcázar Silva (2022) that she grew up speaking, reading, and writing in both Spanish and English (116).

Covid-19 was the central focus of her PSA, but she decided to emphasize other diseases that leave a person at higher risk, namely asthma and diabetes. Her stated core audience, however, was children. Alcázar Silva (2022) speculates that this may have been early enough in the pandemic that it was not yet widely known that children were at a lower risk for developing severe health problems from the virus; however, Yazmin also seems to indicate in the lyrics of the song that she saw children as a conduit for reaching other members of the family. This connected with the marketing strategy she laid out in her pitch, where she indicated that the video would be shared through the platform YouTube,

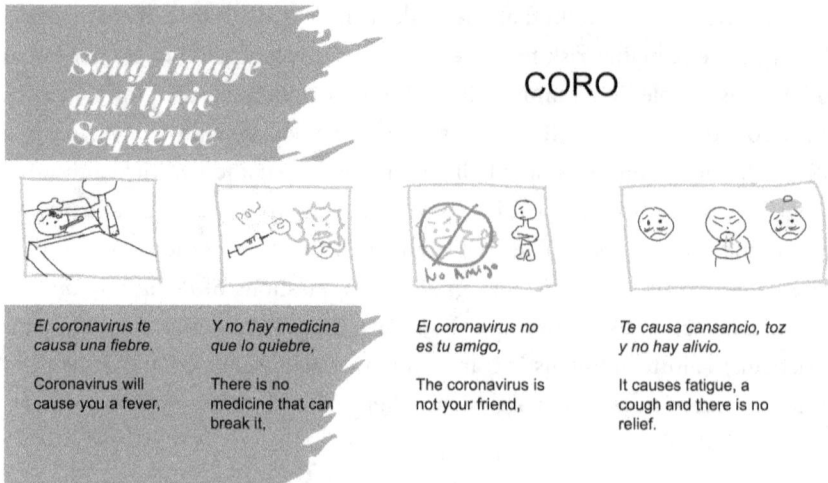

Figure 5 Sample from Yazmin's PSA.

where the catchy song and cartoon-like images would catch children's attention. Because schools were closed, Yazmin also suggested that teachers could be sharing the link with their students to help spread the word.

Yazmin presented her storyboard and both sets of lyrics in horizontal row, as captured in Figure 5. Spanish was clearly the source text, and it was placed in italics. There was a symmetrical relationship between the images and the text, in that both presented parallel information. This makes sense given that the proposed video would accompany a children's song, and the images would reinforce the meaning of the words. Yazmin referred to her chosen musical genre as *canción de cuna*, or lullaby, but given the examples she gives, i.e., "Ten Little Monkeys," and the song lyrics, it seems possible that she was using this term to refer more broadly to any kind of song made to entertain and engage children.

One of the clearest indications that the Spanish song text was the original is the presence of play with form in that version that is absent in the English.

Spanish Text[3]	**English Text**
El Coronavirus No es tu Amigo	*The Coronavirus Is Not Your Friend*
Verso 1	Verse 1
Si estas enfermo con diabetes mellitus,	If you are sick with diabetes mellitus,
Por favor no te infectes con coronavirus,	Please do not get infected with coronavirus,
Dile a tu familia que no estén vagos.	Tell your family to not be roaming around,
Quédate en casa, no vayas por tacos.	Stay at home, don't go for tacos.

Cora El coronavirus te causa una fiebre, Y no hay medicina que lo quiebre, El coronavirus no es tu amigo, Te causa cansancio, toz y no hay alivio.	Chorus The coronavirus will cause you a fever, There is no medicine that can break it, The coronavirus is not your friend, It causes fatigue, a cough and there is no relief.
Verso 2 El coronavirus puede vivir en tus manos, Así que lávatelas bien en los baños, Usa tu codo para saludar, Así para no contaminar.	Verse 2 The coronavirus can live on your hands, So, wash them good in the bathrooms, Use your elbow to greet, That way you do not contaminate.
Cora	Chorus
Verso 3 Si tienes asma y no te estas cuidando, El coronavirus no está jugando, Él se meterá en tus pulmones, Te hará que defunciones.	Verse 3 If you have asthma and not taking care of yourself, The coronavirus is not playing, It will get inside your lungs, It will make you demise.
Cora	Chorus
Verso 4 Los síntomas no se ven hasta en dos semanas, Así que use cloro con muchas ganas. La distancia de 6 pies es lo que protege, Y deja que esta canción te aconseje.	Verse 4 You don't see the symptoms until after two weeks, So, use bleach with enthusiasm, The 6 feet distance is what protects, And let this song give you advice.

The primacy of the Spanish text is most clear in the presence of rhyme and other types of sound play in that version of the text, which are absent in the English. Maintaining rhyme schemes across languages seems to be one of the more difficult forms of language play (see also Warner 2022). Yazmin's Spanish text basically follows the structure of a traditional quatrain, with four lines consisting of two sets of rhyming couplets—a form of poetry found across many languages and often used in children's poems and songs. Yazmin's PSA lyrics include both examples of perfect rhyme, such as "fiebre" and "quiebre" in the first two lines of the chorus, and near or slant rhyme, such as "vagos" and "tacos" at the end of the first verse. In one instance, she crafts a rhyme by pairing the word "pulomes" with "defunciones," by putting the latter noun in the place of a verb. The resulting expression "Te hará que defunciones" (It will make you demise) is nonstandard but completely comprehensible. Yazmin noted in her reflection that the combination of rhyme and repetition would make her song easier for children to remember. The absence of these features furthers the impression that the role of English here is to stand in for the Spanish rather than as a children's song on its own.

In the title and repeated in the chorus of Yazmin's PSA is representational play, through which the coronavirus is personified as "not your friend/no es tu amigo." In the visuals, the virus is depicted having eyes with furrowed brows and a scowling mouth. In the image corresponding to the second line of the chorus, a syringe hovers independently in space, poised to attack a coronavirus wearing red boxing gloves. In the subsequent image, the virus is placed within a red circle with a line running across and a human figure stands, arms crossed, staring it down.

A less overt form of representation play in Yazmin's PSA appears through the echoing or ventriloquation (Bakhtin 1981) of discourses around Covid-19. References to washing hands and using elbows to greet (instead of a handshake) as well as 6-feet that became the standard for social distancing, appeared in spring 2020 in both physical and virtual public spaces. By incorporating these allusions to multiple other PSAs and media reports on how to mitigate disease and rendering them in a catchy verse with vibrant images, Yazmin's children's song refracts ways of making sense of the novel coronavirus that were ubiquitous in the earliest months of the pandemic, channeling a public safety emergency and the ensuing communications struggles into a cartoonish video.

Alcázar Silva (2022, 114) noted that many of Yazmin's choices demonstrate awareness of register and comprehensibility. This is present in the accessibility of "(not) your friend" as a concept, as well as in the concrete appeal, "Dile a tu familia que no estén de vagos/Quédate en casa, no vayas por tacos./Tell your family to not be roaming around/Stay at home, don't go for tacos." The images tend to mirror the words exactly. For example, the line "Te causa cansancio, toz y no hay alivio./It causes fatigue, a cough and there is no relief." is accompanied by three cartoon faces—one with bags under the eyes, one covering its mouth as a spray comes from its mouth, and a third with a water bag held to the forehead. In an actual song video, the visuals would reinforce the comprehension of the verbal text.

The minimalistic drawings are designed to make the text accessible to children, but there is another representational effect at play here, which Yazmin addressed in her reflections. During the earlier conversations about foreignization and domestication strategies in translation, Yazmin had been one of the most outspoken students and she had seen strengths and weaknesses in both approaches. She observed, on the one hand, that domestication better "reaches the heart more," but also that it can also lead to stereotypes (see Alcázar Silva 2022, 100). In the design of her own PSA, it seemed that Yazmin was still grappling with these tensions. In her reflection she wrote the following:

> En el video, no escoji [sic, escogi] una raza. Decidí usar personajes que no tuvieran color como azul. Lo que si puse atención era que mis personajes fueran niños así para que los niños puedan relacionarse con los personajes. También trate de incluir un hombre y una mujer para los personajes, no quería que mi presentación se viera solo hombres y no niñas.
>
> *In the video, I did not choose a race. I decided to use characters that had no color like blue. What I did pay attention to was that my characters were children so that children could relate with the characters. I also tried to include a man and a woman for the characters, I did not want my presentation to only show men and no girls.*
>
> (See Alcázar Silva 2022, 120–122)

Alcázar Silva (2022) speculated that Yazmin's decision to create cartoon figures with no discernible race may have been influenced by the stroke videos, where figures were conspicuously represented with different skin colors and other physical attributes in videos for different languages. However, later in her reflection, Yazmin expressed doubt about whether her choice, pondering whether the "video could have been more effective if more races were depicted so that the child could relate to the characters" [in the original Spanish: video pudiera ser más efectivo si agregara razas así para que el niño pudiera relacionarse con los personajes] (see Alcázar Silva 2022, 122).

Another tension in Yazmin's proposal relates to the framing of the PSA as a lullaby for children. The text is explicitly addressed to a "tu," an informal singular second-person, who is positioned as the messenger for the information about how to mitigate the virus. It is the child who is expected to tell their families to stay home. The gentleness of the lullaby genre is undercut in moments such as the end of verse 3 where the use of personification extends into the cautionary statement that the virus "is not playing," which is followed by the concluding line "Te hará que defunciones/It will make you die." The threat of death is certainly a thematic deviation for the traditional lullaby. In the context of Yazmin's PSA, it points back to another way in which the kinds of emotional response that might *reach the heart* of her audience become complicated.

"I Tried to Have Diversity in My Ideas": Julieta's PSA

According to Alcázar Silva (2022), Julieta had reported at various moments of the class about her experiences growing up bilingually on the US-Mexico border and serving as a language broker for her parents. She was tracked as an English Language Learner in school, which in the state of Arizona could simply reflect that a language other than English was indicated as her home language on school in-take forms (see Jimenez-Silva et al. 2014). Now, at the university, she was enrolled in a Spanish translation and interpretation class alongside many heritage and second-language learners, and while it is not clear how she positioned herself, this was likely a context in which Julieta's bilingualism was met with yet another set of social/symbolic values.

Julieta's pitch was for a PSA on the importance of safe sex, which she associated with both prophylactics, i.e., STI testing and the use of condoms, and with consent. Her intended audience was teenagers and young adults. For the music genre she chose contemporary rap because "es movido y conocido por los jóvenes" ["it is music to dance to that the youth knows"]. She described her PSA in the form of a rap video as "a fun way to learn about sexual education without having to be in the classroom" [una manera divertida de aprender sobre la educación sexual sin tener que estar en un salón (see Alcázar Silva 2022, 126).

English Text	Spanish Text
Verse 1	Verse 1
When you want to have some fun	Cuando te quieres divertir
You know what I'm talking about	Tu sabes de lo que estoy hablando
You must be safe	Te tienes que cuidar
You must have consent	Se requiere consentimiento
You must get checked	Te debes checar
Chorus	Chorus
Wrap it up	Cubrelo
You gotta wrap it up	Lo tienes que cubrir
You can't be silly	No puedes andar de payaso
You gotta wrap your willy	Te tienes que cubrir
Verse 2	Verse 2
You can't forget	No puedes olvidar
No glove no love	Sin condón no hay amor
No push and shove	No empujos[4] ni jalones
Practice safe love	Practica el amor seguro

Chorus	Chorus
Verse 3	Verse 3
Sexually transmitted diseases	Las enfermedades de transmisión sexual
Spread fast	Se contraen rápido
Unwanted pregnancies	Los embarazos no deseados
Don't finish last	No terminan a lo último
Chorus	Chorus

Like Yazmin's, Julieta's original song text included significant amounts of rhyme and other forms of sound play, which were absent in the translated lyrics. The rhyme was also related to the musical genre selected—in this case hip-hop. Julieta's lyrics rely extensively on slant rhymes, using words that sound alike or are assonant—a common feature of rap and hip-hop. For example, the first verse ends with "consent" and "checked." There is also some use of chain rhymes, where rhymes carry over across stanzas, as in the subsequent verse that begins with a line ending in "forget" and then continues with three lines initiating a new chain, "No glove no love/No push and shove/Practice safe love." There are also instances of perfect rhyme, like the couplets ending in "silly" and "willy" that end the chorus.

In his book on the poetics of hip-hop, Bradley (2017) posits that, "[w]hile perfect rhymes satisfy our rhyming mind, slant rhymes tease us a little, denying us the satisfaction of completion and often resulting in a creative tension" (58-9). Julieta plays with this type of rhyming in the translated version of the song in Spanish. She often ends lines with infinitive verbs, which immediately creates resonance in the—ar and—ir endings. Words like "hablando" and "consentimento" in verse one, "amor" and "seguro" in verse 2, and "rápido" and "ultimo" in verse 3 are also used at the ends of line to create assonant effects. She also alters the chorus slightly to create the repetition of the word "cubrir" in lieu of the rhyming between "silly" and "willy."

Despite this attention to language play in the song texts, in the presentation of Julieta's proposal, the visuals dominate. A typical slide includes a large image, taking up between a third and a half of the space. The English language lyrics, labeled "source text," appear above the Spanish translation, labeled "target language." Where word bubbles appear in the comic, the text for these is only in English, which suggests that this is an English-language PSA with a Spanish translation provided. Given the openness of this aspect of the assignment, the matter of what students decided to translate or leave un-translated cannot be understood as a deliberate statement. As Malinowski (2018) argues in connection with the role of translation and translators in linguistic landscapes, "the mutual understandings (or lack thereof), conflicts, and negotiated coexistences among people make language visible as a primary instrument of identity and difference, and it is the translator who occupies a unique place as cultural mediator" (60). In the context of an assignment that effectively invites students to engage in sociodramatic play in the role of professional translators, untranslatedness can thus be seen as an index of the translational, translanguaging space within which this multiliteracy play unfolds.

While the song text largely consists of advice, formulated through the modal verb "must" and directives, i.e., "don't" and "can't," the images provide a parallel but separate narrative of a relationship between a masculine-presenting and a feminine-presenting character. The images in Julieta's safe sex PSA are, in contrast to Yazmin's children's cartoons, highly detailed, comic book-style story frames, generated using the digital application, Pixton.[5] Whereas the objects and actors in Yazmin's storyboard float in space, Julieta's images include backgrounds with details such as furniture and decor. The visual depiction of body language often conveys what is happening in the absence of verbal text. In her reflection, Julieta provided explanations for each of these image choices. For example, in one image the two figures sit on the edge of a bed. The blonde, masculine-presenting character is winking at the viewer and the brunette, feminine-presenting character has brought their hands to their face over an open, smiling mouth (see Alcázar Silva 2022, 136). Julieta described this in her reflection as the moment when you see more intimacy between them. In a later scene, the blonde figure is in a room that is clearly intended to be a doctor's office. There is an examination table in the middle with a standing scale off to the side. A speech bubble reads "I am STI free," and the figure is smiling broadly. Appearing between these two is a second image set in the bedroom, where the feminine-presenting character asks, "Have you been tested before?" (See Figure 6). The reply: ""No … no one has approached that with me" (Alcázar Silva 2022, 137). Julieta explained why she included this scene in her reflection:

> [L]a gente no tiene que tener pena de tener este tipo de discusiones abiertamente ya que son muy importantes y se tiene que promover este tipo de discusiones en un espacio abierto y en un espacio seguro. En teoría esta escena ya sería después de que la persona recibe resultados negativos o resultados positivos, pero tomaron medicamento para um curar su enfermedad y ya que tomaron decisiones responsables están tratando de reconectarse con esa persona.

[P]eople don't have to feel embarrassed for having this type of conversation openly since they are very important, and you have to promote this type of conversation in a space to speak openly and feel safe. In theory, this scene would be after the person receives negative or positive results, but they took medicine to cure their illness and since they made responsible decisions they are trying to reconnect with that person.]

(Alcázar Silva 2022, 140)

Julieta's recognition that this is a difficult social situation, where young people could use models, makes it even more striking that only an English-language version of the dialogue is included.

The premise for Julieta's pitch—a PSA as rap music video—is in itself an example of play with frame. As noted by Alcázar Silva (2022, 128), hip-hop music has historically been used across the globe as a means of disrupting "hegemonic norms" (see also Kitwana 2005), particularly among minoritized groups. She also sees relationships between Julieta's PSA and traditions of comedic rap, which borrows linguistic and musical features from these genres, while also employing parody and humor to challenge social norms—including those that are pervasive in domains of hip-hop culture such as hypermasculinity. Hip-hop is also emblematic as a form of global youth culture. Within sociolinguistics and applied linguistics, the expression of hybrid identities through this musical

Figure 6 Sample from Julieta's PSA.

style has been a focus of interest (Blommaert and Rampton 2011; Pennycook 2007). Helland (2017) uses the example of Japanese Chicana rap artist Mona AKA Sad Girl to show how the interplay of multiple semiotic modes can contribute to the expression of hybrid identities by indexing global and local cultures. Within the context of the US-Mexico border, hip-hop provides a possible re-framing for the untranslated dialogues in Julieta's PSA—a linguistic index of the English-hegemonic context within which she might imagine these conversations taking place.

In the design of the images Julieta intentionally used inclusive representations in terms of race. This can be seen in the design of the figures. One has lighter skin and blonde hair, the other brown hair and skin. She stated in her reflection, "Trate de tener diversidad en mis ideas para incluir a las personas y los conceptos." [I tried to have diversity in my ideas to be able to include people and concepts]. But it can also be seen as a thread running through other design choices in her PSA proposal, where diversity is less about distinct differences or something like *foreignization* and more about the hybridity of translanguaging practices. Although her texts are marked as "source" and "target," the texts themselves each include sound play, such as slant rhyme, which suggests more bidirectional movement in the translation process. Julieta's choice of hip-hop for her musical genre also indexes traditions of translocal cultural production where hybridity and recontextualization are valorized over *cultural appropriateness*. There are moments of tension, such as the use of English alone in the visuals; and yet, Yazmin's emphasis on diversity is a way of thinking into her focal topic—discourses on safe sex among youth—as itself something that does not belong in a particular subset of the population in the United States, but is located in moments of dialogue between individuals who carry with them their own diverse sets of ideas and experiences that can impact one another.

Concluding Thoughts: Translating the Translators

The PSA project described in this chapter took place at a moment when discourses around health safety and disease were foregrounded. Both Yazmin and Julieta chose to focus on public health issues that are, by the nature of their spread, interpersonal rather than individual concerns. Mitigating these diseases protects oneself and others. Through the act of designing these PSAs, students in the class were being pushed to translate public health discourses across languages and modalities, and in so doing to experiment with the play between these different meaning-making systems, that is, the various ways in which they come into contact. This includes moments where the multiplicity of design elements was at harmony with one another and where they seemed to clash. For example, in the chorus of Yazmin's song the meanings of the images and of the two sets of lyrics are mutually reinforcing as is the personification of the virus, but the loss of the rhythm and rhyme in the English texts is at odds with the intended catchiness of a children's song. In Julieta's lyrics, there are moments where the slant rhyming and sound of the two versions are not the same but they are resonant with one another. Meanwhile, the images tell a parallel story, which is linked to but does not directly correspond with the multilingual song text.

In identifying moments of tension between the layers of texts and modes in these PSA, my point is not to suggest *problems* in the design of these texts but rather the ways in which role playing as translators also revealed moments of translation play, in the sense of felicities and infelicities between meaning-making systems that lay bare at least a little of the systems themselves. In the case of Yazmin and Julieta's projects, the binary between *domestication* and *foreignization*, which had been introduced as a conceptual backdrop to the projects, became less a heuristic to think with and more one to think *against* as the students worked to understand how to move between languages and modalities. For Yazmin, this emerged in the attention to affect and aesthetic responses of diverse audiences and how these can be at odds with one another at times. The choice to focus on children at first seemed to simplify some things by offering a way out of certain questions of representation and framing but the impetus to "reach the heart more" remained complicated. Julieta's commitment to representing diversity was realized in the visual depiction of different skin tones and indirectly through the choice of a genre that itself celebrates minoritized identities, but the scenarios in which she imagined her figures were anglophone. The imagined context of the PSA helped to locate translation in the lifeworlds of the students; viewed in this way, Julieta's design choices can be seen as indexical of experiences that are familiar to her living on the US-Mexico border and navigating multilingual spaces where languages are not necessarily allowed to mingle on equal footing.

In her rationale for the larger study within which the PSA project took place, Alcázar Silva (2022) states that she wanted to work with concepts from multiliteracies and symbolic competence to recognize that the translator is "not as a machine that encodes and decodes, but rather a person who embodies the histories, culture, and values in their multilingual expression" (154). In Yazmin's and Julieta's projects, cultural discourses and familiar ways of designing meaning around public health come into play, but also their values in relation to translation and language mediation—and questions about what it means to design particular communities into one's texts as the intended addressees for messages with an aesthetic impact. In their conceptualization of multiliteracies, Cope and Kalantzis (2009) have contended that in the act of redesigning the designer is also redesigned (184; see also Chapter 1 of this book). In the case of the projects discussed in this chapter, it was through the act of translating and the opportunity to engage playfully with translation that the students were re-designed. By navigating but not necessarily resolving the histories, cultures, and values they embody, the students were developing translation competencies and linguistic awareness, but they were translating themselves into multilingual subjects (see also Gramling and Warner 2016, 97).

6

Speculative Play in an Italian Language-Culture Classroom

Introduction

This final chapter takes up the New London Group's central claim that education, and specifically language and literacy education, is most centrally about enabling students to design social futures, while also shifting some of the emphasis from planning to play, and thus also introducing the role of desires. An underlying argument is that designing futures—for oneself and for others—is crucially about world-building, that is, about exploring through new languages and cultures alternative possibilities for the world and one's place within it, which can be other than what is immediately available in one's current reality. Inspired by Mirra and Garcia's (2020) work on speculative civic literacies, I will refer to this dimension of multiliteracies in language-culture learning contexts as *speculative play*. Through designing activities that encourage speculative play, learners are given opportunities to subvert or expand their sense of their own multilingual subjectivities and connect this to imagined future selves. As the examples in this chapter show, designing one's social future is sometimes directly connected to occupational aspirations, but it also can relate more to a broader set of desires related to who students want to be in the world.

Understanding some forms of multiliteracy play as speculative play invites one to take an epistemological and affective stance that deliberately contrasts with one that is predominantly anticipatory. In their anthropological account of technoscience in the modern era, Adams, Murphy, and Clarke (2009) argue that anticipatory logic is woven into contemporary life, such that it often masquerades as common sense; the assumption is that the future is anticipat*able*, if only we could amass enough information. Within educational domains, anticipatory modes of thinking saturate discourses and decisions around course and curriculum development, even down to questions of which programs are worthy of investment (see Gramling and Warner 2016). The imperative to anticipate carries with it an ethical weight; the logic of anticipation dictates that education be optimized with the goal of maximally preparing students for a future that is predetermined (see Warner, Gaspar, Diao 2020; Durand and McAllister 2023).

A speculative stance, in contrast, empowers students to reflect on what matters to them as they imagine what kinds of futures their education might prepare them to design. Speculative play in this sense can be part of what Barrineau, Mendy, and Peters (2022) theorize as an "emergentist education," that is, one that privileges radical futurity over prediction. Radical futurity "assumes that the future does not exist yet, but stretches across from the not-yet known, beyond the not-yet possible to the not-yet imaginable" (Barrineau, Mendy, and Peters 2022, 2). The role of education is to foster designers, not simply "naive thinkers" capable of reproducing designs (see Chapter 1 and Freire 2007).

The field of language and culture education is in itself subject to anticipatory modes of thinking—both from within, where the potential market value of language skills is often cited as a case for language learning, and from without, where parallel arguments about the return on investment are frequently used as a case against language requirements and even as a reason for closing down programs of study (see Warner, Gaspar, and Diao 2020). There is a striking tension between discourses wherein languages are viewed as a means for designing one's professional future by attaining a form of symbolic capital that can be cashed in on the job market, on the one hand, and contemporary enrollments data at US institutions of higher education, on the other. In the United States, the language with the single highest increase over the last twenty years is Korean (Looney and Lusin 2019), not because of potential economic advantages it may garner learners but because of the cultural and aesthetic influence of K-pop and K-drama. Based on case studies of Italian and Mandarin learners, Warner, Gaspar, and Diao (2020) show that learners' ways of imagining their futures are more nuanced and are often grounded in everyday experiences and values that are not captured at all by the typical marketization practices of language programs (123). Anticipatory thinking that posits the value of language learning while neglecting the motivations and desires of language learners has dire negative impacts for the field of second language studies but also for the students that educational institutions are entrusted to serve.

Given the clashing discourses around language learning and its role in education, it is not incidental that the two vignettes featured in this chapter come from an Italian language-culture classroom. Italian, like Korean, tends to fall outside of the bounds of anticipatory arguments for language and culture learning in US-American contexts and is more likely to be promoted based on its cultural history and perceived beauty than the economic advantages it might procure. Perhaps, exactly because the study of Italian is shaped through alternate discourses around the value of language-culture learning, the case studies featured in this chapter thus provide opportunities for considering the desires that drive learners' re-commitments to language learning and how these intertwine with the futures they imagine for themselves.

Course Context

The instructional context for the examples featured in this chapter was a project-based learning unit included in an intermediate (fourth-semester) Italian course taught by Borbala Gaspar in spring 2018.[1] Gaspar was also one of the lead curriculum designers for this course, and she and a colleague, Margherita Berti, had piloted a version of the project-based language learning activities. One of the primary changes initiated in 2018 was to include more overt literacy-based activities leading up to the final presentations. These included models for how to design presentation slides, which the students and instructors assessed together using the rubrics (see Gaspar and Warner 2021, 19–23). Gaspar and Berti also developed a workshop on finding resources in Italian, which emphasized the available designs present in a typical web search. For example, students were presented with a screenshot from a YouTube page in Italian and were told that this was the result of a search for "polenta ricetta come si fa" (polenta recipe how to make). They were then guided to notice the range of visual and verbal resources that a standard YouTube search offers for expanding and developing their own future searches, and to consider how new information might compel them to ask new questions about their topics.

The main objective of the project was broadly defined; students should research a topic of interest to them that relates to Italian language, culture, and society. As a first step, the class participants completed a survey that asked them to brainstorm at least three topics of personal interest to them. They then each met with Gaspar individually to shape their topics, develop guiding questions they potentially wanted to explore for their project, and begin to brainstorm an interactive activity, which they would include in the culminating in-class presentation. Subsequent phases of the project, in which students conducted research and created presentation slides, were each supported through modeling and in-class workshops. Although the presentation was to be conducted in

Italian, students were enabled to move between their languages in the earlier phases of the project, as they formulated their ideas.

The following is the prompt that students were given at the start, which summarizes these phases of the project:

> Throughout the course you will work on a project of your choice that you will research and learn more about. This topic can be based on your personal interest. The first step is to think about a topic that you would like to choose. The following are questions that can help you make this decision: Do you have any hobbies? Do you volunteer anywhere? Do you want to find out if there is a similar group of interest in Italy? Do you want to present to a sorority/fraternity house or connect your project to it somehow? Do you want to connect your major to Italian? Or do you simply want to search and find interesting information?
>
> Before completing, submitting, and presenting your project, you will complete several steps: (a) Scaffolding your topic interest with peers and with me and constructing possible research questions; (b) writing a proposal and finding resources; (c) correcting your proposal based on the received feedback; (d) looking at project example slides and evaluating them with your peers; (e) carry out your research, read, take notes, write and discuss your preliminary findings during class project discussions; (f) create your slides and presentation; (g) create an activity for the class; (h) make corrections to your slides; (i) practice your presentation; (j) present your project.

It is worth noting that students' desires are foregrounded in the language of this prompt, i.e., through the repetition of the phrase "do you want." Both Gaspar's and students' recounts of the projects suggest that this was also reinforced at other stages of the project, especially in the one-on-one conferences.

While a primary objective of the student projects was to develop their research literacy in Italian, both with regard to finding and working with key sources and through the carefully scaffolded design of core academic genres (i.e., research proposals and presentation slides), the two instructors were also inspired by the potential of project-based language learning as a way of engaging learners' "hearts, bodies and senses" (van Lier 2004, xiv). The emphasis on the affective dimensions of knowledge production in a new language found additional conceptual support in multiliteracies scholarship that advocates for multisensory approaches to multiliteracies (e.g., Pahl and Rowsell 2020; see Chapter 2 for additional discussion). This dimension of the projects was most deliberately facilitated through the one-on-one support that students were given; in addition to the scheduled conferences, Gaspar maintained an ongoing conversation with each of the students in the class using the digital communications app GroupMe, where they would share additional resources and talk about new developments in the projects. In recorded interviews carried out by Gaspar's co-teacher after the end of the term, students almost unanimously mentioned Gaspar's guidance as one of the most influential parts of the project; her mentoring and openness seemed to allow the students a space to interpret the presentation and the classroom activity embedded within it in various ways, which certainly will have contributed to the multisensory, playful formats that emerged among the students in this class—two of which (Tommaso and Carla) will serve as the focal case studies discussed in the remainder of this chapter.

Designing Multilingual Futures through Multiliteracy Play: The Cases of Tommaso and Carla

To present the vignettes from Tommaso and Carla, I am drawing from a range of data sources that were collected as part of the larger study. My sources include learner artifacts created at various phases of the project as well as a post-project survey. In addition, consenting students were invited for a semi-structured interview after the end of the term. Because both Tommaso and Carla were students in Gaspar's class, her teaching colleague, Margherita Berti, conducted these interviews. The interviews were conducted primarily in English, although there was some code-switching. The conversations focused on the experience of the project, as well as the students' future hopes and plans in relation to Italian. As an additional form of data, I draw upon Gaspar's reflections as the instructor of the course and my co-investigator on a previous research study (Gaspar and Warner 2020).

Like the students featured in the previous two chapters, Tommaso and Carla are arguably exemplary but not necessarily typical. They were two of only six consenting students in a class of thirteen to complete every phase of the project. Both also participated in an optional departmental undergraduate showcase at the end of the semester, which suggests that they were highly engaged not only inside but outside of the class. Coincidentally, both Tommaso and Carla were double majoring in both Italian and archaeology, a shared interest that shows up in the topics they selected, but manifests in quite different ways. For Carla, who shared in her post-semester interview that she had been accepted into a graduate program for archaeology and hoped to one day teach and research in this field, her imagined self as a future archaeology professor was a core element in the kinds of world-building she engaged in her presentation. Tommaso described archaeology as less a professional field and more a key influence on his worldview. Explaining what he had learned through the study of archaeology, Tommaso explained in the interview, "We just view the world as if it's different and we kind of interpret it differently, but at the, like, same base level we're all the same and it kind of helps." Although it is not directly relevant to their projects, it is also noteworthy that both Carla and Tommaso had family ties to Italy, which they mentioned in their interviews: Carla's father was Sicilian but had never taught her his first language; Tomasso's family came from Romania, and his grandfather had spent time in a refugee camp in Italy after fleeing the Communist regime.

While both Tommaso and Carla made connections between their Italian projects and their major, in neither case were their choices instrumentally directed toward something like career advancement. Instead, the academic literacy activities from the proposal to the research to the presentation were transformed into "hopeful" literacy practices (Pahl and Pool 2020, 92)—that is, imaginative ways of making sense of what could be. In the next two sections, I will look at each of these case studies in turn and how forms of multiliteracy play seemed to enable this speculative relationship to Italian.

"Have That Experience and See That Beauty": Carla's Project

In her proposal, Carla listed "the Etruscans" as an intended thematic focus for her project. This was not only in line with her interest in archaeology, but also drew from recent experiences; the summer before this class, Carla had been able to conduct fieldwork in Orvieto, Italy, as part of a university summer abroad program. Describing her plan for the presentation, Carla offered an outline in three parts:

> The first component is to show the students how charming and historically authentic this city is. My intent is to show my fellow students how wonderful it is to study Italian in this hilltop village. The second part of my presentation will be an exploration of the Etruscan culture since Orvieto was an Etruscan strong holding in the Classical world. The third section of my presentation will be to show the students something about how archaeologists work.

Of note here is that Carla was not positioning herself primarily as a researcher or even a student here but rather as an educator and advocate—both for archaeology but also for study abroad in Italy. Words like "charming and historically authentic" or "quaint" (as she described Orvieto later in the proposal) echo the language of study abroad websites or promotional materials. The repetition of the phrase "show the students," along with her stated intentions to include photos from her own fieldwork experience and reconstruct archaeological work for the others in class, immediately placed her in the role of instructor—but it was importantly her desire to convey her lived experience working and studying in Italy that is the primary focus of her project rather than information about the Etruscans per se.

Carla enacted a first-person point of view through creative play with perspective in both the visual and verbal design of her presentation. She first began the presentation from a distance; her opening slide included a zoomed-out panoramic view of Orvieto with the text "Alta su un enorme blocco di tufo c'è una città storica, Orvieto" (High on a huge block of tuff is a historic city, Orvieto). The next slide consisted of three images, two of which include close-ups of Carla clearly at sites in Orvieto. These appeared along with three autobiographical statements:

• Ho vissuto ad Orvieto, in Umbria	• I lived in Orvieto, in Umbria
• Ho studiato la cultura etrusca	• I studied the Etruscan culture
• Ho lavorato allo scavo delle tombe etrusche	• I worked on the excavation of the Etruscan tombs

Although first-person pronouns were absent from the remainder of the slides up until the beginning of the activity, this introduction to the topic connected the contents of the rest of the presentation with Carla's experience.

Across the next twelve slides, facts about the Etruscans were conveyed in an impersonal third-person perspective more typical to an academic talk; however, multiliteracy play entered in via the images and in the spoken language Carla adopted when presenting. As she moved into the second slide, Carla used the phrase, "Ok andiamo ad Orvieto" (let's go to Orvieto)." Not only did this maintain the first-person perspective exactly at the moment when she shifted into the more informational, less experiential part of her talk, but it also expanded into the plural, inviting the rest of the class to come with her on a virtual tour of the city. This effect was also referenced by Carla in the interview after the end of the semester, when she was asked why she also included images of herself. Carla answered, "I wanted to show them this is what I did, and I also wanted to inspire them that you too can do this. You can go to Italy for summer and speak Italian." Carla was, in other words, engaging her fellow students in a bit of speculative play.

Throughout the presentation, Carla opted for photographs that were composed with a one-point perspective, such that the viewer was positioned

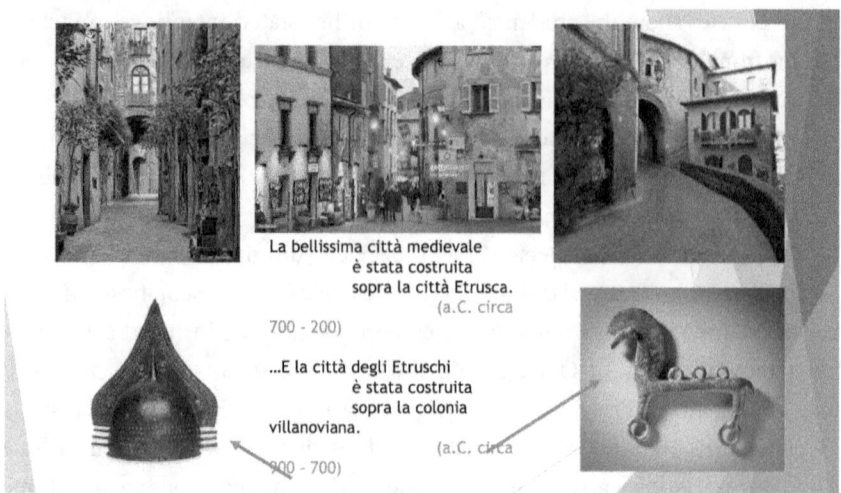

Figure 7 Sample from Carla's presentation slides.

looking straight down a street or into another space in the city. This created an almost first-person point of view, inviting viewers to imagine themselves in the space represented by the image (see also Serafini 2014, 63–5). The top-left and top-right images in Figure 7 are representative of these one-point perspective images in Carla's presentation. As Carla moved between these slides, she described the streets that she followed as she moved from the outskirts of Orvieto to downtown, where the Etruscan tombs are, creating a sense that she was walking the class through a virtual tour of the town.

Carla's presentation culminated in a whole-class activity, which she had planned carefully from almost the beginning of the project. The transition from presentation to activity was marked by a slide where the language again reflected the first-person plural. Above the two images of students working at dig sites and next to a single close-up photograph of a pottery shard was the following text:

> Di solito noi non troviamo pentole, ciotole o piatti completi; troviamo i pezzi!!!
> Usually we don't find pots, bowls or complete dishes; let's find the pieces!!!

As the images shifted to group activities at the dig site, the verbal text once again addressed the students directly. This is also carried through to the next slide, which featured objects from the excavation. Above the images was a text in the first-person plural, which provided some additional context about the activity to come:

Allo Scavo	At the Excavation
Noi mettiamo insieme i pezzi della ceramica.	We put the pieces of pottery together.
È come un puzzle tridimensionale.	It's like a three-dimensional puzzle.
Perchè tutti i pezzi?	Why all the pieces?
• gli animali	• animals
• i terremoti	• earthquakes
• i ladri	• thieves
• il passaggio del tempo	• the passage of time

With funds from a mini grant, which Gaspar had helped to write, Carla had gone to a secondhand shop, had purchased an assortment of miscellaneous dishes (bowls, plates, cups), and then broken them into pieces. The class was divided into small groups and each group received a bag of shards, which they were instructed to reassemble to the best of their abilities. To further create the effect that the students were in Orvieto on a dig, Carla played a video in the background, showing the archeological site of Orvieto and an interview with the Italian director of the archeological site in Orvieto. The ambient noise of Italian and pieces of broken shards clanging along with the images of Orvieto in the video gave the classroom the feel of a bustling archaeological site. At the end of this activity, Carla displayed a slide with two images taken from the point of view of someone sitting at a cafe table—one looking down at a piece of cake and cup of coffee and one gazing down the street ahead. Carla again invited the students in the class to imagine themselves in this scene. The accompanying text read: "Dopo una giornata allo scavo, si può bere un caffè con una fetta della torta al limone!" (After a day of excavation, you can have a coffee with a slice of lemon cake!). In her interview Carla explained her choices in this part of the presentation, sharing, "I wanted them to, like, go through walking that course and have that experience and see that beauty."

"A Whole New World to Myself": Tommaso's Project

In comparison to Carla, Tommaso stumbled into his topic. His initial interests for the project teetered between broad, i.e., "Ancient Rome" and highly specific, e.g., "making masquerade masks." When he met with Gaspar in her office for the one-on-one conference, he spotted a poster from a previous student's presentation about one of the characters from the commedia dell'arte, a form of masked theater originating in Italy during the sixteenth century, and with Gaspar's encouragement decided this could be a way to explore the making of masquerade masks within a specific context. Before submitting the proposal,

Tommaso did some initial research on the commedia dell'arte, and narrowed his focus once again to one of the classical characters from this theatrical tradition—Pulcinella. Pulcinella, who represents a witty everyman type characterized through contradictions (e.g., poor/rich, smart/stupid, noble/base), evolved into a stock figure in Neopolitan puppetry and has survived in the modern day as an icon of Naples. By the proposal, this connection between Pulcinella and Naples has become a central part of Tommaso's project, although he also emphasized his interest in how this fictional figure had appeared in different cultural and historical contexts up to the modern day. Framing his project in the proposal, he wrote:

> I chose my topic because I like to better understand cultures and their motivations. The carnival within Venice has peaked [sic] my interest and how the masks originated. The main focus will be behind a single character from la Commedia dell'arte. I chose Pulcinella, because use [sic] in popular culture not just in Venetian masks, but even in Naples pizza.

Tommaso's working title for the project, "Pulcinella: Naples' Hermes," pointed to this focus on Neapolitan culture, but also, through the reference to the Olympian deity with whom Pulcinella is sometimes compared, to a cultural-historical trajectory that extends beyond the confines of that city or even of Italy.

The tension between the particular and the broad or even universal came to characterize Tommaso's project at every phase, as Pulcinella became for him more a transcultural concept than a classical Italian figure. At one point during in-class work, Gaspar heard Tommaso comment to fellow students that "Pulcinella is everywhere." This sentiment—and what it helped Tommaso to understand about culture and humanity—became in many ways the core message of his project.

Leading up to the presentations, Tommaso used the class GroupMe chat to share his discoveries related to Pulcinella. For example, shortly before the due date, he shared a link to a TedX Talk titled "Make Em Laugh,"[2] which discusses elements of comedy that are said to transverse national and historical boundaries; the speaker, a noted expert in the commedia dell'arte, cites Pulcinella as one of his core examples. Tommaso's comment attached to the post reads: "This will help you guys understand my presentation better tomorrow." Tommaso had also not lost his original interest in mask making. Over the course of a couple of days, Tommaso posted three images, in which he shared different stages of the creation of his Pulcinella mask (see Figure 8). On the day of the presentation, he brought the mask and passed it around in the class, while he explained the process of

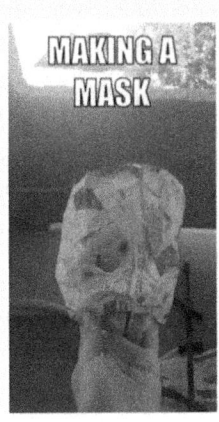  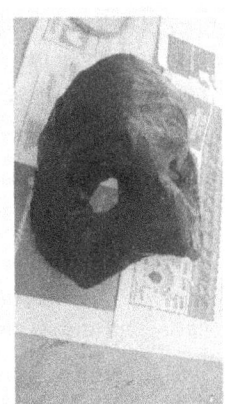

Figure 8 Tommaso's masks.

production. In his end of the semester interview, Tommaso mentioned YouTube videos, including performances and puppetry, and the experience of making the mask as ways in which he developed a "deeper" relationship to his research.

In the presentation itself, Tommaso oscillated between treating Pulcinella as a cultural object and as a kind of role model. At the start of the talk, the emphasis was clearly on the former. He opened with a series of nine slides introducing the commedia dell'arte, including individual slides for six of the traditional characters. The final character in this sequence was Pulcinella. Also, in his presentation style, he positioned himself in the role of scholar; he was the only student to dress in a suit for his presentation, creating an air of formality, and he maintained an academic register by using impersonal language. The focus was on the cultural content and history, not on his relationship to the topic.

Although the slide introducing Pulcinella initiated the transition from the broad introduction to his focal figure, this shift in scope was momentarily delayed because this was the point where Tommaso introduced his interactive activity. The class was put in small groups, where they were asked to take turns pantomiming something through gestures, while the others guessed what they were trying to express. Tommaso was in effect asking them to play with the pantomime theater, which characterized the early commedia dell'arte, but in conversations with Gaspar he had further explained that an additional goal was to help his classmates to better understand Pulcinella, who was well known for his excessive use of gestures.

Much of the rest of the presentation was devoted to contextualizing Pulcinella within Italian culture and history from ancient Rome to the present and to showing connections to other parts of the world. This again was delivered in a largely academic register, both in his oral presentation and in the language used in the slides, which were accompanied by images, primarily of Pulcinella in his various manifestations. In several moments, Tommaso associated Pulcinella's character with the history of Naples. One of the most direct examples of this appeared toward the end of the presentation. On a slide with the header "The City of Contradictions," Tommaso included an image with a topographical map of the region where Naples is situated with an arrow pointing to Mount Vesuvius, an active volcano near the coast, and the label "l'inferno" or "hell." The adjacent text on the slide read:

Napoli è un paradiso che è proprio vicino all'inferno!	**Naples is a paradise that is right next to hell!**
Pulcinella sfida il senso e il non senso; osa il buon senso e il non senso; sfida la ragione e l'irragionevolezza. È un imbroglione, un burlone, un provocatore. È preoccupato a provocare le autorità e le persone. Lui infrange le leggi, tuttavia non promuove il caos; lui vuole il caos, ma non l'illegalità.	Pulcinella challenges sense and nonsense; he dares common sense and nonsense; he defies reason and unreason. He is a trickster, a prankster, a provocateur. He is preoccupied with provoking the authorities and people. He breaks the laws, yet he does not promote chaos; he wants chaos, but not lawlessness.

That the qualities of Pulcinella are shared with the city of Naples was also implied at other moments in Tommaso's project presentation; however, the final slide expanded beyond that local context to suggest a universality to Pulcinella:

Pulcinella è nelle nostre barzellette pervertite. Lui esiste nelle culture di tutto il mondo. Può essere visto nei nostri comici, cartoni animati, persino nei libri. Può essere Homer Simpson negli Stati Uniti o Mario in Giappone.	Pulcinella is in our perverted jokes. He exists in cultures all over the world. He can be seen in our comedians, cartoons, even books. He can be Homer Simpson in the US or Mario in Japan.

The introduction of the first-person plural here—a departure from impersonal pronouns outside of the pantomime activity—directly implicated his audience, but the second and last sentence seemed to convey a much broader "we" that encompasses not only the US-American culture of the local context but humanity at large.

In these instances, where the spirit of Pulcinella rather than cultural history shifted into focus, Tommaso broke frame from the academic talk. This was likewise the case when he initiated the pantomime activity and shared the masks he had created. The connection between these moments, where personal response was foregrounded, and Tommaso's earlier comment that "Pulcinella is everywhere" becomes clearer in the end of the semester interview. Although he seemed resistant in some moments, when questioned about the academic aspects of the presentation, such as his strategies for conducting research or designing his slides, Tommaso became excited when asked what he was most proud of, replying "Honestly, it was just … the most proud thing was honestly what I learned. Okay. I kind of like opened up a whole new world to myself." He then went on to describe how he wanted to share what he had learned with everyone he knew, not only his classmates, but also family and friends, and noted that this became somewhat of an "obsession." When asked, "So, what is the meaning of Pulcinella to you today," Tommaso responded at length, echoing some of the statements about Pulcinella that he had made in his closing slides:

> Looking at what is terrible in life and laughing at it. It is saying oh, yeah, you know, I got a flat tire. You know, I might as well go drinking tonight, you know not taking life too seriously … I have all these bills but, you know, I'm still alive. What's the big deal? At least I still have my health or if I don't have my health, at least I'm still alive. Someone passes, you know, at least they're not suffering anymore. Going from either [sic] the negative and just laughing at it. And saying who cares?

He went on to explain that although he was originally focused on the historical and cultural references, only later he was able to "feel the symbolic meaning" and to view it as something he could carry with him in his life. For Tommaso, Pulcinella became more than an object of study; instead, it evolved into a philosophy of life.

Conclusion: Projecting New Worlds

Through their projects in Gaspar's Italian language-culture class, Carla and Tomasso were orienting themselves toward multilingual futures in ways that were speculative and hopeful rather than expeditious. For Tomasso, his exploration of the Pulcinellean spirit in Neapolitan, Italian, and other cultures around the world opened up a "whole new world," in which he could bricolage a set of attitudes toward life and ways of being in the world. Carla used her presentation to position herself in the roles of scholar and educator—an imagined future life that was connected to her plans to attend graduate school after the end of the semester and continue her work as an archaeologist. She also created a speculative space for other students in the class to envision themselves as study abroad students taking part in an archaeological dig and treating themselves to a slice of cake at the end of the day.

Through an assemblage of different types of multiliteracy play, Carla and Tomasso, in cahoots with their classmates and instructor, transformed the classroom into a space for imagining lives that were other than ordinary. Both student-creators engaged play with form drawing on multisensory resources, for example, in the whole class activities, where they engaged the audio and tactile dimensions. Tomasso's presentation engaged extensively in play with representation, drawing upon the playfulness that was already a part of Pulcinella's traditional characterization as a paradoxical figure, and showing how the character could function as an available design for regional identities and more transcultural motifs. Carla's playful re-framing of the presentation as a virtual tour allowed her to not only recount but to re-imagine her trip to Orvieto for her fellow students.

In their presentations, Carla and Tomasso demonstrated academic literacy skills and language abilities that are part of more familiar teaching and assessment models; there was evidence of extensive research into their chosen topics, and they were designing meaning effectively, based on the responses of their classmates and instructors. Simultaneously, they were engaging affectively and aesthetically with the lifeworlds within which these themes were entangled, and they were inviting the rest of the class into their world building and play. Through the projects, they were given the opportunity to envision and design social, professional, and personal futures for themselves that could not have been anticipated by an instructor or curriculum designer. Through the speculative play that was enabled through the various phases of the project, language and literacy were not experienced as disembodied skills but were deeply ensconced in the students' social, emotional, and moral lives—which were themselves quite significantly multilingual lives.

Conclusion

A Critical-Aesthetic Multiliteracy Pedagogy for the Language-Culture Classroom

In this book, I have made the case that what I am calling multiliteracy play can help in realizing the paradigm shifts encouraged by contemporary scholarship in second language education and applied linguistics around the so-called *multi*-turn (see Introduction), especially those inspired by multiliteracies theories (see Chapter 1). Multiliteracy play, as I have defined it, is a shorthand for modes of engaging with language, language learning, and language teaching that attend to both those aspects of meaning that can be pinned down, analyzed, and conceptualized, and those dimensions of being in the flow of languaging activities, which do not fit tidily into thesis statements or even reflections, but make these same activities meaningful. The proposed ideal is a balance between **designs**, the repertoires of meaning-making resources available for communication and expression, and **desires**, the affective pushes and pulls that are in excess of those designed meanings, as well as the impressions and epiphanies that can come from engaging with designs in aesthetic ways (see also Ros i Solé 2016, 37).

Underlying the discussions of multiliteracy play brought together in this book, a core argument has been that contemporary second language-culture education requires a greater emphasis on critical-aesthetic perspectives and pedagogies to support them. In this concluding chapter, I pull the threads of that argument together into three proposed principles for what such a pedagogy for language-culture classrooms might entail. Because these are building on existing multiliteracies pedagogies, what I am offering is not a new model but rather a set of perspectives that can inform those existing frameworks, i.e., those described at length in Chapter 1 and summarized in my adapted version for fostering multiliteracy play at the end of Chapter 3.

Centering the Redesigners

Chapter 1 focused on multiliteracies frameworks as they have been developed in education and as they have been taken up in second language-culture teaching and learning. Across these fields, multiple theoretical models have emerged in recent decades, which act as helpful heuristics for noticing how elements of language and other modalities can be brought together to make meaning. These models are complemented by pedagogical frameworks, many taking direct inspiration from the four dimensions of learning identified in the New London Group's (1996) multiliteracies manifesto (and later re-worked by Cope and Kalantzis, e.g., 2000, 2009): situated practice (experiencing), overt instruction (conceptualizing), critical framing (analyzing), and transformed practice (applying) (see also Chapter 1). While they vary in their chosen metalanguages for both meaning designs and pedagogical acts of designing, they share in common an attention to language learners as agentful *designers*, who through the learning of new language and culture are expanding their own repertoires of *available designs*, as they engage in meaning-focused *designing* activities, through which they expand the scope of available designs and are also themselves potentially transformed, i.e., *redesigned*.

In exemplary curricula and models for teaching languages and culture as multiliteracies, the redesigned—the transformative potential of literacy activities—is the least theorized component (as I have argued in Chapter 1); one of the primary reasons for this is that the human subjectivities of learners/designers have been somewhat sidelined in many discussions of multiliteracies and language-culture education. While the notion of design does assume agency on the part of learners as designers of meaning themselves, agency is assumed to be largely synonymous with intention or purpose. In this purview, meanings are crafted because of goal-oriented design processes, and these directed language practices are the locus of language learning. Agency is enabled but bounded. Leander and Boldt (2018) drew attention to this effect of design as a metaphor, writing:

> [W]e are concerned that teachers and students are most idealized—or at least recognized—when they are unproblematically rational, unified and driven in a clearly goal-directed way. Teachers seem to have a general idea of where students need to end up, even if they don't know the particular content of that product. […]. In the relationship to the student, the teacher is static, already known and knowing, while the student continues to matter primarily as an object to be transformed along a preferred pathway …
>
> (35–6)

Teaching practices that idealize design in this way risk leaving little space for the kinds of meandering off the beaten path that can be truly transformative.

Language-culture learners are readers not only of words, but also of worlds and moreover they are voicers, actors, dreamers, feelers, and builders of worlds. I have borrowed Phipps and Gonzalez's term, *languagers*, throughout this book to try to capture the agentful view of the learner shared with multiliteracies frameworks, but also to recognize that the lived experience of stepping into others' ways of speaking, acting, and engaging in the world is, to use their phrase, often a "risky business" (Phipps and Gonzalez interview with Crosbie 2005, 295). The competencies and semiotic awareness that go into crafting the most well-designed texts are not—nor should they be—wards against the ontological and affective vulnerability that comes with redesigning meanings. As a notion for language teaching and learning, agency can empower learners, but it can also create a myopic view of learners as *those who design*, thereby neglecting the rich complexity of their multilingual subjectivities.

Making a related case, Kramsch (2006) reminds us that learners are "not just communicators and problem solvers, but whole humans with hearts, bodies, and minds, with memories, fantasies, loyalties, and identities" (251). Viewing learners holistically as thinking, feeling, sensing human beings enables educators to acknowledge an often-understated reality that truly transformative practice is really quite hard; transformation is intellectually as well as emotionally inflected, and the uncharted symbolic landscapes we enter into along the way are sometimes overspread with affective and ontological minefields. As they make their way in these new spaces, learners may occupy a range of different positions, from affect aliens to flaneurs to mediators to jokesters. These may not always appear to align with educators' understandings of overtly critical or conscious awareness, but we should also bear in mind that (trans)languaging is not only risky business but also a messy business, which cannot always be contained tidily in pedagogical maps and curricular pathways.

In reminding language educators of the complexity of learners' multilingual subjectivities, Kramsch is not offering educators a new checklist of individual factors, which can be checked off in the pursuit of the perfect classroom experience, if only we get things right. Instead, I read her emphasis on multilingual subjectivities as a reminder that as teachers, curriculum designers, and scholars we are always getting it a little wrong, in the sense that it is always going to be incomplete. In the student examples in Chapters 4–6, I have worked to show some of the glimpses that we, as educators and scholars, may get of the affective and aesthetic dimensions of students' engagements with texts and their designs; however, the discussions of Jaden and Klara in Chapter 2 are a reminder that our access to student experiences and what makes a series of languaging activities meaningful and perhaps even transformative over time can only ever be partially reassembled through the access points available to us (see also Johnson 2022). At best, educators can design a multiplicity of such points through in-class and out-of-class activities, including the kinds of designing and reflective activities showcased in Chapters 4–6.

Desire—as conceptualized in this book—can be understood as what we forget to pay attention to when we view meaning as most primarily or most significantly driven toward communicative purposes or intents. Making space for affect and aesthetics in language-culture learning does not require that we abandon completely the attention to available designs or communicative functions that often shape many curricula and learning objectives. The potential to foster effective intercultural, multilingual mediators may indeed be one of the most important lessons that second language teaching can impart. However, a multiliteracies pedagogy that attends to both designs and desires also recognizes that the complexity, precarity, and indeterminability of students' future lives call for capacities that well-designed utterances alone are insufficient to navigate. Attending to desires thus asks educators to infuse the activities through which students are asked to design and redesign meanings with space for movement, for learners and ourselves to be moved through thoughts, feelings, and relations that are shared and unshared, and for meaning making to be as much in the moment-to-moment experiences of living in relation to texts as in the destination.

Making Space: Language Teaching and Learning as an Open System

Centering learners as redesigners also has implications for how teachers think about themselves and their work. It requires what Cochran-Smith and Lytle (2015) describe as a *stance of inquiry*, which involves "a continual process of making current arrangements problematic" (121). As students are given room to engage in acts of redesigning meanings and relations, they will also take the texts and learning activities designed into language-culture curricula to task—sometimes deliberately and overtly, and sometimes in quieter, even sneakier ways that might be reminiscent of de Certeau's reading as poaching (see Chapter 3).

The implication for pedagogy is that planning is only part of the work of language-culture educators; how to be responsive and when to allow learners to follow desire lines that deviate from our carefully designed curriculum paths are a whole lot of the rest of it. The goal is not necessarily to reconcile the learning environments we have built and the wishful, even willful routes that students take, but rather to allow them to sit in productive tension, and in doing so to acknowledge there was never only one path, there was never only one way of designing.

One way of making space already implied in multiliteracies theories involves taking a more radical approach to the concept implied in the prefix *multi-*, i.e., one that sees multiplicity as fundamentally qualitative rather than quantitative. Viewing language and languaging in this way entails a recognition that texts, as they are encountered in the flow of life, are complex assemblages of modes, materialities, discourses, histories, responses, dialogues, and forces. This is what Leander and Ehret (2019), in their theorization of affective literacy studies, described as a shift from *with* to *and*. In language education, there is power in the *with*, to our careful attention to the functions of particular forms, how they are conventionally and thus recognizably used to make meaning. (See Chapter 1 for models of this in contemporary second language teaching and learning.) However, focusing, analyzing, and conceptualizing the resources *with* which meaning is made can at times seem to squeeze out the *and*—the in-the-moment-ness, the aesthetic, the sensations that make language meaningful (see Chapter 2).

In her conceptual treatise on the personal in language learning, Ros i Solé (2016) makes a related argument for the importance of viewing language learning as "art for art's sake" (37), that is, making space for aesthetic experiences with, in, and through new languages that are not immediately directed toward an instrumental or even developmental objective. One of the challenges for language and culture educators is thus how to reconcile an approach that prioritizes desires with institutionalized or at least institutionalizable assessment practices. As an example of current conversations around this topic, The Diversity, Decolonization, and the German Curriculum (DDGC) Collective, an association of educators and scholars working together to recognize the forms of systemic oppression inherent in fields of language-culture education such as German Studies, held a symposium in spring of 2023 on outcomes and assessment, where deliberate attention was paid to the personal dimensions of language learning.[1] In the opening discussion, one of the lead organizers, David Gramling, reminded participants of the relationship between teachers and learners implied by the Latin root of the word *assessment*, *assidere*, "to sit by," as in to sit by and evaluate or judge. In subsequent conversations, we ruminated on other ways of *sitting by* or even *sitting with* students. In one small group conversation where I was present, we considered the value of allowing learners to sometimes sit *by themselves* or even *in themselves*. Toying with the metaphor that is already built into educational discourses, we reflected on what it means to give students space—for their own sensations, perceptions, and emotions—and at what distance. The aesthetic modes of engaging with language and languaging encouraged through multiliteracy play, as it has been theorized in this book, are an attempt to build in moments, in which teachers and learners sit differently with one another and with others encountered through literacy activities, including reading, responding to, composing, and redesigning texts.

While recognizing the importance of the personal dimensions, it is simultaneously the case that learners, these social systems of meaning making, are never truly by themselves with new languages and cultures. The affective/aesthetic task at hand in the language-culture classroom is that of entering another's text and another's semiotic landscape. This is not only necessarily social but also an inherently political act. Making a case for affective ways of learning and knowing, Hickey-Moody (2013) notes that "[a]rt—film, games, dance, music, images—teaches us to feel in certain ways and those feelings have politics. The aesthetics of everyday life choreograph connections and resistance to people, situations and events" (83). Making space for the reader and text to dance together, to borrow another of de Certeau's reading metaphors (2014, 160), allows learners and teachers alike to view language as art for art's sake and then to step back and notice the feeling rules and emotions they assign to different ways of designing and being in the world, as well as how these may differ from those of others, whose sensations and perceptions are centered by particular designs, and whose are treated as most accessible or even universal. This is akin to what Spivak (2012) describes as holding several scripts open at once, and is essential, she insists, if one is to avoid erasing otherness as one enters another's text. The ethical implication is that the playful position of reading as poaching, suggested by de Certeau (2014), slides readily into a form of reappropriation or effacement, obscuring rather than revealing the forms of power that are also always at play in our affective and aesthetic entanglements with language and literacy. One of the most important questions for teachers and learners to explore through second language literacy is what it means to step into the symbolic spaces of others—and how to create hospitality for others in our own spaces.

Language-Culture Learning as Hopeful

As a pedagogical principle, *making space* may seem a little tenuous for a field such as language pedagogy, whose discourses are saturated with anticipatory notions like planning, outcomes, and curriculum. A point made in Chapter 2 bears repeating here—this book is not a rejection of pedagogical designs any more than it is a rejection of semiotic designs. All of these babies should sit cozily in their bathwater; this is, to torture a metaphor, a provocation to consider what else is happening during the bath besides the imminent and important act of getting the child clean—perhaps the parent sings, tickles toes, shares a giggle, soothes a cry, and all of this because they are nurturing a future for the baby that stands wide open, even if most pressingly they need to get through with bedtime and bath. Viewing the same activity on multiple timescales reveals that a measurable outcome can be important without it being the only matter at hand. The question is, what gets lost when we neglect our equivalents of songs, giggles, and cries? What dimensions of languaging are we missing out on in the classroom when the process of designing meaning is short circuited rather than open?

Hope is an affective attunement that recognizes what is happening here and now as only ever partial, dispersed, and plural (see Anderson 2006, 733–4). A hopeful stance toward language and culture teaching and learning aligns well with the notion of languages and language learning as open systems, by encompassing both the complex multiplicity of design and the unforeclosable nature of designing meaning. A text, an utterance, is only ever partially complete in the here and now exactly because it holds the potential to be redesigned—perhaps even by a language learner, whose playful acts of recreation (in both senses of the word) reveal available designs, possibilities for bricolage, that the composer never intended. Recognizing this play in language does not require us to dismiss perhaps more immediate curricular concerns for, say, the preterit, causal expressions, narrative genres or the many other available designs featured in second language learning objectives, but it asks us to allow a little room for the imagination. Writing on the role of imagination in education more broadly, Greene (2000) described imagination as a way of breaking with what is fixed and finished, through which a person may be "freed to glimpse what might be, to form notions of what should be, and what is not yet" even as that person may "at the same time, remain in touch with what presumably is" (19). Play, as defined in this book, is a mode of engaging with exactly this potential in language and other systems for designing meaning (see Chapter 3; see also Pahl and Poole 2020, 76).

To declare that language-culture learning is a hopeful activity is for me a way of acknowledging that learning outcomes, assessments, and grade reports are pressing and, in some cases, essential, but they are not the primary thing being nurtured through the experiences of the language classroom. And they should not be allowed to edge out the kinds of delighting, dreaming, imagining, transforming, and resignifying that feed language teaching and learning, as whole human activities. Hope is likewise a form of pedagogical humility, an acknowledgment that educators cannot anticipate all the desires and experiences of the learners who might enter their classrooms—and yet there should be space for all of them. Because hope is about potentials rather than outcomes, it can enable pedagogies that respond not to foregone conclusions about the social and work lives students might wish to design but to their capabilities for redesigning the world that exceed these expectations.

While no perfect pedagogy exists for the kind of teaching and learning by designs and desires that has been theorized in this book, through multiliteracy play we can attend to critical feeling as a way of knowing and languaging, and to our aesthetic capacity as humans with hearts, minds, and bodies to affect and to be affected by others. This may indeed be the more important gift of second language-culture teaching at exactly this historical moment where effectively designing meaning in different languages and modalities at the push of a button increasingly seems to be only just outside the reach of our fingertips. The capacities to reflect on our most favored forms of making sense of the world and to be open to the possibility of feeling and sensing otherwise, which language and culture learning can facilitate, are now perhaps more important than ever (see also Lemieux et al. 2022). While we may not know what the future holds, the challenges that are likely to face students in the coming decades will call upon them to consider not only what gets a meaning across but what makes something meaningful—and to recognize that in this they and the other humans with whom they share this planet are led as much by desires as we are by designs.

Notes

Introduction

1. This and all student names used throughout this book are pseudonyms.
2. Humbly borrowed from Mary Oliver's much-quoted line: "Doesn't everything die at last, and too soon? / Tell me, what is it you plan to do / with your one wild and precious life?"

Chapter 1

1. A summary of the debate around Amanda Gorman's poem can be found in the *New York Times* article "Amanda Gorman's Poetry United Critics. It's Dividing Translators," by Alex Marshall (March 26, 2021) https://www.nytimes.com/2021/03/26/books/amanda-gorman-hill-we-climb-translation.html.
2. The New London Group members were (in alphabetical order): Courtney Cazden (US), Bill Cope (Australia), Norman Fairclough (UK), James Gee (United States), Mary Kalantzis (Australia), Gunther Kress (UK), Allan Luke (Australia), Carmen Luke (Australia), Sarah Michaels (US), and Martin Nakata (Australia).
3. Cope and Kalantzis (2011) offer a more detailed discussion of this sociopolitical moment. See especially pages 49–52.
4. The terminology in second language studies fields tends to be a little looser in this regard, so terms like multiliteracies and multiple literacies or even literacy-oriented are used somewhat interchangeably. For the sake of consistency, I will tend toward the term "multiliteracies" throughout this section, indicating terminological differences only in instances where it feels key to understanding a particular scholar or concept.
5. See also Flores and Rosa (2022) for a critique of appropriateness in language education.
6. It is worth noting, however, that Bourdieu was critical of phenomenology, because he felt it over-emphasized cognitivist views of agency and consciousness and did not account sufficiently for the internalization of externalized "structuring structures" through which lived experience is always partly socially shaped (see Bourdieu 1977). This tension between structure and emergence also runs through the notion of design, especially when put into dialogue with desire and affect in later chapters of this book.

Chapter 2

1. These two names are pseudonyms.
2. This seminar was heavily inspired by a course I took with Claire Kramsch as a graduate student at the University of California, Berkeley.
3. It is worth noting here that Lantolf and Swain (2019) also distinguish between affect and feelings in their discussion of sociocultural theory and perezhivanie; however, the contrast they make is more a difference of timescale. For them affect is the more bounded term, because it is connected to a given situation, whereas feelings are unbounded and denote a general emotional orientation toward a person or circumstance. A parallel can be drawn here to Norton's concept of investment, which she proposes in part to account for the reality that a person can be motivated to learn a given language but not be invested in the particular practices of a given classroom and community (Norton and Darvin 2015, 37).
4. See Ahmed (1999) for her critical rereading of Deleuze and Guattari's book *A Thousand Plateaus*.
5. For an earlier discussion of Klara's case study see Warner (2023).
6. All student work in German is presented as it was written, including any deviations from standard spelling and grammar they may have contained.
7. For a previous discussion of Jaden see Warner and Richardson (2017).

Intermezzo

1. The translated poem "Intermezzo," from which this excerpt is borrowed, was published as part of an in memoriam collection of Janina Degutytė's works. (See Gražina M. Slavėnas (trans.), "Poems of Janina Degutytė," *Lituanus: Lithuanian Quarterly Journal of Arts and Sciences* 38, no. 4 (1992): n.p.)

Chapter 3

1. This and all names used in the subsequent chapters in this section are pseudonyms, unless otherwise specified.

Chapter 4

1. Some of the lessons developed as part of this curriculum development project are included as part of the *Foreign Languages and the Literary in the Everyday Project*, which can be found at fllite.org. A previous study from this curriculum, which includes some of the examples of the poems, was published by me in 2022 under the title "Playful designs: Multiliteracies and literariness in the beginning language classroom" in the journal *Foreign Language Annals*. Additional studies from the fourth semester course, which underwent a parallel curriculum reform, can be found in Richardson (2017) and Timlin et al. (2021).
2. The *Foreign Languages and the Literary in the Everyday (FLLITE) Project* can be found at https://fllite.org/. This particular lesson was published under a Creative Commons Attribution-ShareAlike as "Taking Inventory" ©2021 Chelsea Timlin and Chantelle Warner.
3. In American English "school" is used colloquially for university and college education as well as earlier grade levels.
4. Song's German text includes a dative construction, albeit using the wrong grammatical category for the word for freedom "Freiheit." This is not a grammatical concept students will have focused on intensely at this point, although they will have seen it in use. Given the context of the poem and the potential meaning of the dative in German, I have chosen to translate this as "for my freedom" but it is also possible that Song meant to just express "my freedom."

Chapter 5

1. The data in the chapter comes from a larger study conducted by Sara Alcazar as part of her dissertation research. Her full dissertation is titled *Symbolic Competence as a Means of Empowering Heritage Spanish Learners as Language Mediators* (2022).
2. These videos can be found at the Massachusetts Department of Public Health's YouTube channel, https://www.youtube.com/channel/UChbld2EgNwTyn7yuUjJIg6A.
3. As in other chapters, the student examples are presented here as they were submitted, including any typographical, orthographical, and grammatical errors and irregularities. For example, Spanish speakers will note instances where accent marks are missing or the verbs for "to be," *ser* and *estar* are switched. I will comment on these only when they are relevant to the analysis or when they might prove difficult to understand.

4 This is likely meant to be the word "empujones" (shoves). The structure used here, *no + noun*, is also a carryover from English.
5 Pixton can be found at https://www.pixton.com/

Chapter 6

1 My colleague Borbala Gaspar and I published a previous analysis of Tomasso and Clara's work in this class in 2021 under the title "Project-based learning and the development of translingual/transcultural subjectivities: Case studies from the Italian classroom" in the journal *Second Language Research and Practice*. This research served as a foundation for the discussion here.
2 This video can be found on YouTube at https://www.youtube.com/watch?v=PZFcl3MfgE0.

Conclusion

1 The symposium was "DDGC 2023: The Hotcomes Conference," and took place virtually from March 31 to April 1, 2023. Reports and shared outcomes from this event were published online at https://www.ddgccollective.org/ddgc-blog/working-toward-more-just-outcomes-in-language-and-culture-studies-a-report-and-resources-from-the-2023-ddgc-conference.

Bibliography

Adams, Vincanne, Michelle Murphy, and Adele E. Clarke. "Anticipation: Technoscience, life, affect, temporality." *Subjectivity* 28 (2009): 246–65.

Ahmed, Sara. "Phantasies of becoming (the Other)." *European Journal of Cultural Studies* 2, no. 1 (1999): 47–63.

Ahmed, Sara. *Cultural Politics of Emotion*. Edinburgh: Edinburgh University Press, 2004.

Ahmed, Sara. "Happy objects." In *The Affect Theory Reader*, edited by Melissa Gregg and Gregory J. Seigworth, 29–51. Durham, NC: Duke University Press, 2010.

Ahmed, Sara. *The Promise of Happiness*. New York: Duke University Press, 2020.

Alcázar Silva, Sara Melissa. *Symbolic Competence as a Means of Empowering Heritage Spanish Learners as Language Mediators*. Ph.D diss. Tucson: University of Arizona, 2022.

Allen, Heather Willis. "Embracing literacy-based teaching: A longitudinal study of the conceptual development of novice foreign language teachers." In *Research on Second Language Teacher Education. A Sociocultural Perspective on Professional Development*, edited by Karen Johnson and Paula Golombek, 86–101. New York: Routledge, 2011.

Allen, Heather Willis, and Beatrice Dupuy. "Evolving notions of literacy-based foreign language teaching: A qualitative study of graduate student instructors." In *Educating the Future Foreign Language Professoriate for the 21st Century*, edited by Heather Willis Allen and Hiram Maxim, 171–91. Boston: Heinle, 2013.

Allen, Heather Willis. "Redefining writing in the foreign language curriculum: Toward a design approach." *Foreign Language Annals* 51, no. 3 (2018): 513–32.

Allen, Heather Willis, and Kate Paesani. "Exploring the feasibility of a pedagogy of multiliteracies in introductory foreign language courses." *L2 Journal* 2, no. 1 (2010): 119–42.

Allen, Heather Willis, and Lauren Goodspeed. "Textual borrowing and perspective-taking: A genre-based approach to L2 writing." *L2 Journal* 10, no. 2 (2018): 87–110.

Álvarez Valencia, José Aldemar, and Kristen Michelson. "A design perspective on intercultural communication in second/foreign language education." *Journal of International and Intercultural Communication* 16, no. 4 (2022): 1–20.

Anderson, Ben. "Becoming and being hopeful: towards a theory of affect." *Environment and Planning: Society and Space* 24, no. 5 (2006): 733–52.

Anya, Uju. "African Americans in world language study: The forged path and future directions." *Annual Review of Applied Linguistics* 40 (2020): 97–112.

Anya, Uju. "The unbearable whiteness of communicative competence research: A commentary on 'Undoing competence: coloniality, homogeneity, and the overrepresentation of whiteness in applied linguistics.'" *Language Learning* (2022): 1–4.

Anya, Uju, and L.J. Randolph. "Diversifying language educators and learners." *The Language Educator* 10, no. 3 (2019): 23–27.

Arens, Katherine. "When comparative literature becomes cultural studies: Teaching cultures through genre." *The Comparatist* 29 (2005): 123–47.

Arnold, Jane, ed. *Affect in Language Learning*. Cambridge: Cambridge University Press, 1999.

Arnold, Jane, and H. Douglas Brown. "A map of the terrain." In *Affect in Language Learning*, edited by Jane Arnold, 8–12. Cambridge: Cambridge University Press, 1999.

Athanasiou, Athena, Pothiti Hantzaroula, and Kostas Yannakopoulos. "Towards a new epistemology: the 'affective turn.'" *Historein* 8 (2008): 5–16.

Bakhtin, Mikhail Mikhailovich. *The Dialogic Imagination: Four essays by M. M. Bakhtin*, edited by Michael Holquist. Translated by Caryl Emerson and Michael Holquist. Austin: University of Texas Press, 1981.

Barrette, Catherine M., Kate Paesani, and Kimberly Vinall. "Toward an Integrated curriculum: Maximizing the use of target language literature." *Foreign Language Annals* 43, no. 2 (2010): 216–30.

Barrineau, Susanna, Laila Mendy, and Anne-Kathrin Peters. "Emergentist education and the opportunities of radical futurity." *Futures* 144 (2022): 103062.

Barton, David. "Understanding textual practices in a changing world." In *The Future of Literacy Studies*, edited by Mike Baynham and Mastin Prinsloo, 38–53. London: Palgrave Macmillan, 2008.

Barton, David, and Mary Hamilton. *Local Literacies: Reading and Writing in One Community*. London: Routledge, 1998.

Barton, Georgina, and Margaret Baguley. "Learning through story: A collaborative, multimodal arts approach." *English Teaching: Practice and Critique* 13, no. 2 (2014): 93–112.

Bateson, Gregory. *Steps to an Ecology of Mind: Collected Essays in Anthropology, Psychiatry, Evolution, and Epistemology*. Chicago: University of Chicago, 1972.

Becker, Alton L. "The linguistics of particularity: Interpreting subordination in a Javanese text." In *Proceedings of the Tenth Annual Meeting of the Berkeley Linguistics Society*, edited by Claudia Brugman and Monica Macaulay, 425–36. Berkeley: Berkeley Linguistics Society, 1984.

Bell, Nancy D. "Exploring L2 language play as an aid to SLL: A case study of humour in NS–NNS interaction." *Applied Linguistics* 26, no. 2 (2005): 192–218.

Bell, Nancy. "Formulaic language, creativity, and language play in a second language." *Annual Review of Applied Linguistics* 32 (2012): 189–205.

Belz, Julie A. "Second language play as a representation of the multicompetent self in foreign language study." *Journal of Language, Identity, and Education* 1, no. 1 (2002): 13–39.

Benesch, Sarah. *Considering Emotions in Critical English Language Teaching*. New York: Routledge, 2012.

Benesch, Sarah. *Emotions and English Language Teaching: Exploring Teachers' Emotion Labor*. New York: Routledge, 2017.

Benson, Phil. "Learner-centered teaching." In *The Cambridge Guide to Pedagogy and Practice in Second Language Teaching*, edited by Anne Burns and Jack C. Richards, 30–37. Cambridge: Cambridge University Press, 2012.

Bensoussan, Marsha. "Beyond vocabulary: Pragmatic factors in reading comprehension—Culture, convention, coherence and cohesion." *Foreign Language Annals* 19, no. 5 (1986): 399–407.

Berg, William, and Laurey K. Martin-Berg. "A stylistic approach to Foreign language acquisition and literary analysis." In *SLA and the Literature Classroom: Fostering Dialogues*, edited by Virginia Scott and Holly Tucker, 186–204. Boston: Heinle, 2001.

Bernhardt, Elizabeth. *Reading Development in a Second Language: Theoretical, Research, and Classroom Perspectives*. Norwood, NJ: Ablex, 1991.

Bernstein, Basil. "On the classification and framing of educational knowledge." In *Knowledge and Control*, edited by Michael Young, 47–69. London: Collier-Macmillan, 1971.

Bialystok, Ellen. *Bilingualism in Development: Language, Literacy, and Cognition*. Cambridge: Cambridge University Press, 2001.

Bigelow, Martha. "Exploring social justice in world language education through the lens of pain." *The Modern Language Journal* 100 (2016): 554–5.

Bigelow, Martha. "(Re) considering the role of emotion in language teaching and learning." *The Modern Language Journal* 103, no. 2 (2019): 515–16.

Blommaert, Jan. *The Sociolinguistics of Globalization*. Cambridge: Cambridge University Press, 2010.

Blommaert, Jan, and Ben Rampton. "Language and superdiversity." *Diversities* 13, no. 2 (2011): 1–22.

Blyth, Carl. "Designing meaning and identity in multiliteracies pedagogy: From multilingual subjects to authentic speakers." *L2 Journal* 10, no. 2 (2018): 62–86.

Blyth, Carl, Chantelle Warner, and Joanna Luks. "The role of OER in promoting critical reflection and professional development: The Foreign Languages and the Literary in the Everyday Project. In *Open Education and Foreign Language Learning and Teaching: The Rise of a New Knowledge Ecology*, edited by Carl Blyth and Joshua Thoms, 158–82. Bristol: Multilingual Matters, 2021.

Boler, Megan, and Michalinos Zembylas. "Discomforting truths: The emotional terrain of understanding difference." In *Pedagogies of Difference*, edited by Peter Trifonas. New York: Routledge, 2003.

Bolter, Jay David. *Writing Space: the Computer, Hypertext, and the History of Writing.* New York/London: Routledge, 1990.

Bourdieu, Pierre. *Outline of a Theory of Practice.* Cambridge: Cambridge University Press, 1977.

Bourdieu, Pierre. *Le sens pratique.* Paris: Minuit, 1980.

Bradley, Adam. *Book of Rhymes: The Poetics of Hip Hop.* Philadelphia: BasicCivitas, 2017.

Bradley, Jessica, and Lou Harvey. "Creative inquiry in applied linguistics: Language, communication and the arts." In *Voices and Practices in Applied Linguistics: Diversifying a Discipline,* edited by Clare Wright, Lou Harvey, and James Simpson, 91–107. York: White Rose University Press, 2019.

Bredella, Lothar, and Werner Delanoy, eds. *Challenges of Literary Texts in the Foreign Language Classroom.* Tübingen: Gunter Narr Verlag, 1996.

Breen, Michael, and Christopher Candlin. "The essentials of a communicative curriculum in language teaching." *Applied Linguistics* 1, no. 2 (1980): 89–112.

Broner, Maggie A., and Elaine E. Tarone. "Is it fun? Language play in a fifth-grade Spanish immersion classroom." *The Modern Language Journal* 85, no. 3 (2001): 363–79.

Brussig, Thomas. *Helden wie wir.* Berlin: Volk and Welt, 1995.

Budach, Gabriele, Gohar Sharoyan, and Daniela Loghin. "'Animating objects': Co-creation in digital story making between planning and play." In *Liberating Language Education,* edited by Vally Lytra, Vicky Macleroy, Cristina Ros i Solé, Jim Anderson, 277–97. Multilingual Matters, 2022.

Busch, Brigitta. "Expanding the notion of the linguistic repertoire: On the concept of Spracherleben—The lived experience of language." *Applied Linguistics* 38, no. 3 (2017): 340–58.

Busch, Brigitta. "The language portrait in multilingualism research: Theoretical and methodological considerations." *Working Papers in Urban Language and Literacies* 236 (2018): 1–13.

Busch, Brigitta. "The linguistic repertoire revisited." *Applied Linguistics* 33, no. 5 (2012): 502–23.

Byram, Michael. "'Cultural awareness' as vocabulary learning." *Language Learning Journal* 16, no. 1 (1997): 51–57.

Byram, Katra, and Claire Kramsch. "Why is it so difficult to teach language as culture?" *The German Quarterly* 81, no. 1 (2008): 20–34.

Byrd Clark, Julie, and Fred Dervin. *Reflexivity in Language and Intercultural Education.* London and New York: Routledge, 2014.

Byrnes, Heidi. "Constructing curricula in collegiate foreign language departments." In *Learning Foreign and Second Languages: Perspectives in Research and Scholarship,* edited by Heidi Byrnes, 262–95. New York: MLA, 1998.

Byrnes, Heidi, ed. *Advanced Language Learning: The Contribution of Halliday and Vygotsky.* London: Continuum, 2006.

Byrnes, Heidi. "Articulating a foreign language sequence through content: A look at the culture standards." *Language Teaching* 41, no. 1 (2008): 103–18.

Byrnes, Heidi. "What kind of resource Is language and why does it matter for German studies?" *The German Quarterly* 81, no. 1 (2008): 8–19.

Byrnes, Heidi, and Katherin Sprang. "Fostering advanced L2 literacy: A genre-based, cognitive approach." In *Advanced Foreign Language Learning: A Challenge to College Programs*, edited by Heidi Byrnes and Hiram Maxim, 47–85. Boston: Heinle, 2004.

Byrnes, Heidi, and Susanne Kord. "Developing literacy and literary competence: Challenges for Foreign language departments." In *SLA and the Literature Classroom: Fostering Dialogues*, edited by Virginia Scott and Holly Tucker, 35–72. Boston: Heinle, 2001.

Byrnes, Heidi, Hiram Maxim, and John Norris. "Realizing advanced foreign language writing development in collegiate education: Curricular design, pedagogy, assessment." *Modern Language Journal* 94 (2010): 1–235.

Byrnes, Heidi, Cori Crane, Hiram H. Maxim, and Katherine A. Sprang. "Taking text to task: Issues and choices in curriculum construction." *International Journal of Applied Linguistics* 152, no. 1 (2006): 85–110.

Callois, Roger. *Man, Play and Games*, translated by Meyer Barash. Urbana and Chicago, IL: University of Illinois Press, 2001[1958].

Canagarajah, Suresh. "Code meshing in academic writing: Multilingual translanguaging strategies." *Modern Language Journal* 95, no. 3 (2006): 401–7.

Canagarajah, Suresh. *Translingual Practice: Global Englishes and Cosmopolitan Relations*. New York: Routledge, 2013.

Canale, Michael, and Merrill Swain. "Theoretical bases of communicative approaches to second language teaching and testing." *Applied Linguistics* 1 (1980): 1–47.

Carr, Jo. "From 'sympathetic' to 'dialogic' imagination: Cultural study in the foreign language classroom." In *Striving for the Third Place: Intercultural Competence through Language Education*, edited by Joseph Lo Bianco, Anthony J. Liddicoat, and Chantal Crozet, 103–12. Melbourne: Language Australia, 1999.

Carrell, Patricia. "Schema theory and ESL reading: Classroom implications and applications." *Modern Language Journal* 68, (1984): 332–43.

Carroli, Piera. *Literature in Second Language Education: Enhancing the Role of Texts in Learning*. London/New York: Continuum, 2008.

Carter, Ronald. "Language awareness." *ELT Journal* 57, no. 1 (2003): 64–5.

Carter, Ronald, and John McRae, eds. *Language, Literature and the Learner*. London/New York: Routledge, 2014.

Cazden, Courtney. *Classroom Discourse: The Language of Teaching and Learning*. Portsmouth, NH: Heinemann, 1988.

Chen, Hsin-I. "Identity practices of multilingual writers in social networking spaces." *Language Learning and Technology* 17, no. 2 (2013): 143–70.

Choi, Jayoung. "A heritage language learner's literacy practices in a Korean language course in a US university: From a multiliteracies perspective." *Journal of Language and Literacy Education*, 11, no. 2 (2015): 116–33.

Clough, Patricia, and Jean Hailey, eds. *The Affective Turn: Theorizing the Social*. Durham, NC: Duke University Press, 2007.

Cochran-Smith, Marilyn, and Susan L. Lytle. *Inquiry as Stance: Practitioner Research for the Next Generation*. New York: Teachers College Press, 2008.

Coda, James. "Disrupting standard practice: queering the world language classroom." *Dimension* 74 (2017): 89.

Cole, David R. "Affective literacies: Deleuze, discipline and power." In *Deleuze and Education*, edited by Inna Semetsky, 94–112. Edinburgh: Edinburgh University Press, 2013.

Colombi, María Cecilia, and Mariana Achugar. "Systemic functional linguistic explorations into the longitudinal study of advanced capacities: The case of Spanish heritage language learners." In *The Longitudinal Study of Advanced L2 Capacities*, edited by Lourdes Ortega and Heidi Byrnes, 36–57. New York: Routledge, 2008.

Colombi, María Cecilia, and Mary J. Schleppegrell, eds. *Developing Advanced Literacy in First and Second Languages: Meaning with Power*. London: Taylor and Francis, 2002.

Cook, Guy. "Language play in English." In *Using English: From Conversation to Canon*, edited by Janet Maybin and Neil Mercer, 224–31. London: Routledge, 1996.

Cook, Guy. "Language play, language learning." *ELT Journal* 51, no. 3 (1997): 224–31.

Cook, Guy. *Language Play, Language Learning*. Oxford: Oxford University Press, 2000.

Cope, Bill, and Mary Kalantzis. *Multiliteracies: Literacy Learning and the Design of Social Futures*. London/New York: Routledge, 2000.

Cope, Bill, and Mary Kalantzis. "Designs for social futures." In *Multiliteracies*, edited by Bill Cope and Mary Kalantzis, 201–32. London/New York: Routledge, 2005[1999].

Cope, Bill, and Mary Kalantzis, eds. *Multiliteracies in Motion*. London /New York: Routledge, 2009.

Cope, Bill, and Mary Kalantzis. "'Design' in principle and practice: A reconsideration of the terms of design engagement." *The Design Journal* 14, no. 1 (2011): 45–63.

Cope, Bill, and Mary Kalantzis. *A Pedagogy of Multiliteracies: Learning by Design*. London: Palgrave, 2015.

Council of Europe. *Common European Framework of Reference for Languages: Learning, Teaching, Assessment*. Cambridge: Cambridge University Press, 2001.

Council of Europe. *Common European Framework of Reference for Languages: Learning, Teaching, Assessment. Companion Volume with New Descriptors*. Strasbourg: Council of Europe, 2018.

Creese, Angela, and Adrian Blackledge. "Translanguaging and identity in educational settings." *Annual Review of Applied Linguistics* 35 (2015): 20–35.

Crosbie, Veronica. "Future directions for modern languages in the higher education landscape: An interview with Alison Phipps and Mike Gonzalez." *Language and Intercultural Communication* 5, no. 3–4 (2005): 294–303.

Crystal, David. *Language Play*. Chicago: University of Chicago Press, 2001.
Darvin, Ron, and Bonny Norton. "Identity and a model of investment in applied linguistics." *Annual Review of Applied Linguistics* 35 (2015): 36–56.
De Certeau, Michel. *The Practice of Everyday Life*, translated by Steven Rendall. Berkeley: University of California Press, 1984.
De Certeau, Michel. "Reading as poaching." In *Readers and Reading*, edited by Andrew Bennett, 150–63. London/New York: Routledge, 2014.
De Costa, Peter. "Elite multilingualism, affect and neoliberalism." *Journal of Multilingual and Multicultural Development* 40, no. 5 (2019): 453–60.
Deleuze, Gilles. *Spinoza: Practical Philosophy*. San Francisco: City Lights Books, 1988.
Deleuze, Gilles. "Spinoza and the three ethics." In *Essays Critical and Clinical*, trans. Daniel W. Smith and Michael A. Greco, 138–51. London/New York, Verso, 1997.
Deleuze, Gilles, and Félix Guattari. *A Thousand Plateaus: Capitalism and Schizophrenia*, translated by Brian Massumi. Minneapolis: University of Minnesota, 1987[1980].
Deleuze, Gilles, and Félix Guattari. *What Is Philosophy?* New York: Columbia University Press, 1994.
Derrida, Jacques. "Structure, sign, and play in the discourse of the human sciences." In *Writing and Difference*, edited by Alan Bass, 278–93. London/New York: Routledge, 2007[1967].
Dervin, Fred. "Towards post-intercultural teacher education: Analysing 'extreme 'intercultural dialogue to reconstruct interculturality." *European Journal of Teacher Education* 38, no. 1 (2015): 71–86.
Dervin, Fred, and Karen Risager, eds. *Researching Identity and Interculturality*. London/New York: Routledge, 2014.
Dewaele, Jean-Marc. "Investigating the psychological and emotional dimensions in instructed language learning: Obstacles and possibilities." *The Modern Language Journal* 89, no. 3 (2005): 367–80.
Dewaele, Jean-Marc, and Chengchen Li. "Emotions in second language acquisition: A critical review and research agenda." *Foreign Language World* 196, no. 1 (2020): 34–49.
Diaz, Adrianna. *Developing Critical Languaculture Pedagogies in Higher Education: Theory and Practice*. Bristol: Multilingual Matters, 2013.
Dörnyei, Zoltán. "New themes and approaches in second language motivation research." *Annual Review of Applied Linguistics* 21 (2001): 43–59.
Dornyei, Zoltán. *The Psychology of the Language Learner: Individual Differences in Second Language Acquisition*. London/New York: Routledge, 2005.
Dörnyei, Zoltán. "Individual differences: Interplay of learner characteristics and learning environment." *Language Learning* 59 (2009): 230–48.
Dörnyei, Zoltán, and Ema Ushioda. *Teaching and Researching Motivation*. London/New York: Routledge, 2021.
Douglas Fir Group. "A transdisciplinary framework for SLA in a multilingual world." *Modern Language Journal* 100 (2016): 19–47.

Dubreil, Sebastien, and Steven Thorne. "Social pedagogies and entwining language with the world." In *Engaging the World: Social Pedagogies and Language Learning*, edited by Sebastien Dubreil and Steven Thorne, 1–11. Boston: Cengage, 2017.

Ducate, Lara, and Lara Lomicka. "Adventures in the blogosphere: From blog readers to blog writers." *Computer Assisted Language Learning* 21, no. 1 (2008): 9–28.

Dulay, Heidi, and Marina Burt. "Remarks on creativity in language acquisition." In *Viewpoints on English as a Second Language in Honor of James E. Alatis*, edited by Marina Burt and Mary Finocchiaro, 95–126. New York: Regents Publishing Company, 1977.

Dupuy, Beatrice, and Kristen Michelson, eds. *Pathways to Paradigm Change: Critical Examinations of Prevailing Discourses and Ideologies of Second Language Education*. Boston: Cengage, 2019.

Durand, Alain-Philippe, and Ken S. McAllister. "Humanities= Jobs: The tactics of contrarian entrepreneurial humanists." *ADFL Bulletin* 47, no. 2 (2022): 82–98.

Duranti, Alessandro. "Performance and encoding of agency in historical-natural languages." *Texas Linguistic Forum* 44, no. 2 (2001): 266–87.

Ehret, Christian. "Propositions from affect theory for feeling literacy through the event." In *Theoretical Models and Processes of Literacy*, edited by Donna Alvermann, Norman Unrau, Misty Sailors and Robert B. Ruddell, 563–81. New York: Routledge, 2018.

Ehret, Christian, and Jennifer Rowsell. "Literacy, affect, and uncontrollability." *Reading Research Quarterly* 56, no. 2 (2021): 201–6.

Eich, Gunter. "Inventur." In *Gesammelte Werke in vier Bänden 1*, edited by Axel Vieregg. Frankfurt am Main: Suhrkamp Verlag, 1991[1945].

Elsner, Daniela, Sissy Helff, and Britta Viebrock, eds. *Films, Graphic Novels and Visuals: Developing Multiliteracies in Foreign Language Education: An Interdisciplinary Approach*, Vol. 2. Münster: LIT Verlag, 2013.

Embeywa, Richmond. *Ideologies on Learner Subjectivity in the German Integration Course*, Ph.D diss. Tucson: University of Arizona, 2023.

Fairclough, Norman. *Discourse and Social Power*. London: Polity Press, 1992.

Finke, Ronald A. "Imagery, creativity, and emergent structure." *Consciousness and Cognition* 5, no. 3 (1996): 381–93.

Firth, Alan, and Johannes Wagner. "On discourse, communication, and (some) fundamental concepts in SLA research." *The Modern Language Journal* 81, no. 3 (1997): 285–300.

Flores, Nelson. "The unexamined relationship between neoliberalism and plurilingualism: A cautionary tale." *TESOL Quarterly* 47, no. 3 (2013): 500–20.

Freire, Paulo. *Pedagogy of the Oppressed*, translated by Myra Bergman Ramos. New York: Continuum, 2007[1970].

Freire, Paulo. *Pedagogy of the Heart*. New York/London: Bloomsbury Publishing, 2021[1988].

Freire, Paulo, and Donaldo Macedo. *Literacy: Reading the Word and the World*. London/New York: Routledge, 2005[1987].

Flores, Nelson, and Jonathan Rosa. "Undoing competence: Coloniality, homogeneity, and the overrepresentation of whiteness in applied linguistics." *Language Learning* (2022): 1–26.

Frei, Chistina, Bridget Levine-West, and Glenn Levine-West. *Augenblicke: German Through Film, Media and Texts*. Ann Arbor, MI: XanEdu, 2021.

Futro, Dobrochna. "Translanguaging art: Exploring the transformative potential of contemporary art for language teaching in the multilingual context." In *Liberating Language Education*, edited by Vally Lytra, Cristina Ros i Solé, Jim Anderson and Vicky Macleroy, 226–247. Bristol Multilingual Matters, 2022.

Garcia, Antero, and Robyn Seglem. "Twenty years of multiliteracies: Moving from theory to social change in literacies and beyond," special volume of *Theory in Practice* 57, no. 1 (2018).

Garcia, Antero, Allan Luke, and Robyn Seglem. "Looking at the next 20 years of multiliteracies: A discussion with Allan Luke." *Theory into Practice* 57, no. 1 (2018): 72–8.

García, Ofelia, and Claire E. Sylvan. "Pedagogies and practices in multilingual classrooms: Singularities in pluralities." *The Modern Language Journal* 95, no. 3 (2011): 385–400.

Gaspar, Borbala. *Shifting Goals in Italian Learning: Imagination, Multilingualism, and Agency in the Narratives of Underrepresented Foreign Language Learners*. Ph.D diss. The University of Arizona, 2020.

Gavins, Joanna. "Text-worlds." In *The Bloomsbury Companion to Stylistics*, edited by Violeta Sotirova. London: Bloomsbury, 2016.

Gavins, Joanna, and Ernestine Lahey, eds. *World Building: Discourse in the Mind*. London: Bloomsbury Publishing, 2016.

Gee, James. *The New Work Order*. London/New York: Routledge, 2018.

Gee, James Paul. "Literacies, identities, and discourses." In *Developing Advanced Literacy in First and Second Languages: Meaning with Power*, edited by Maria Cecilia Colombi, Mary J. Schleppegrell, 159–75. London: Taylor and Francis, 2002.

Gee, James Paul. *Social Linguistics and Literacies: Ideology in Discourses*, 3rd ed. London: Routledge, 2007[1990].

Gee, James Paul. *New Digital Media and Learning as an Emerging Area and "Worked Examples" As One Way Forward*. Cambridge, MA: The MIT Press, 2009.

Geertz, Clifford. *The Interpretation of Cultures*. New York: Basic Books, 1973.

Geisler, Michael, Claire Kramsch, Scott McGinnis, Peter Patrikis, Mary Louise Pratt, Karin Ryding, and Haun Saussy. "Foreign languages and higher education: New structures for a changed world: MLA ad hoc committee on foreign languages." *Profession* (2007): 234–45.

Goffman, Erving. *Frame Analysis: An Essay on The Organization of Experience*. Cambridge, MA: Harvard University Press, 1974.

Goffman, Erving. *Forms of Talk*. Philadelphia, PA: University of Pennsylvania Press, 1981.

Golombek, Paula and Karen Johnson. "Narrative inquiry as a mediational space: examining emotional and cognitive dissonance in second language teachers' development." *Teachers and Teaching* 10, no. 3 (2004): 307–27.

Gramling, David. *The Invention of Monolingualism*. London: Bloomsbury, 2016.

Gramling, David. *The Invention of Multilingualism*. Cambridge: Cambridge University Press, 2021.

Gramling, David. "Building a new public idea about Multilingualism." *Cadernos de Tradução* 40, no. 3 (2020): 15–32.

Gramling, David, and Chantelle Warner. "Toward a contact pragmatics of literature: habitus, text, and the advanced L2 classroom." In *Critical and Intercultural Theory and Language Pedagogy*, edited by Glenn Levine and Alison Phipps, 57–75. Boston, MA: Heinle, 2011.

Gramling, David J., and Chantelle Warner. "Whose 'crisis in language'? Translating and the futurity of foreign language learning." *L2 Journal* 8, no. 4 (2016).

Greene, Maxine. "Curriculum and consciousness." *Teachers College Record* 73, no. 2 (1971): 253–69.

Greene, Maxine. *Releasing the Imagination: Essays on Education, the Arts, and Social Change*. Hoboken, NJ: Wiley, 2000.

Gregg, Melissa, and Gregory J. Seigworth, eds. *The Affect Theory Reader*. Durham, NC: Duke University Press, 2010.

Guattari, Felix. *The Guattari Reader*, edited by Gary Genosko. Oxford; Cambridge, MA: Blackwell Publishers, 1996.

Hall, Geoff. *Literature in Language Education*. Basingstroke: Springer, 2005.

Hallet, Wolfgang. "Literature and Literacies: Literarische Bildung als Paradigma für Standardisierung, Differenz und Heterogenität." In *Bildung zwischen Standardisierung und Heterogenität*, edited by Carl-Peter Buschkühle, Ludwig Duncker, Vadim Oswalt, 53–80. Wiesbaden: Springer, 2009.

Halliday, M. A. K. *Language as Social Semiotic: The Social Interpretation of Language and Meaning*. London: Edward Arnold, 1978.

Halliday, M.A.K. "Spoken and written modes of meaning." *Media Texts: Authors and Readers* 7 (1994): 51–73.

Halliday, M.A.K. "On grammar and grammatics." *Amsterdam Studies in the Theory and History of Linguistic Science Series* 3 (1996): 1–38.

Halliday, M.A.K. *On Grammar: Volume 1*. London/New York: Continuum, 2002.

Hanna, Barbara and Juliana de Nooy. "A funny thing happened on the way to the forum: Electronic discussion and foreign language learning." *Language Learning and Technology* 7, no. 1 (2003): 71–85.

Harris, Roy. *Introduction to Integrational Linguistics*. Oxford: Pergamon, 1998.

Hasan, Ruqaiya. "Semiotic mediation and mental development in pluralistic societies: Some implications for tomorrow's schooling." In *Learning for Life in the 21st Century: Socio-Cultural Perspectives on The Future of Education*, edited by Gordon Wells and Guy Claxton, 112–26. Oxford, England: Blackwell, 2002.

Heath, Shirley Brice. *Ways with Words: Language, Life and Work in Communities and Classrooms*. Cambridge, England: Cambridge University Press, 1983.

Hedgock, John S., and Dana R. Ferris. *Teaching Readers of English*. New York: Routledge, 2009.

Heine, Heinrich. "Heimkehr". In *Lieder und Gedichte*, edited by C.A. Buchheim, 71–72. London: Macmillan, 1924.

Helland, Kristin I. "Mona AKA Sad Girl: A multilingual multimodal critical discourse analysis of music videos of a Japanese Chicana rap artist." *Discourse, Context and Media* 23 (2018): 25–40.

Heller, Monica. "The commodification of language." *Annual Review of Anthropology*, 39 (2010): 101–14.

Heller, Monica, and Bonnie McElhinny. *Language, Capitalism, Colonialism: Toward a Critical History*. Toronto: University of Toronto Press, 2017.

Hickey-Moody, Anna. "Affect as method: Feelings, aesthetics and affective pedagogy." In *Deleuze and Research Methodologies*, edited by Rebecca Coleman, 79–95. Edinburgh: Edinburgh University Press, 2013.

Hollett, Ty. "The felt-force of literacy." *Reading Research Quarterly* 56, no. 2 (2021): 369–72.

Huizinga, Johan. *Homo Ludens: A Study of the Play Element in Culture*. Boston, MA: Beacon Press, 1955 [1938].

Hymes, Dell. "On communicative competence." In *Sociolinguistics. Selected Readings*, edited by J.B. Pride and Janet Holmes, 269–93. Harmondsworth: Penguin, 1972.

Jewitt, Carey. *Introduction*. In *The Routledge Handbook of Multimodal Analysis*, edited by Cary Jewitt, 1–7. Abingdon: Routledge, 2009.

Jimenez-Silva, Margarita, Gomez Laura, and Jesus Cisneros. "Examining Arizona's policy response post Flores v. Arizona in educating K–12 English language learners." *Journal of Latinos in Education* 13, no. 3 (2014): 181–95.

Johnson, Karen, and Paula Golombek. "'Seeing' teacher learning." *TESOL Quarterly* 37, no. 4 (2003): 729–37.

Johnson, Stacey Margarita. "Who is at the center of our language teaching?" *Second Language Research and Practice* 3, no. 1 (2022): 116–27.

Johnson, Stacey Margarita. "Authentic resources and written reflection as contributors to transformative learning." In *Transformative Language Learning and Teaching*, edited by Betty Lou Leaver, Dan E. Davidson, and Christine Campbell, 71–9. Cambridge: Cambridge University Press, 2021.

Kaiser, Mark. "Teaching a film clip in a multiliteracies framework." *L2 Journal* 10, no. 3 (2018): 47–57.

Kearney, Erin. "A high-leverage language teaching practice: Leading an open-ended group discussion." *Foreign Language Annals* 48, no. 1 (2015): 100–23.

Kell, Catherine. "Ariadne's thread: Literacy, scale and meaning-making across space and time." In *Language, Literacy and Diversity*, edited by Christopher Stroud and Mastin Prinsloo, 88–107. New York/London: Routledge, 2015.

Kern, Richard. *Literacy and Language Learning*. Oxford: Oxford University Press, 2000.

Kern, Richard. "Technology as Pharmakon: The promise and perils of the internet for foreign language education." *The Modern Language Journal* 98, no. 1 (2014): 340–57.

Kern, Richard, and Jean Marie Schultz. "Beyond orality: Investigating literacy and the literary in second and foreign language instruction." *The Modern Language Journal* 89, no. 3 (2005): 381–92.

Kirsch, Sarah. "Naturschutzgebiet." In *Erdreich. Gedichte*, 181. Stuttgart: DVA, 1982.

Kitwana, Bakari. *Why White Kids Love Hip-Hop: Wankstas, Wiggers, Wannabes, and The New Reality of Race in America*. New York: Civitas Books, 2005.

Knisely, Kris Aric. "Le français non- binaire: Linguistic forms used by non- binary speakers of French." *Foreign Language Annals* 53, no. 4 (2020): 850–76.

Knisely, Kris Aric. "L/G/B and T: Queer excisions, entailments, and intersections." In *Intersectional Perspectives On LGBTQ+ Issues in Modern Language Teaching and Learning*, edited by Joshua M. Paiz and James E. Coda, 153–82. Cham, Switzerland: Palgrave Macmillan, 2021.

Knisely, Kris Aric, and Joshua M. Paiz "Bringing trans, non-binary, and queer understandings to bear in language education." *Critical Multilingualism Studies* 9, no. 1 (2021): 23–45.

Knobel, Michele, and Colin Lankshear, eds. *A New Literacies Sampler*. New York: Peter Lang, 2007.

Kramsch, Claire. *Context and Culture in Language Teaching*. Oxford: Oxford University Press, 1993.

Kramsch, Claire. The language teacher as go-between." *Utbildning & Demokrati- tidskrift för didaktik och utbildningspolitk* 13, no. 3 (2004): 37–60.

Kramsch, Claire. "From Communicative Competence to Symbolic Competence." *Modern Language Journal* 90, no. 2 (2006): 249–52.

Kramsch, Claire. "Ecological perspectives on foreign language education." *Language Teaching* 41 (2008): 389–408.

Kramsch, Claire. *The Multilingual Subject*. Oxford: Oxford University Press, 2009.

Kramsch, Claire "The symbolic dimensions of the intercultural." *Language Teaching* 44, (2011): 354–67.

Kramsch, Claire, and Thomas Nolden. "Redefining literacy in a foreign language." *Die Unterrichtspraxis: Teaching College German* 27, no. 1 (1994): 28–35.

Kramsch, Claire, and Sune Vork Steffensen. "Ecological perspectives on second language acquisition and socialization." *Encyclopedia of Language and Education* 8 (2008): 17–28.

Kramsch, Claire, and Anne Whiteside. "Language ecology in multilingual settings. Towards a theory of symbolic competence." *Applied Linguistics* 29, no. 4 (2008): 645–71.

Kramsch, Claire, Geneviève Zarate, and Danielle Levy. *Handbook Multilingualism and Multiculturalism*. Paris: Éd. des Archives contemporaines, 2008.

Kramsch, Claire, and Lihua Zhang. *The Multilingual Instructor*. Oxford: Oxford University Press, 2017.

Krashen, Stephen. *Principles and Practice in Second Language Acquisition*. New York: Pergamon Press, 1982.

Krashen, Stephen D., and Tracy Terrell. *Natural Approach*. New York: Pergamon, 1983.

Krashen, Stephen D., Tracy D. Terrell, Madeline E. Ehrman, and Martha Herzog. "A theoretical basis for teaching the receptive skills." *Foreign Language Annals* 17, no. 4 (1984): 261.

Kress, Gunther. *Linguistic Process and Sociocultural Change*. Oxford: Oxford University Press, 1990.

Kress, Gunther. "Multimodality: Challenges to thinking about language." *TESOL Quarterly* 34, no. 2 (2000): 337–40.

Kress, Gunther. *Literacy in the New Media Age*. London: Psychology Press, 2003.

Kress, Gunther. "Design: The rhetorical work of shaping the semiotic world." In *Multimodal Approaches to Research and Pedagogy*, edited by Arlene Archer and Denise Newfield, 149–78. London: Routledge, 2014.

Kress, Gunther, and Theo van Leeuwen. *Reading Images: The Grammar of Visual Design*, 3rd ed. London: Routledge, 2021[1996].

Kristeva, Julia. *Desire in Language: A Semiotic Approach to Literature and Art*. New York: Columbia University Press, 1980.

Krueger, Cheryl. "Form, content, and critical cistance: The role of 'creative personalization' in language and content courses." *Foreign Language Annals* 34, no. 1 (2001): 18–25.

Kubota, Ryuko. "Learning a foreign language as leisure and consumption: Enjoyment, desire, and the business of *eikaiwa*." *International Journal of Bilingual Education and Bilingualism*, 14, no. 4 (2011): 473–88.

Kubota, Ryuko. "The multi/plural turn, postcolonial theory, and neoliberal multiculturalism: Complicities and implications for applied linguistics." *Applied Linguistics*, 37, no. 4 (2016): 474–94.

Kubota, Ryuko, and Angel Lin, eds. *Race, Culture, and Identities in Second Language Education: Exploring Critically Engaged Practice*. London/New York: Routledge, 2009.

Kumagai, Yuri, Keiko Konoeda, Miyuki Nishimata (Fukai), and Shinji Sato. "Fostering multimodal literacies in the japanese language classrooms: Digital video projects." In *Multiliteracies in World Language Education*, edited by Ana López-Sánchez, Yuri Kumagai and Sujane Wu, 153–75. London/New York: Routledge, 2016.

Lankshear, Colin, and Michele Knobel. *New Literacies: Everyday Practices and Social Learning*. New York: McGraw-Hill Education/Open University Press, 2011.

Lantolf, James P. "The function of language play in the acquisition of L2 Spanish." In *Contemporary Perspectives on the Acquisition of* Spanish, edited by Ana Teresa Pérez-Leroux and William R. Glass, 3–24. Somerville, MA: Cascadilla Press, 1997.

Lantolf, James P. "Motivational dialogue in the second language setting." *International Journal of TESOL Studies* 3, no. 3 (2021): 1–22.

Lantolf, James P., and Merrill Swain. "Perezhivanie: The cognitive–emotional dialectic within the social situation of development." *Contemporary Language Motivation Theory* 60 (2019): 80–105.

Lantolf, James P., and María-del-Carmen Yáñez. "Talking yourself into Spanish: Intrapersonal communication and second language learning." *Hispania* 86 (2003): 97–109.

Lau, Sunny Man Chu. "Language, identity, and emotionality: Exploring the potential of language portraits in preparing teachers for diverse learners." *The New Educator* 12, no. 2 (2016): 147–70.

Leander, Kevin, and Gail Boldt. "Rereading 'A Pedagogy of Multiliteracies' bodies, texts, and emergence." *Journal of Literacy Research*, 45, no. 1 (2013): 22–46.

Leander, Kevin, and Gail Boldt. "Design, desire, and difference." *Theory Into Practice* 57, no. 1 (2018): 29–37.

Leander, Kevin and Christian Ehret, eds. *Affect in Literacy Learning and Teaching: Pedagogies, Politics and Coming to Know*. London/New York: Routledge, 2019.

Leander, Kevin, and Deborah Wells Rowe. "Mapping literacy spaces in motion: A rhizomatic analysis of a classroom literacy performance." *Reading Research Quarterly* 41, no. 4 (2006): 428–60.

Lee, James, and Bill VanPatten. *Making Communicative Language Teaching Happen*. Boston: McGraw-Hill, 1995.

Lemieux, Amélie, Kelly Johnston, and Fiona Scott. "Attending to our response-abilities: Diff/reading data through pedagogies of the other-wise." In *Unsettling Literacies: Directions for Literacy Research in Precarious Times*, edited by Claire Lee, Chris Bailey, Cathy Burnett and Jennifer Rowsell 67–81. Singapore: Springer, 2022.

Leung, Constance, and Angela Scarino. "Reconceptualizing the nature of goals and outcomes in language/s education." *The Modern Language Journal* 100, no. S1 (2016): 81–95.

Levi-Strauss, Claude. *The Savage Mind*. Chicago: University of Chicago Press, 1966[1962].

Levine, Glenn. "A human ecological language pedagogy." *Modern Language Journal* 104, no. 1 (2020): 1–130.

Levine, Glenn, and Alison Phipps. *Critical and Intercultural Theory and Language Pedagogy*. Boston: Cengage, 2011.

Li Wei. "Moment analysis and translanguaging space: Discursive construction of identities by multilingual Chinese youth in Britain." *Journal of Pragmatics* 43, no. 5 (2011): 1222–35.

Li Wei. "Translanguaging as a practical theory of language." *Applied Linguistics* 39, no. 1 (2018): 9–30.

Li Wei. "Translanguaging as method." *Research Methods in Applied Linguistics* 1, no. 3 (2022): 1–4.

Liddicoat, Anthony. "Language planning for literacy: Issues and implications." *Current Issues in Language Planning* 5, no. 1 (2004): 1–17.

Liddicoat, Anthony J. "Culture for language learning in Australian language-in-education policy." *Australian Review of Applied Linguistics* 28, no. 2 (2005): 28–43.

Liddicoat, Anthony J. "Sexual identity as linguistic failure: Trajectories of interaction in the heteronormative language classroom." *Journal of Language, Identity, and Education* 8, no. 2–3 (2009): 191–202.

Liddicoat, Anthony, and Chantal Crozet. "Teaching culture as an itegrated part of language teaching: An introduction." *Australian Review of Applied Linguistics* 14: 1–22.

Liddicoat, Anthony, and Richard Kern. "From the learner to the speaker/social actor." In *Handbook of Multilingualism and Multiculturalism*, edited by Geneviève Zarate, Danielle Lévy and Claire Kramsch, 17–23. Paris: Editions des Archives Contemporaines, 2011.

Liddicoat, Anthony, and Angela Scarino. *Intercultural Language Teaching and Learning*. Oxford: Wiley-Blackwell, 2013.

Lightbown, Patsy, and Nina Spada. *How Languages are Learned*. Hong Kong: Oxford University Press, 1993.

Lim, Fei Victor. "Developing a systemic functional approach to teach multimodal literacy." *Functional Linguistics* 5, no. 13 (2018): 1–17.

Looney, Dennis, and Natasha Lusin. "Enrollments in languages other than English in United States institutions of higher education, Summer 2016 and Fall 2016." Modern Language Association, 2019.

Lotherington, Heather, and Jennifer Jenson. "Teaching multimodal and digital literacy in L2 settings: New literacies, new basics, new pedagogies." *Annual Review of Applied Linguistics* 31 (2011): 226–46.

López-Sánchez, Ana, Yuri Kumagai, and Sujane Wu. *Multiliteracies In World Language Education*. London/New York: Routledge, 2016.

Luke, Allan. "Genres of power: Literacy education and the production of capital." In *Critical Literacy, Schooling, and Social Justice*, 143–67. New York: Routledge, 2018.

Lytra, Vally, Cristina Ros i Solé, Jim Anderson, and Vicky Macleroy, eds. *Liberating Language Education*. Bristol: Multilingual Matters, 2022.

Makoni, Sinfree, and Alastair Pennycook. "Disinventing and (re) constituting languages." *Critical Inquiry in Language Studies: An International Journal* 2, no. 3 (2005): 137–56.

Malinowksi, David. "Learning to translate the linguistic landscape." In *Expanding the Linguistic Landscape: Linguistic Diversity, Multimodality and the Use of Space as a Semiotic Resource*, edited by Martin Pütz and Neele Mundt, 58–71. Bristol: Multilingual Matters, 2018.

Mandzunowski, Damian, and Lena Henningsen. "Why poach when you can wander?: Michel de Certeau's concept of reading-as-poaching revisited." *READCHINA* 2 (2021): n.p.

Martin, James R. "Meaning beyond the clause: SFL perspectives." *Annual Review of Applied Linguistics* 22 (2002): 52–74.

Martin, J.R., and David Rose. *Genre Relations. Mapping Culture*. London/Oakville: Equinox, 2008.

Masny, Diana, and David R. Cole. "Applying multiple literacies in Australian and Canadian contexts." In *Future Directions in Literacy: International Conversations Conference Proceedings*, edited by Alyson Simpson, 190–211. Sydney: Sydney University Press, 2007.

Masny, Diana, and David R. Cole. *Multiple Literacies Theory: A Deleuzian Perspective*. Leiden: Brill, 2009.

Massumi, Brian. *Parables for the Virtual: Movement, Affect, Sensation*. Duke University Press, 2002.

Maxim, Hiram H. "Integrating textual thinking into the introductory college-level foreign language classroom." *The Modern Language Journal* 90, no. 1 (2006): 19–32.

Maxim, Hiram H. "Developing advanced formal language abilities along a genre-based continuum." In *Conceptions of L2 Grammar: Theoretical Approaches and Their Application in the L2 Classroom*, edited by Stacey L. Katz and Johanna Watzinger-Tharp, 172–88. Boston: Cengage, 2008.

Maxim, Hiram. "'It's made to match': Linking L2 reading and writing through textual borrowing." In *Crossing Languages and Research Methods: Analyses of Adult Foreign Language Reading*, edited by Cindy Brantmeier, 97–122. Charlotte, NC: Information Age Publishing, 2009.

May, Stephen, ed. *The Multilingual Turn: Implications for SLA, TESOL, and Bilingual Education*. London/New York: Routledge, 2013.

McKee, Lori, and Rachel Heydon. "'Enabled to play, enabled to explore': children's civic engagement, literacies, and teacher professional learning." *Discourse: Studies in the Cultural Politics of Education* 41, no. 5 (2020): 782–98.

McIntyre, Lee. *Post-Truth*. Cambridge, MA: MIT Press, 2018.

McNamara, Tim. "Poststructuralism and its challenges for applied linguistics." *Applied Linguistics* 33, no. 5 (2012): 473–82.

McRae, John. *Literature with a Small "l."* Basingstoke: MEP/Macmillan, 1991.

McRae, John. "Representational language learning: from language awareness to text awareness." In *Language, Literature and the Learner*, edited by Ronald Carter and John McRae, 16–40. London/New York: Routledge, 2014.

Merleau-Ponty, Maurice. *Phenomenology of Perception*, translated by Donald A. Landes. London/New York: Routledge, 2012[1945].

Michelson, Kristen. "Teaching culture as a relational process through a multiliteracies-based global simulation." *Language, Culture and Curriculum* 31, no. 1 (2018): 1–20.

Michelson, Kristen, and Beatrice Dupuy. "Multi-storied lives: Global simulation as an approach to developing multiliteracies in an intermediate French course." *L2 Journal* 6, no. 1 (2014).

Michelson, Kristen, and Elyse Petit. "Becoming social actors: Designing a global simulation for situated language and culture learning." In *Engaging the World: Social Pedagogies and Language Learning*, edited by Sebastien Dubreil and Steven Thorne, 138–67. Boston: Cengage, 2017.

Mills, Kathy A. *The Multiliteracies Classroom*. Clevedon: Multilingual Matters, 2010.

Mirra, Nicole, and Antero Garcia. "'I hesitate but I do have hope': Youth speculative civic literacies for troubled times." *Harvard Educational Review* 90, no. 2 (2020): 295–321.

Moore, Danièle, Sunny Man Chu Lau, and Saskia van Viegen. "Mise en écho des perspectives on plurilingual competence and pluralistic pedagogies: A conversation with Danièle Moore." In *Plurilingual Pedagogies: Critical and Creative Endeavors for Equitable Language in Education*, edited by Sunny Man Chu Lau and Saskia van Viegen, 23–45. Cham, Switzerland: Springer, 2020.

Motha, Suhanthie and Angel Lin. "'Non-coercive rearrangements': Theorizing desire in TESOL." *TESOL Quarterly* 48, no. 2 (2014): 331–59.

Murphie, Andrew. "Affect—a basic summary of approaches." *Adventures in Jutland*. 30 January 2010. http://www.andrewmurphie.org/blog/?p=93.

NCSSL and ACTFL. NCSSFL-ACTFL Can-do statements. 2017. https://www.actfl.org/publications/guidelines-and-manuals/ncssfl-actfl-can-do-statements.

Negrón, Rosalyn. "Spanish as a Heritage Language and the Negotiation of Race and Intra-Latina/o Hierarchies in the US." In *The Routledge Handbook of Spanish as a Heritage Language*, edited by Kim Potowski and Javier Muñoz-Basols, 107–123. London/New York: Routledge, 2018.

New London Group. "A pedagogy of multiliteracies: Designing social futures." *Harvard Educational Review* 66, no. 1 (1996): 60–93.

Nibelungenlied, Das, edited and translated by Ursula Schulze. Düsseldord/Zürich: Artemis & Winkler Verlag, 2005.

Nordström, Alexandra, Kristiina Kumpulainen, and John Potter. "Positive affect in young children's multiliteracies learning endeavors." In *Multiliteracies and Early Years Innovation: Perspectives from Finland and Beyond*, edited by Kristiina Kumpulainen and Julian Sefton-Green, 166–82. London/New York: Routledge, 2019.

Norton, Bonny. *Identity and Language Learning: Gender, Ethnicity and Educational Change*. Boston: Allyn and Bacon, 2000.

Norton, Bonny. "Non-participation, imagined communities, and the language classroom." In *Learner Contributions to Language Learning: New Directions in Research*, edited by Michael Breen, 159–71. Harlow: Pearson Education, 2001.

Norton, Bonny. "Identity as a sociocultural construct in second language education." *TESOL in Context* (2006): 22–33.

Norton, Bonny. *Identity and Language Learning: Extending the Conversation*. Bristol: Multilingual Matters, 2013.

Nunan, David. "Content familiarity and the perception of textual relationships in second language reading." *RELC Journal* 16, no. 1 (1985): 43–51.

Nunan, David. *Learner-Centered English Language Education: The Selected Works of David Nunan*. London/New York: Routledge, 2012.

Omaggio-Hadley, Alice. *Language Teaching in Context*. Boston: Heinle, 1986.

Ong, Walther. *Orality And Literacy: The Technologizing of the Word*. London: Methuen, 1982.

Ortega, Lourdes, and Heidi Byrnes, eds. *The Longitudinal Study of Advanced L2 Capacities*. New York: Routledge, 2008.

Oskoz, Ana, and Idoia Elola. "Digital stories: overview." *CALICO Journal* 33, no. 2 (2016): 157–73.

Otsuji, Emi, and Alastair Pennycook. "Metrolingualism: Fixity, fluidity and language in flux." *International Journal of Multilingualism* 7, no. 3 (2010): 240–54.

Oxford, Rebecca L., María Matilde Olivero, Melinda Harrison, and Tammy Gregersen, eds. *Peacebuilding in Language Education: Innovations in Theory and Practice*. Bristol: Multilingual Matters, 2020.

Paesani, Kate. "Investigating connections among reading, writing, and language development: A multiliteracies perspective." *Reading in a Foreign Language* 28, no. 2 (2016): 266–89.

Paesani, Kate, Heather Willis Allen and Beatrice Dupuy. *A Multiliteracies Framework for Collegiate Foreign Language Teaching*. London: Pearson, 2016.

Paesani, Kate, and Heather Willis Allen. "Teacher development and multiliteracies pedagogy: Challenges and opportunities for postsecondary language programs." *Second Language Research and Practice* 1, no. 1 (2020): 124–38.

Paesani, Kate, and Mandy Menke. *Literacies in Language Education: A Guide for Teachers and Teacher Educators*. Washington DC: Georgetown University Press, 2023.

Pahl, Kate and Steven Pool. "Hoping: the literacies of the 'not yet.'" In *Living Literacies: Literacy for Social Change*, edited by Kate Pahl and Jennifer Rowsell. Cambridge, MA: MIT Press, 2020.

Pahl, Kate, and Jennifer Rowsell. *Living Literacies: Literacy for Social Change*. Cambridge, MA: MIT Press, 2020.

Paiz, Joshua M. "Queering ESL teaching: Pedagogical and materials creation issues." *TESOL Journal* 9, no. 2 (2018): 348–67.

Paiz, Joshua M. "Queering practice: LGBTQ+ diversity and inclusion in English language teaching." *Journal of Language, Identity & Education* 18, no. 4 (2019): 266–75.

Paran, Amos. "The role of literature in instructed foreign language learning and teaching: An evidence-based survey." *Language Teaching* 41, no. 4 (2008): 465–96.

Parra, María Luisa, Araceli Otero, Rosa Flores, and Marguerite Lavallée. "Designing a comprehensive curriculum for advanced Spanish heritage learners: Contributions from the multiliteracies framework." In *Multiliteracies Pedagogy and Language Learning: Teaching Spanish to Heritage Speakers*, edited by Gabriela C. Zapata and Manel Lacorte, 27–66. Cham, Switzerland: Palgrave Macmilla, 2017.

Pavlenko, Aneta. "The affective turn in SLA: From 'affective factors' to 'language desire' and 'commodification of affect.'" In *The Affective Dimension in Second Language Acquisition*, edited by Danuta Gabryś-Barker and Joanna Bielska, 3–28. Bristol: Multilingual Matters, 2013.

Peirce, Bonny Norton. "Social identity, investment, and language learning." *TESOL Quarterly* 29, no. 1 (1995): 9–31.

Pennycook, Alastair. "Language, localization, and the real: Hip-hop and the global spread of authenticity." *Journal of Language, Identity, and Education* 6, no. 2 (2007): 101–15.

Pennycook, Alastair. *Language as a Local Practice*. London/New York: Routledge, 2010.

Pennycook, Alastair. "Translanguaging and semiotic assemblages." *International Journal of Multilingualism* 14, no. 3 (2017): 269–82.

Pennycook, Alastair. "Posthumanist applied linguistics." *Applied linguistics* 39, no. 4 (2018): 445–61.

Pennycook, Alastair. "Translingual entanglements of English." *World Englishes* 39, no. 2 (2020): 222–35.

Perry, Kristen. "What Is literacy?—A critical overview of sociocultural perspectives." *Journal of Language and Literacy Education* 8, no. 1 (2012): 50–71.

Phillips, June K. "Reading is communication, too!" *Foreign Language Annals* 11, no. 3 (1978): 281–7.

Phillips, June K. "Practical implications of recent research in reading." *Foreign Language Annals* 17, no. 4 (1984): 285–96.

Phipps, Alison. "Drawing breath: Creative elements and their exile from higher education." *Arts and Humanities in Higher Education* 9, no. 1 (2010): 42–53.

Phipps, Alison, and Mike Gonzalez. *Modern Languages: Learning and Teaching in an Intercultural Field*. Thousand Oaks, CA: Sage, 2004.

Pomerantz, Anne, and Nancy D. Bell. "Learning to play, playing to learn: FL learners as multicompetent language users." *Applied Linguistics* 28, no. 4 (2007): 556–78.

Porto, Melina and Michalinos Zembylas. "Linguistic and artistic representations of trauma: The contribution of pedagogies of discomfort in language education." *The Modern Language Journal* 106 (2022): 328–50.

Pritchard, Robert. "The effects of cultural schemata on reading processing strategies." *Reading Research Quarterly* 25, no. 4 (1990): 273–95.

Quist, Gerdi. "Cosmopolitan imaginings: creativity and responsibility in the language classroom." *Language and Intercultural Communication* 13, no. 3 (2013): 330–42.

Rampton, Ben. "Deutsch in Inner London and the animation of an instructed foreign language." *Journal of Sociolinguistics* 3, no. 4 (1999): 480–504.

Reinhardt, Jonathon. "Social media in second and foreign language teaching and learning: Blogs, wikis, and social networking." *Language Teaching* 52, no. 1 (2019): 1–39.

Reinhardt, Jonathon, and Steven Thorne. "Digital literacies as emergent multifarious repertoires." In *Engaging Language Learners in CALL: From Theory and Research* to *Informed Practice*, edited by Nike Arnold and Lara Ducate, 208–239. London: Equinox, 2019.

Reinhardt, Jonathon, Chantelle Warner, and Kristin Lange. "Digital games as practices and texts: New literacies and genres in an L2 German classroom." *Digital Literacies in Foreign and Second Language Education* 12 (2014): 159–77.

Richardson, Diane. "Beyond a tolerance of ambiguity: Symbolic competence as creative uncertainty and doubt." *L2 Journal* 9, no. 2 (2017): 12–34.

Risager, Karen. *Language and Culture: Global Flows and Local Complexity*. Clevedon: Multilingual Matters, 2006.

Risager, Karem. *Language and Culture Pedagogy: From a National to a Transnational Paradigm*. Clevedon: Multilingual Matters, 2007.

Rosa, Jonathan, and Nelson Flores. "Unsettling race and language: Toward a raciolinguistic perspective." *Language in Society* 46, no. 5 (2017): 621–47.

Rose, David, and James R. Martin. *Learning to Write, Reading to Learn: Genre, Knowledge and Pedagogy in the Sydney School*. London: Equinox, 2012.

Rosenblatt, Louise M. "The literary transaction: evocation and response." *Theory into Practice* 21, no. 4 (1982): 268–77.

Rosenblatt, Louise M. "The aesthetic transaction." *Journal of Aesthetic Education* 20 (1986): 122–7.

Rosenblatt, Louise M. *The Reader, the Text, the Poem: The Transactional Theory of the Literary Work*. Carbondale, IL: Southern Illinois University Press, 1994[1978].

Rosenblatt, Louise M. "The transactional theory of reading and writing." In *Theoretical Models and Processes of Reading*, edited by Donna E. Alvermann, Norman J. Unrau and Robert B. Ruddell, 1057–92. Newark, De: International Reading Association, 1994.

Ros i Solé, Cristina. *The Personal World of the Language Learner*. New York: Springer, 2016.

Ros i Solé, Cristina, Jane Fenoulhet, and Gerdi Quist. "Vibrant identities and finding joy in difference." *Language and Intercultural Communication* 20, no. 5 (2020): 397–407.

Ross, Andrew. "Beyond empathy and compassion: Genocide and the emotional complexities of humanitarian politics." In *Emotions and Mass Atrocity: Philosophical and Theoretical Explorations*, edited by Thomas Brudholm and Johannes Lang, 185–208. Cambridge: Cambridge University Press, 2018.

Rothery, Joan. "Making changes: Developing an educational linguistics." In *Literacy in Society*, edited by Ruqaiya Hasan and Geoff Williams, 86–123. London: Longman, 1996.

Rowsell, Jennifer. "Toward a phenomenology of contemporary reading." *Australian Journal of Language and Literacy* 37, no. 2 (2014): 117–27.

Rowsell, Jennifer, and Peter Vietgen. "Embracing the unknown in community arts zone visual arts." *Pedagogies: An International Journal* 12, no. 1 (2017): 90–107.

Rumelhart, David. "On evaluating story grammars." *Cognitive Science* 4, no. 3 (1980): 313–6.

Rusch, Claudia. *Meine freie deutsche Jugend*. Frankfurt am Main: Fischer, 2003.

Ryshina Pankova, Marianna. "Understanding 'Green Germany' through images and film: A critical literacy approach." *Die Unterrichtspraxis/Teaching German* 46, no. 2 (2013): 163–84.

Samaniego, Malena, and Chantelle Warner. "Designing meaning in inherited languages." In *Innovative Strategies for Heritage Language Teaching: A Practical Guide for the Classroom*, edited by Marta Fairclough and Sara M. Beaudrie, 191–213. Washington DC: Georgetown, 2016.

Sarkozy, Nicolas. "Lettre aux éducateurs." *Le Monde*, September 4, 2007. https://www.lemonde.fr/societe/article/2007/09/04/l-integralite-de-la-lettre-aux-educateurs-de-m-sarkozy_950952_3224.html

Sauro, Shannon. "Investigating language learning in the digital wilds." In *The Routledge Handbook of Language Learning and Teaching Beyond the Classroom*, edited by Hayo Reinders, Chun Lai, and Pia Sundqvist, 327–39. London/New York: Routledge, 2022.

Scollon, Ron and Suzanne Scollon. *Narrative, Literacy, and Face in Interethnic Communication*. Norwood, NJ: Ablex, 1981.

Schiller, Friedrich. *On the Aesthetic Education of Man*, translated by Keith Tribe, edited by Alexander Schmidt. London: Penguin, 2016[1795].

Schmidt, Richard W. "Attention." In *Cognition and Second Language Instruction*, edited by Peter Robinson, 3–32. Cambridge: Cambridge University Press, 2001.

Schufflebarger, Amanda. "Poetry as design in community-based adult ESL classrooms: Meaning-making with creative/aesthetic texts." *L2 Journal* 14, no. 3 (2022): 1–11.

Schulz, Renate A. "Second language reading research: From theory to practice." *Foreign Language Annals* 17, no. 4 (1984): 309.

Scott, Sally, and Wade Edwards. *Disability and World Language Learning: Inclusive Teaching for Diverse Learners*. Lanham and London: Rowman and Littlefield, 2018.

Scott, Virginia, and Holly Tucker, eds. (2001). *SLA and the Literature Classroom: Fostering Dialogues*. Boston: Cengage, 2001.

Scribner, Sylvia, and Michael Cole. *The Psychology of Literacy*. Cambridge, MA: Harvard University Press, 1981.

Schleppegrell, Mary J. *The Language of Schooling: A Functional Linguistics Perspective*. New York/London: Routledge, 2004.

Schufflebarger Snell, Amanda. *Subversive Survival Through Critical Creativity in Community-Based Adult Second Language Contexts*. Ph.D diss. Tucson: University of Arizona, 2019.

Schufflebarger Snell, Amanda. "Play and bricolage in adult second language classrooms." *Working Papers in Educational Linguistics* 31, no. 2 (2016): 77–92.

Schufflebarger, Amanda. "Poetry as design in community-based adult ESL classrooms: Meaning-making with creative/aesthetic texts." *L2 Journal* 14, no. 3 (2022): 1–11.

Selinker, Larry. "Interlanguage." *IRAL: International Review of Applied Linguistics in Language Teaching* 10 (1972): 209–32.

Serafini, Frank. *Reading the Visual: An Introduction to Teaching Multimodal Literacy*. New York: Teachers College Press, 2014.

Simpson, Paul. *Stylistics: A Resource Book for Students*. London: Psychology Press, 2004.

Smith, Blaine E. "Beyond words: A review of research on adolescents and multimodal composition." In *Exploring Multimodal Composition and Digital Writing*, edited by Richard E. Ferdig, 1–19. Hershey, PA: IGI Global, 2014.

Smith, Blaine E. "Composing for affect, audience, and identity: Toward a multidimensional understanding of adolescents' multimodal composing goals and designs." *Written Communication* 35, no. 2 (2018): 182–214.

Smith, Blaine E., Natalie Amgott, and Irina Malova. "'It made me think in a different way': Bilingual students' perspectives on multimodal composing in the English language arts classroom." *TESOL Quarterly* 56, no. 2 (2022): 525–51.

Smith, Cheryl Hogue. "Interrogating texts: From deferent to efferent and aesthetic reading practices." *Journal of Basic Writing* 31, no. 1 (2012): 59–79.

Song, Juyoung. "Emotions and language teacher identity: Conflicts, vulnerability, and transformation." *TESOL Quarterly* 50, no. 3 (2016): 631–54.

Souto-Manning, Mariana. "Honoring and building on the rich literacy practices of young bilingual and multilingual learners." *The Reading Teacher* 70, no. 3 (2016): 263–71.

Spinoza, Baruch. *The Essential Spinoza: Ethics and Related Writings*. Indianapolis, IN: Hackett Publishing, 2006.

Spivak, Gayatari. *An Aesthetic Education in the Era of Globalization*. Cambridge, MA: Harvard University Press, 2012.

Stornaiuolo, Amy. "Literacy as worldmaking: Cosmopolitanism, creativity, and multimodality." In *The Routledge Handbook of Literacy Studies*, edited by Kate Pahl and Jennifer Rowsell, 561–72. London: Routledge, 2015.

Stornaiuolo, Amy, Glynda Hull, and Mark Evan Nelson. "Mobile texts and migrant audiences: Rethinking literacy and assessment in a new media age." *Language Arts* 86, no. 5 (2009): 382–92.

Stornaiuolo, Amy, and Erin Hope Whitney. "Writing as worldmaking." *Language Arts* 95, no. 4 (2018): 205–17.

Street, Brian. *Literacy in Theory and Practice*. Cambridge, MA: Harvard University Press, 1984.

Suh, Joowon and Ji-Young Jung. "Literacy and multiliteracies in Korean language learning and teaching." In *Teaching Korean as a Foreign Language*, edited by Joowon Suh and Ji-Young Jung, 127–46. New York/London: Routledge, 2020.

Svalberg, Agneta. "Language awareness and language learning." *Language Teaching* 40, no. 4 (2007): 287–308.

Svalberg, Agneta. "Language awareness in language learning and teaching: A research agenda." *Language Teaching* 45, no. 3 (2012): 376–88.

Swaffar, Janet. "The case for foreign languages as a discipline." *Profession* Annual volume (1999): 155–67.

Swaffar, Janet. "A template for advanced learner tasks: Staging genre reading and cultural literacy through the précis." In *Advanced Foreign Language Learning: A Challenge to College Programs*, edited by Heidi Byrnes and Hiram Maxim, 19–45. Boston: Heinle, 2004.

Swaffar, Janet, and Katherine Arens. *Remapping The Foreign Language Curriculum: An Approach Through Multiple Literacies*. New York: Modern Language Association, 2005.

Swaffar, Janet, Katherine Arens, and Heidi Byrnes. *Reading For Meaning: An Integrated Approach to Language Learning*. Englewood Cliffs, NJ: Prentice Hall, 1991.

Swain, Merrill. "The inseparability of cognition and emotion in second language learning." *Language Teaching* 46, no. 2 (2013): 195–207.

Swain, Merrill, and Yuko Watanabe. "Languaging: Collaborative dialogue as a source of second language learning." In *The Encyclopedia of Applied Linguistics*, edited by Carol Chapelle, 3218–25. London: Blackwell, 2013.

Swales, John M. *Genre Analysis: English in Academic and Research Settings*. Cambridge: Cambridge University Press, 1990.

Sykes, Julie E., and Jonathon Reinhardt. *Language at Play: Digital Games in Second and Foreign Language Teaching and Learning*. London: Pearson, 2012.

Takahashi, Kimie. *Language Desire: Gender, Sexuality and Second Language Learning*. Clevedon: Multilingual Matters, 2013.

Tardy, Christine M. "Researching first and second language genre learning: A comparative review and a look ahead." *Journal of Second Language Writing* 15, no. 2 (2006): 79–101.

Tardy, Christine M. "The potential power of play in second language academic writing." *Journal of Second Language Writing* 53 (2021): 1–12.

Thorne, Steven L. "Epistemology, politics, and ethics in sociocultural theory." *The Modern Language Journal* 89, no. 3 (2005): 393–409.

Thorne, Steven L., and Jonathon Reinhardt. "'Bridging activities,' new media literacies, and advanced foreign language proficiency." *Calico Journal* 25, no. 3 (2008): 558–72.

Thorne, Steven L., Ingrid Fischer, and Xiaofei Lu. "The semiotic ecology and linguistic complexity of an online game world." *ReCALL* 24, no. 3 (2012): 279–301.

Thorne, Steven L., Shannon Sauro, and Bryan Smith. "Technologies, identities, and expressive activity." *Annual Review of Applied Linguistics* 35 (2015): 215–33.

Timlin, Chelsea, Chantelle Warner, Laurie Clark and Patrick Ploschnitzki. "Living literacies in a *Märchenwelt*: World building and perspective taking in a fairy tale simulation project." *Unterrichtspraxis: Teaching College German*, 54, no. 1 (2021): 5–19.

Tin, Tan Bee. "Freedom, constraints and creativity in language learning tasks: New task features." *Innovation in Language Learning and Teaching* 6, no. 2 (2012): 177–86.

Tin, Tan Bee. "Language creativity and co-emergence of form and meaning in creative writing tasks." *Applied Linguistics*, 32, no. 2 (2011): 215–35.

Tin, Tan Bee. "Towards creativity in ELT: The need to say something new." *ELT Journal* 67, no. 4 (2013): 385–97.

Tin, Tan Bee. *Unpacking Creativity for Language Teaching*. London/New York: Routledge, 2022.

Tomasello, Michael. *The Cultural Origins of Human Cognition*. Cambridge, MA: Harvard University Press, 1999.

Troyan, Francis J. "Leveraging genre theory: A genre- based interactive model for the era of the Common Core State Standards." *Foreign Language Annals* 47, no. 1 (2014): 5–24.

Troyan, Francis. "Learning to mean in Spanish writing: A case study of a Genre-based pedagogy for standards-based writing instruction." *Foreign Language Annals* 49 (2016): 317–35.

Tschirner, Erwin, Brigitte Nikolai, and Tracy D. Terrell. *Kontakte: A Communicative Approach*, 7th ed. New York: McGraw-Hill, 2013.

Unsworth, Len. *Teaching Multiliteracies Across the Curriculum Changing Contexts of Text and Image in Classroom Practice*. Buckingham: Buckingham Open University Press, 2001.

Unsworth, Len. "Towards ametalanguage for multiliteracies education: Describing the meaning making." *English Teaching: Practice and Critique* 5, no. 1 (2006): 55–76.

Upton, Brian. *The Aesthetic of Play*. Cambridge, MA: MIT press, 2015.

Ushioda, Ema. "A person-in-context relational view of emergent motivation, self and identity." In *Motivation, Language Identity and the L2 Self*, edited by Ema Ushioda and Zoltán Dörnyei, 215–28. Clevedon: Multilingual Matters, 2009.

van Leeuwen, Theo. "Genre and field in critical discourse analysis." *Discourse and Society* 4 (1993): 193–223.

van Lier, Leo. *The Ecology and Semiotics of Language Learning: A Sociocultural Perspective*. Dordrecht: Kluwer Academic, 2004.

Vygotsky, Lev Semenovich. *Mind in Society: Development of Higher Psychological Processes*, edited by Michael Cole. Cambridge, MA: Harvard University Press, 1978.

Vygotsky, Lev Semenovich. "The problem of the environment." In *The Vygotsky Reader*, edited by René van der Veer and Jaan Valsiner, 347–384. Oxford: Blackwell, 1994.

Vygotsky, Lev Semenovich. *The Collected Works of L. S. Vygotsky. Volume 4. The History of the Development of Higher Mental Functions*. New York: Plenum, 1997.

Vygotsky, Lev Semenovich. "Play and Its role in the mental development of the child." *International Research in Early Childhood Education* 7, no. 2 (2016[1966]): 3–25.

Vygotsky, Lev Semenovich. *The Psychology of Art*. Cambridge, MA: MIT Press, 1971[1925].

Vytniorgu, Richard. "An ethical ideal? Louise Rosenblatt and democracy—a personalist reconsideration." *Humanities* 7, no. 29 (2018): 1–13.

Walsh, Maureen. "Multimodal literacy: What does it mean for classroom practice?" *Australian Journal of Language and Literacy* 33, no. 3 (2010): 211–39.

Wagner, Daniel A. "What happened to literacy? Historical and conceptual perspectives on literacy in UNESCO." *International Journal of Educational Development* 31 (2011): 319–23.

Warner, Chantelle. "It's just a game, right?: Types of play in foreign language CMC." *Language Learning and Technology* 8, no. 2 (2004): 69–87.

Warner, Chantelle. "Rethinking the role of language study in internationalizing higher education." *L2 Journal* 3, no. 1 (2011).

Warner, Chantelle. "Mapping new classrooms in literacy-oriented foreign language teaching and learning: The role of the reading experience." In *Transforming the Foreign Language Curriculum in Higher Education: New Perspectives from The United States*, edited by Katherine Arens, Janet Swaffar and Per Urlaub, 157–76. Heidelberg, Germany: Springer, 2014.

Warner, Chantelle. "Transdisciplinarity across two-tiers: The case of applied linguistics and literary studies in US foreign language departments." *AILA Review* 31, no. 1 (2018): 29–52.

Warner, Chantelle. "Retelling stories across foreign languages and cultures: Literary imagination and symbolic competence." In *Narrative Retellings: Stylistic Approaches*, edited by Marina Lambrou, 199–215. London: Bloomsbury, 2020.

Warner, Chantelle. "Playful designs: Multiliteracies and literariness in the beginning language classroom." *Foreign Language Annals*, 55, no. 3 (2022): 704–24.

Warner, Chantelle. "Response, aesthetics, and deep learning in the German language-culture classroom." In *Transformation, Embodiment, and Well-Being in Foreign Language Pedagogy: Enacting Deep Learning*, edited by Troy McConachy and Joseph Shaules, 53–174. London: Bloomsbury, 2023.

Warner, Chantelle, and Beatrice Dupuy. "Moving towards multiliteracies in foreign language teaching: Past and present perspectives … and beyond." *Foreign Language Annals*, 51 (2018): 116–28.

Warner, Chantelle, Borbala Gaspar, and Wenhao Diao. "Enterprising and imagining multilingual subjects: Beyond commodity-centered discourses of language learning in the US." *Critical Multilingualism Studies* 9, no. 1 (2021): 103–27.

Warner, Chantelle, and David Gramling. "'Gerade Dir hat er eine Botschaft gesendet': Contact pragmatics and the teaching of foreign language texts." In *Traditions and Transitions: Curricula for German Studies*, edited by John Plews and Barbara Schmenk, 209–26. Waterloo, Belgium: Wilfrid Laurier University Press, 2013.

Warner, Chantelle, and David Gramling. "Kontaktpragmatik: fremdsprachliche Literatur und symbolische Beweglichkeit." *Deutsch als Fremdsprache* 51 (2014): 67–76.

Warner, Chantelle, and Diane Richardson. "Beyond participation: Symbolic struggles with(in) digital social media in the L2 classroom." In *Engaging the World: Social Pedagogies and Language Learning*, edited by Sebastien Dubreil and Steven Thorne, 199–226. Boston, MA: Cengage, 2017.

Warner, Chantelle, Diane Richardson, and Kristin Lange. "Realizing multiple literacies through game-enhanced pedagogies: Designing learning across discourse levels." *Journal of Gaming & Virtual Worlds* 11, no. 1 (2019): 9–28.

Warner, Chantelle, Borbala Gaspar, and Wenhao Diao. "Enterprising and imagining multilingual subjects: Beyond commodity-centered discourses of language learning in the US." *Critical Multilingualism Studies* 9, no. 1 (2021): 103–27.

Warren, Mackenzie, and Winkler Claudia. "Developing multiliteracies through genre in the beginner German classroom." In *Multiliteracies in World Language Education*, edited by Yuri Kumagai, López-Sánchez Ana, Wu Sujane, 29–57. New York: Routledge, 2016.

Weedon, Chris. *Feminist Practice and Post-Structuralist Theory*. Oxford: Basil Blackwell, 1987.

Widdowson, Henry. *Teaching Language as Communication*. Oxford: Oxford University Press, 1978.

Zapata, Gabriela. *Learning By Design and Second Language Teaching: Theory, Research, And Practice*. London/New York: Routledge, 2022.

Zapata, Gabriela C., and Manel Lacorte, eds. *Multiliteracies Pedagogy and Language Learning: Teaching Spanish to Heritage Speakers*. College Park, MD: Palgrave Macmillan, 2017.

Zaidi, Rahat and Jennifer Rowsell, eds. *Literacy Lives in Transcultural Times*. London/New York: Routledge, 2017.

Zapata, Gabriela, and Manel Lacort. *Multiliteracies Pedagogy and Language Learning Teaching Spanish to Heritage Speakers*. Berlin: Springer, 2017.

Zembylas, Michalinos. "'Pedagogy of discomfort' and its ethical implications: The tensions of ethical violence in social justice education." *Ethics and Education* 10, no. 2 (2015): 163–74.

Zimmerman, Eric. "Gaming literacy: Game design as a model for literacy in the twenty-first century." In *The Video Game Theory Reader 2*, edited by Bernard Perron and Mark J. P. Wolf, 45–54. London/New York: Routledge, 2008.

Zimmerman, Eric. "Jerked around by the magic circle-clearing the air ten years later." *Gamasutra*, February 7, 2012. https://www.gamedeveloper.com/design/jerked-around-by-the-magic-circle---clearing-the-air-ten-years-later#close-modal

Zimmerman, Eric, and Katoe Salen. *Rules of Play: Game Design Fundamentals*. Boston, MA: MIT Press, 2003.

Zournazi, Mary. *Hope: New Philosophies for Change*. London: Psychology Press, 2003.

Index

Adams, Vincanne 169
aesthetic education 3–4, 81
aesthetic experience 71, 81, 91, 109, 125, 150, 187
affect/affect theory 4, 68, 69, 192 n.3
    and desire 74–9
    emotions and 69–71
    as experience/lived experience 71
    holistic/cognitive humanistic approach 70
    lesson planning and 84
    motivation and 72–4
    sociocultural models and 71
Affect in Language Teaching (Arnold) 70
affective filter hypothesis 69–71
affective literacy studies 76, 187
    in language-culture classroom 84–97
Ahmed, Sara 78
Alcázar Silva, Sara Melissa 40–1, 151–5, 157, 161, 165, 167
Allen, Heather Willis 43–6, 55–6, 59
American Council on the Teaching of Foreign Languages (ACTFL) 48, 51
Amgott, Natalie 41
analyzing design 31–3, 48–54
Anderson, Jim 73
anticipatory logic/thinking 169–71
anxiety 1, 70, 72
Arens, Katherine 52
assemblages 77, 82, 98–9, 140, 182, 187
associated pedagogy 1, 4, 33, 44, 48, 54

Barrineau, Susanna 170
Baruch, Spinoza 75
Bateson, Gregory 117–18, 121–2
Bell, Nancy D. 112
Belz, Julie A. 112
Benesch, Sarah 78
Bensoussan, Marsha 10
Berti, Margherita 171, 173
Bialystok, Ellen 83
Boldt, Gail 68, 76, 184

Bolter, Jay David 26–7
Bourdieu, Pierre 14
bricolage (creative assemblage) 113–20
Broner, Maggie A. 109–10
Burt, Marina 69–70
Byram, Michael 13, 88

Callois, Roger 115–16
Carr, Jo 128
Cazden, Courtney 67
Clarke, Adele E. 169
Claudia, Winkler 46–7, 55
cognitive models 69–71
Common European Framework 13, 48
communicative competence 1, 3, 13–14, 48, 59
communicative language teaching 9–10, 12, 35–6, 41, 48, 64
comprehension-oriented models 10
computer-mediated communication 121–4
conceptualizing design 31–3, 48–54
consciousness 25, 71, 101
contact pragmatics, imperial readings 57
Cope, Bill 27, 30–1, 36, 43–4, 59–62, 131–2, 168, 184
cosmopolitan imaginings 128–9
creative personalization 58–9, 108, 130
critical framing, pedagogical act 31–2, 44–8, 132
critical literacy 31, 40, 42, 46, 53
culture learning. *See* second language and culture learning

De Certeau, Michel 126, 188
deconstruction 46–7
Deleuze, Gilles 7, 18
    affect theory 75–7
Derrida, Jacques 115
descriptive and interpretive tasks 63–4
designers 17, 19, 56–60, 103, 131, 133, 157, 168, 170–1, 184–6

designing 43
	classroom activities 63–9, 83–4
	metalanguages, conceptualizing and analyzing 48–54
	pedagogical sequences for 43–8
	textual borrowing 54–6
design/meaning design 29–30, 39–43, 68, 101–3. *See also* knowledge processes
	conceptualizing and analyzing 31–3, 48–54
	film and media 42
	multimodality and digital technologies 39–40
	poetry writing 41–2
desire 74–9, 101–3, 186
	design/redesign space for 97–9
	economies of 81
	in language-culture classroom 86–97
	multilingual subjectivities and 79–82
	multiliteracies-based curriculum 85–6
dialogic imagination 128
Diao, Wenhao 170
digital literacy 12, 26–7, 39–40
discourse approaches. *See* meaning-oriented teaching
diversity 4, 16
Dornyei, Zoltán 72–3
double subjectivity 4
Dulay, Heidi 69–70
Dupuy, Beatrice 44, 46
Duranti, Alessandro 56

Ehret, Christian 77, 83–4, 90–1, 187
elaborated code 51
Elsner, Daniela 41–2
emergentist education 170
emotions, learners 69–71
	and feelings 78
	motivation and 72–4
	sociocultural approaches to 71
epistemic assemblages 7. *See also* assemblages
experience/lived experience 2, 9, 15–16, 43, 54, 58–9, 61, 71–2, 90–1, 97–9, 121, 170, 185–6
	felt experience, literacy 63–9, 82–5

Fairclough, Norman 33
Fenoulhet, Jane 77–8

Flores, Nelson 8, 16
form play 118–19
frame play 118–19
Freire, Paolo 5–6, 24–5, 59

game theory 115–16
Garcia, Antero 34, 169
Gaspar, Borbala 170, 171–3, 177–9
Gee, James Paul 51
genre-based pedagogies 50–3, 55
Goffman, Erving 14, 118, 122
Gonzalez, Mike 8, 16
Goodspeed, Lauren 55–6, 59
Gramling, David 9, 129
grammar as design
	and communication 9
	communicative *vs.* multiliteracies 49
	SFL models 34, 53
Greene, Maxine 101
Guattari, Félix 7, 18
	affect theory 75–7

Halliday, M. A. K. 11, 33–4, 49
Hasan, Ruqaiya 25–6
Heath, Shirley Brice 25
Helff, Sissy 41–2
Henningsen, Lena 127
heritage language learners 40, 59, 151, 153–4
Heydon, Rachel 131
Hickey-Moody, Anna 188
Hull, Glynda 61–2
human ecological approach 8
humanistic approach 2–3, 70, 107–8
Hymes, Dell 1, 11, 14

Ideal L2 Self 73
ideational metafunctions 50
identity/identity construction 14–16, 72–5, 81–2, 108, 139–40, 145, 164
imagination 14–15, 74, 90–1, 146, 189–90
	and constitution of self 15–16
	cultural imaginations 61
	dialogic imagination 128
	literary imagination 127
	sympathetic imagination 128
	and world building 117
independent construction 46–7
intercultural learning 13, 48
interpersonal metafunctions 50

"Inventur" (Inventory) (Eich) 136–40
IRE (initiation-response-evaluation) format 67

James R. Martin 34
Jenson, Jennifer 39
joint construction 46–7

Kaiser, Mark 42
Kalantzis, Mary 27, 30–1, 36, 59–62, 131–2, 168, 184
Kern, Richard 14, 16, 44, 49, 56
keying/rekeying 90–1, 118, 122–4
Knobel, Michele 26, 28–9, 40, 43–4
knowledge-focused learning 31–2, 64
Kramsch, Claire 9–11, 61, 88, 114, 185
    on communicative competence 2
    on language learning 7
    on multilingual subjectivities and desire 4, 15, 79–82
    on symbolic competence 3, 17, 61, 80–2, 153
    third space concept 15, 81
Krashen, Stephen D. 10
    on affective filter 1, 69–70
    on motivation 72
Kress, Gunter 30, 33–4, 52–3
Kristeva, Julia 78
Krueger, Cheryl 58–9
Kubota, Ryuko 8, 81

Lange Kristin 40
language figure 102–3
language goals 3, 12–13, 46–8, 108–9, 141–2, 153–4
language ideologies 6–9, 24
language play 110–12, 116, 118–19, 121, 159
Language Play, Language Learning (Cook) 109, 111–12, 116–17, 119, 121
languagers 16–17, 112, 185
languages other than English (LOTEs) 35, 50, 82
languaging 6, 67, 78, 80–1, 98
Lankshear, Colin 26, 28–9, 40
Lantolf, James P. 73, 109–11
Leander, Kevin 68, 76, 83–4, 184, 187
learner-centered teaching 13–17
learner ideologies 13–17
Learning by Design and Language Teaching (Zapata) 59

learning ideologies 9–13
Levine, Glenn 8, 113–14
Levi-Strauss, Claude 114
Liddicoat, Anthony 6, 14, 16
Lin, Angel 81
Literacy and Language Teaching (Kern) 36
literacy crises 24
literacy-oriented language teaching. *See* multiliteracy/multiliteracies
literature 12, 41–2, 52, 89, 91, 135
Lotherington, Heather 39
Luke, Allan 34–5

magic circle play 122–4
Malova, Irina 41
Mandzunowski, Damian 127
Martin, James R. 50
Massumi, Brain 75–6
Maxim, Hiram H. 55
McKee, Lori 131
McNamara, Tim 8
McRae, John 130
meaning-oriented teaching 1–2, 11–12, 17, 49, 51–2, 60
Mendy, Laila 170
Menke, Mandy 48–9
metafunctions 50
    linguistic and visual 54 (*see also* systemic functional linguistics (SFL))
metalanguage (for teaching literacy) 48–9
    of genres 50–3
    grammatical forms 49
    lesson planning and 84
    metafunctions 50, 54
    of systemic functional linguistics 49, 51, 53
Michelson, Kristen 57
Mirra, Nicole 169
monolingualism 7
Motha, Suhanthie 81
motivation 7, 62, 70, 72–4, 170–1
multilingual game 17, 61, 153. *See also* symbolic competence
The Multilingual Instructor (Kramsch and Zhang) 140
multilingualism 4–5, 7–9, 16, 27–8, 129
multilingual subjectivities 4, 15, 79–82
multilingual turn 5, 8

multiliteracies-based curriculum, lesson planning 63–9, 85–6
multiliteracies pedagogies 35
  language goals 64
  photographs and video clip lesson plan 63–9
  teaching by design 38–9, 41, 43, 68
multiliteracy/multiliteracies 4, 17, 23
  communicative teaching vs. 35–6, 39, 41, 48
  critiques of 76
  felt experience 82–4
  literacy play 125–9
  New London Group's model of 27–35
  reading activities 45–6
  in second language studies 35–9
  sociocultural models 23–7
multiliteracy play 4, 113–20, 183
  bricolage (creative assemblage) 113–20
  designing 120–5
  model of 130–1
  pedagogies/learning activities in 132–4
  redesigning through literacy play 125–9
multimodality 27–8, 34, 63, 153
  and digital technologies 39–40
multiple literacies theory (MLT) 76
Murphie, Andrew 75
Murphy, Michelle 169

native speaker/non-native speakers 6
Nelson, Mark Evan 61–2
neoliberalism 16
New Literacies: Everyday Practices and Social Learning (Lankshear and Knobel) 23–4
New London Group (NLG) 3–99, 101–5, 107–32, 169, 184, 191 n.2
Norton, Bonny 14–15, 192 n.3

Ostalgie 87–91
Ought-to L2 Self 73
overt instruction, pedagogical act 31, 44–8, 132

Paesani, Kate 43–6, 48
Pahl, Kate 126
pedagogical acts 30–2, 45
Pennycook, Alastair 7, 77–8

perezhivanie 9–80, 82
Peters, Anne-Kathrin 170
Petit, Elyse 57
Phipps, Alison 8, 16
photography/images lesson plan 63–9
play (language play) 109. *See also* multiliteracy play
  behavior/activity 117
  and creativity 115–17
  designing meaning playfully 120–5
  design types 118–19
  as fun/rehearsal 109–11, 120–1
  and game theory 115
  imaginary play 117
  with language and literacy activities 107–9, 125–9, 132
  magic circle 122–4
  oppositional practice 126–7
  and private speech 110
  symbolic play 110–11
pluralizing literacy 6, 8, 27–35
poetic texts/poetry 41–2, 116–17, 135–6. *See also* literature
  classroom activities 136–40
  "Freedom to Play" 147–9
  "It Represented Other Stuff" 141–3
  "Unimportant, but Significant" 143–7
Pomerantz, Anne 112
Pool, Steven 126
private speech 110–11
proficiency-based language teaching 1

Quist, Gerdi 77–8, 128–9

Rampton, Ben 123
reading activities and pedagogical acts 45–6
reading-as-poaching 126–7
recognition literacy 46–7
redesigners 60–2, 184–6. *See also* designers
redesign/redesigning 29–30, 60–2
Reinhardt, Jonathon 40
relational transformation 90–1
representational texts 117
representation play 118–19
reproduction literacy 46
Richardson, Diane 40
Rose, David 34, 50

Rosenblatt, Louise M. 80–1
Ros i Solé, Cristina 15, 77–8, 187
Ross, Andrew 96–7
Rothery, Joan 46–7

sanctioned play tasks 136
Scarino, Angela 6
Schiller, Friedrich 3
Schufflebarger (Snell), Amanda 42, 108, 114, 115
Schultz, Jean Marie 56
second language and culture learning 2, 35–9
  affect in 69–71
  critical-aesthetic approach 97–9
  designs/designers 39–43, 56–60
  emotions in 69
  genre-based pedagogies in 50–3, 55
  metalanguages, designing 48–54
  motivation 72–4
  multilingual subjectivities, aesthetics, and desire 79–82
  pedagogical sequences for designing 43–8
  sociocultural models 71
  textual borrowing 54–6
Seglem, Robyn 34
semiotic mediation 4, 6–8, 25–6, 57–8, 68, 79
Silva, Sara Alcázar 151–2
situated practice, pedagogical act 31, 44–8, 132
Smith, Blaine E. 41–2
social situation of development (SSD) 73
sociocultural theories of literacy 3, 8, 10, 12–13, 23–7, 31, 59, 71, 73, 110
speaker/actor, learner 14, 79
speculative play 169
  anticipatory logic 169–71
  "A Whole New World to Myself" 177–81
  designing multilingual futures 173–4
  "Have That Experience and See That Beauty" 174–7
  multiliteracy play as 169
  project-based learning 171–3
Spivak, Gayatari 3, 81, 128, 188
Stornaiuolo, Amy 61–2
Swaffar, Janet 50–2

symbolic capital 14–15, 79, 170
symbolic competence 3, 17, 61, 80–2, 152–3, 167
  bricolage and 114
symbolic play 110–11
sympathetic imagination 128
systemic functional linguistics (SFL) 33–4, 49, 52–3
  and visual metafunctions 53–4

Takahashi, Kimie 81
Tarone, Elaine E. 109–10
technology-mediated practices 26
textual borrowing design 54–6
textual metafunctions 50
Thorne, Steven 40
Timlin, Chelsea 58, 137
Tin, Tan Bee 116, 125, 136
transformation, literacy. *See* redesign/redesigning
transformative intercultural learning 128
transformed practice, pedagogical act 32, 44–8, 132, 140
translanguaging/translanguaging space 7–8, 17, 108, 129, 164, 166
translation competence 152
translation play 152
  curriculum for 152–5
  "It Reaches the Heart More" 157–61
  "I Tried to Have Diversity in My Ideas" 162–6
  medical PSAs (public service announcements) project 155–7
Troyan, Francis 50–2

Unsworth, Len 46
Ushioda, Ema 72

van Leeuwen, Theo 33–4, 52–3
verbal-visual multimodality 41–2
vibrant identities 77
video lesson plan 63–6
Viebrock, Britta 41–2
Vygotsky, Lev Semenovich 31
  on experience/lived experience (*perezhivanie*) 71, 80
  on motivation 73–4
  on sociocultural theory 31, 71, 110

Warner, Chantelle 8, 14, 16, 37, 40, 48, 58–61, 82, 86, 96, 98, 101, 108, 118–19, 121, 123–4, 129, 135–6, 159, 168, 170, 173
Warren, Mackenzie 46–7, 55
Weedon, Chris 14–15
Wei, Li 7–8

Whiteside, Anne 114
Widdowson, Henry 11
world building 117, 169–70

Yáñez, María-del-Carmen 110

Zimmerman, Eric 114

www.ingramcontent.com/pod-product-compliance
Lightning Source LLC
Chambersburg PA
CBHW071833300426
44116CB00009B/1529